NEGOTIATING SOCIALISM IN RURAL CHINA

NEGOTIATING SOCIALISM IN RURAL CHINA

Mao, Peasants, and Local Cadres
in Shanxi, 1949–1953

XIAOJIA HOU

East Asia Program
Cornell University
Ithaca, New York 14853

The Cornell East Asia Series is published by the Cornell University East Asia Program (distinct from Cornell University Press). We publish books on a variety of topics relating to East Asia as a service to the academic community and the general public. Address submission inquiries to CEAS Editorial Board, East Asia Program, Cornell University, 140 Uris Hall, Ithaca, New York 14853-7601.

Cover image: Chen Zihua. *Illustrated Book of Chen Zihua (Zhongyang wenxian chubanshe (Beijing), 2015.* Used with permission from Zhongyang wenxian chubanshe.

ISSN 1050-2955
ISBN 978-1-939161-59-8 hardcover
ISBN 978-1-939161-79-6 paperback
ISBN 978-1-942242-79-6 e-book
Library of Congress Control Number: 2016933707
Printed in the United States of America

Contents

Acknowledgments

I began work on this book while still a graduate student at Cornell University. Sherman Cochran, my teacher, did everything one could ask from an adviser, and more. He showed me how to become a better scholar, and a better person. Peter Holquist taught me how to read and think critically, and to appreciate coffee. Chen Jian and Allen Carlson have also been particularly helpful, even after I graduated. My friends there, especially Amy Pozza, read my earliest draft, edited it, and accompanied me to complete the PhD degree. My indebtedness to them goes beyond this simple acknowledgment.

After graduate school, I joined the Department of History at University of Colorado Denver. My colleagues there encouraged me to expand the dissertation. To name a few, Pam Laird, my mentor, guided me through my first job and trained me how to write a book prospectus. Carl Pletsch and Gabriel Finkelstein's positive comments on the manuscript encouraged me to pursue further. The department coordinator Tabitha Fitzpatrick's sunny smile lightened those intense archival-reading days. My current institute, the Department of History at San Jose State University, and my new colleagues here continue to encourage me to turn the research into a book.

Many scholars in the field of modern China have consistently shared their resources and insights with me. Among those to whom I owe a debt of gratitude are Niu Dayong, Yang Kuisong, Wang Hai-guang, Cao Shuji, James Gao, Chen Yixin, Zhang Ming, Gao Wangling, Zhang Baijia, and Xin Yi.

The research has involved a great deal of archives and restricted circulations. I thank Changzhi Municipal Archive, Jincheng Municipal Archive, Shanxi Provincial Archive, Shanxi Local History Office Library, Sichuan

Provincial Archive, and Wuxiang County Archive for allowing me to access their archives. The Universities Service Center in Hong Kong offered access to many restricted circulated journals and ample opportunities to chat with scholars from the world. Academia Sinica in Taiwan hosted my summer research to learn the story from the other side of the strait; for that I am indebted to Hsiung Ping-chen, Chen Yung-fa and Yu Ming-ling. In the United States, I found rare materials and local chronicles at the Kroch Library (Cornell), Starr East Asian Library (University of California Berkeley), and the Stanford East Asia Library.

Over the years, this project has received substantial financial support. Sage Fellowship, Hu Shih Memorial, Lee Teng-hui Fellowship, Lam Family Fellowship, Sicca Fellowship, and Starr Fellowship, all from Cornell University, funded my dissertation research in China, Hong Kong, Taiwan, and Russia. The History Department and the Faculty Development Center of University of Colorado Denver supported further research travels in Asia.

Along the way, many people have provided useful comments on parts or the whole of this manuscript. The ones who stand out are Thomas Bernstein, Li Hua-yu, Paul Pickowicz, and Mark Selden. Not only have their own scholarship inspired me, they also read parts of the manuscript and made invaluable suggestions. Special thanks are due to Felix Wemheuer, Roger des Forges, and Paul Sorrell. They read the manuscript in draft thoroughly, commented it in detail, and helped me with the revision. Their committment of time and energy led to a much stronger final version. In the actual production of this work, Managing Editor Mai Shaikhanuar-Cota provided the kind of support that only a dedicated professional could. I am deeply indebted to them.

Finally, I wish to express my immense appreciation to my family. Lexi, my daughter, has grown along with the project. My husband, Qianfan Xu, is always the first audience of my ideas and the harshest critic. Our discussions have been a source of stimulation. An immeasurable degree of thanks goes to my parents who have been unfailing in their trust and support, and always made me feel like a spoiled daughter.

Introduction

In the fall of 1953, the Chinese Communist Party (CCP) launched a nation-wide movement to encourage peasants to form agricultural producers' cooperatives (APCs). In these new organizations, peasants pooled their private landholdings, farmed together, and distributed the harvest in proportion to the participants' contributions of land and labor. This movement was officially labeled agricultural cooperativization, but in many crucial respects, it resembled Soviet collectivization.[1] China's agricultural cooperativization movement reached a "High Tide" in 1955–1956, when Chinese peasants were forced to join APCs and to hand over their private property. Ultimately, it led to the utopian commune movement in 1958, which was followed by a famine unprecedented in human history: estimates of the death toll range from twenty to forty million. The initial agricultural cooperativization movement began the process of ending the private peasant economy, which had existed in China for more than two millennia, transformed the lives of hundreds of millions of people, and culminated in calamity. Surprisingly, however, the movement's beginnings are poorly understood.

Researchers have shown some interest in the High Tide of 1955–1956. Scholars ask why agricultural cooperativization went wrong in 1955 and what factors influenced it. In 1966, Kenneth Walker published a brief ten-year retrospective of China's collectivization experiment.[2] In the following decade, Thomas Bernstein published several important articles comparing cooperativization in China with Soviet collectivization, giving a good deal

---

1. Gao Huamin, *Nongye hezuohua yundong shimo.*
2. Kenneth R. Walker, "Collectivization in Retrospect."

1

of attention to the High Tide.[3] In 1993, Frederick C. Teiwes and Warren Sun published a documentary collection focusing on the same limited period.[4] In 2006, *China Quarterly* published a High Tide Symposium.[5] More scholarship has been published on the Great Famine, which is becoming a hot topic in Western academia and on the popular book market.[6] Yet the obvious question, "How did the movement start in 1953?" has not been properly addressed: there is no monograph in English devoted to the origins of China's agricultural cooperativization movement.

This lack of attention to the events that preceded the High Tide reflects the conventional wisdom on the origins of agricultural cooperativization. With few exceptions,[7] U.S. scholars assume that Chinese Communist leaders, particularly Mao Zedong, carefully planned the movement and implemented it from the center. These commentators generally regard cooperativization as China's "primitive accumulation," a precursor to industrialization and a method of extracting grain from the countryside.[8] Most scholars have believed that agricultural cooperativization went smoothly between 1953 and 1954, until the High Tide of 1955–1956, when the party accelerated it recklessly. As Christopher Howe summarizes, "the judgment now is that the movement of co-operatives was a success, but that the accelerated shift in early 1956 to the higher level collectives was a huge mistake."[9]

In the United States, more has been written on agricultural cooperativization by economists and political scientists than by historians. Economists, naturally, tend to assess the movement with respect to its impact on China's economy, especially on industrialization. Political scientists, on the other hand, have sought to explain why Chinese peasants did not violently

---

3. Thomas Bernstein, "Keeping the Revolution Going"; "Stalinism, Famine, and Chinese Peasants"; "Leadership and Mass Mobilization."

4. Frederick C. Teiwes and Warren Sun, eds., *Politics of Agricultural Cooperativization.*

5. *China Quarterly* 187 (2006).

6. The most recent monographs include Frank Dikötter, *Mao's Great Famine;* Yang Jisheng, *Tombstone;* Kimberley Ens Manning and Felix Wemheuer, eds., *Eating Bitterness.*

7. For example, Thomas Bernstein, in the articles cited in footnote 3, points out that primitive accumulation was not the CCP's sole aim in agricultural collectivization. He underscores the fact that in the early 1950s the party was losing control over local cadres.

8. Y.Y. Kueh, "Mao and Agriculture." The other articles in the volume take a similar stance.

9. Christopher Howe, "China's High Tide of Socialism."

resist, to the extent that Soviet peasants had, when the government expropriated their property.[10] Both economists and political scientists have focused on the movement's results, rather than its beginnings. They treat the unfolding of cooperativization as a historical "given," which they attribute to Mao Zedong.[11] The paucity of historians' input on this subject, sadly, can be attributed to the scarcity of reliable sources.

The CCP's censorship regime has helped to shape the popular view. In 1981, the party released *The Resolution on Certain Questions on the History of Our Party since the Founding of the People's Republic of China* (*Resolution*), which prescribed authoritative responses to the historical questions raised. The *Resolution* concludes that 1949–1952 was a "good" period, that in 1953 the party made a wise decision to launch agricultural cooperativization, and that prior to 1955 peasants supported the movement.[12] Although the CCP could not control how researchers outside China have interpreted its history, it certainly has had the ability to decide what materials could be published in China. By providing "correct" answers to questions and publishing only documents consistent with those answers, the government indirectly limited the interpretations that were possible. With few sources suggesting a contrary viewpoint, researchers outside China have had to work with whatever materials they could lay their hands on. That led many of them to at least acquiesce in the CCP's master narrative.

Recent Chinese scholarship has moved in a different direction. With better access to local archives and unpublished documents, Chinese historians have uncovered many details of how agricultural cooperativization operated on the ground before 1955. Gao Huamin carefully examines the whole agricultural cooperativization movement and compares it with Soviet collectivization. Despite the different nomenclature and a few operational differences, he argues that in China agricultural cooperativization amounted to collectivization. However, constrained by the limits imposed on him as a

---

10. Yu Liu, "Why Did It Go So High?"

11. From the economic perspective, a few Chinese scholars hold similar views. Lin Yifu, a leading economist in China, explicitly regards cooperativization as China's primitive accumulation, i.e., as a precursor to industrialization (Lin Yifu, Cai Fang, and Li Zhou, *Zhongguo de qiji*). Wen Tiejun, *Zhongguo nongcun*, explains the cooperativization movement as a vehicle for the nationalization of the grain market in 1953.

12. Central Committee of the CCP, *Guanyu jianguo yilai dang de ruogan lishi wenti de jueyi*.

historian by the party, Gao chooses to justify the movement, especially its inception, and proceeds to dwell on why things went wrong in 1955. Mostly concerned with elite politics in Beijing, Gao's book is weakest when it comes to telling what happened to the peasants and how they reacted.[13] In 2002, Du Runsheng, a senior party official who personally participated in and supervised the cooperativization movement, edited a book on the general cooperative movement in China in the twentieth century. Benefiting from special permission to access the Central Party Archives, this volume is a valuable collection of documents. It serves well as a sourcebook, but fails to analyze the documents collected within its covers, as its purpose is to defend cooperativization. According to Du, the CCP's agricultural cooperativization movement was not a mere copy of the Soviet model but was derived from the cooperatives that were widespread in China in the 1930s and 1940s—an explanation that the CCP put forward to appease Chinese peasants and that later became a normative approach in Chinese scholarship.[14] As I argue in this book, this interpretation is misleading. A 2003 study by Xing Leqin focuses on high politics and offers few new insights.[15] Luo Pinghan's work concentrates heavily on the High Tide, and fails to address the origins of cooperativization in 1953.[16]

In 2006, Ye Yangbing published probably the best monograph to date on the subject. Drawing on many local archives across different provinces, Ye explores the beginnings of agricultural cooperativization in detail, discussing how the movement fluctuated over the years and how the peasants reacted. This last topic is the subject of an exhaustive study. However, by focusing solely on the movement itself, Ye overlooks how agricultural cooperativization interacted with the wider political landscape. Like other Chinese scholars, Ye concludes that agricultural cooperativization as a whole was a success.[17] Unfortunately, restricted by the *Resolution*, all the authors mentioned above have had to defend the party's handling of the origins of the movement and to confirm the master narrative. They have clearly not been in a position to challenge the paradigm that agricultural cooperativization was a necessary stage and an effective strategy in the de-

---

13. Gao Huamin, *Nongye hezuohua yundong shimo*.
14. Du Runsheng, *Dangdai zhongguo de nongye hezuo zhi*.
15. Xing Leqin, *20 shiji 50 niandai*.
16. Luo Pinghan, *Nongye hezuohua yundong shi*.
17. Ye Yangbing, *Zhongguo nongye hezuohua yundong yanjiu*.

velopment of the Chinese economy. As a result, Chinese historians and American scholars have continued to embrace a similar conclusion: that agricultural cooperativization began as a well-conceived policy originating at the top level of the CCP and that up to 1955 it was a success.

However, a close reading of contemporary documents and access to county, prefectural, and provincial archives in Shanxi Province have led me to challenge this conventional wisdom and rewrite the history of the early agricultural cooperativization in China. Foremost, in terms of the origins of the movement, it was not only Mao Zedong who started this radical social transformation from above, but also, as early as 1950, Shanxi's provincial leaders who played a crucial role in bringing cooperativization to the national agenda. It appears that those Shanxi leaders cared little about industrialization; rather, they were deeply involved in regional factional fights. To gain an upper hand in political struggles, they invented the form of agricultural producers' cooperatives, established experimental cases, fabricated statistics, exploited splits in the central leadership, and in the end successfully promoted their agenda. Between 1951 and 1952, early experiments in agricultural cooperatives underwent a long, dynamic process of development. Cadres of lower ranks and peasants in Shanxi had different versions of the APCs that would better serve their interests, and thus they pushed forward. Their experimental activities, in turn, reoriented the thinking of higher-ranking cadres. During the course of these experiments, information was filtered, data was inflated, communications were manipulated, and perfect cases were presented by the Shanxi leaders, as I demonstrate in Chapter 3. Regardless, APCs did not go well, even at the experimental stage. Abuses of power, impetuosity, and the disruption of rural productivity clearly plagued the movement, but they have largely escaped scholars' attention. The early cooperativization (1951–1953) caused long-lasting problems that would be repeated in the High Tide; the CCP went down a path toward famine earlier than most scholars have imagined.

Agricultural cooperativization was not simply an adjunct to industrialization. It was part of a broad socialist modernization project that aimed to transform cultural, social, and political relationships in the countryside; it was as much about the redistribution of skill, knowledge, and technical control as it was about the redistribution of land and political power.[18] In nature it reflected the struggle of Chinese leaders, particularly Mao Zedong, to bal-

18. Jacob Eyferth, *Eating Rice from Bamboo Roots*.

ance their intertwined goals of revolution and modernization. As Jeremy Brown points out, on the one hand, Mao wanted to build a strong, prosperous, and modern nation; on the other hand, he sought to make China a more equal and fair society by eliminating class exploitation and redistributing property.[19] The two goals were not easily reconciled, but the Soviet model of collectivization conveniently offered a solution. In theory, it promised to deliver socialism by abolishing private property. As Karl Marx had famously asserted in the *Communist Manifesto*, "The theory of the Communists may be summed up in the single sentence: Abolition of private property."[20] Then Stalin promised and proved on his own terms that collectivization would reduce inequality, integrate the dispersed, small-scale peasant economy into a centralized planned economy, and increase productivity. Even many noncommunist agrarian specialists in the 1930s and 1940s touted the benefits of economies of scale and called for increasing the size of farms to facilitate mechanization.[21] Hence, why not do it?

The beginning of China's agricultural cooperativization is also of great academic significance because it links two heavily researched subjects of modern China: the CCP's peasant policies before 1949 and the collective system that developed after 1953. A great deal of scholarship has been published on the "peasant role" in the Chinese revolution.[22] There is an equally rich literature on the agricultural economy under the collective system.[23] Nevertheless, developments between these two periods have been largely overlooked.[24] The study of the development of China's agricultural cooperativization drive between 1949 and 1953 promises to fill this gap.

Although this book focuses on a single rural policy, that policy was

---

19. Jeremy Brown, *City versus Countryside*, 2.

20. Karl Marx, *Communist Manifesto*, 68.

21. Miao Xinyu, *Jianguo qian 30 nian*.

22. A great deal of material has been published on the pre-1949 era, such as the work of Lucien Bianco, Jean Chesneaux, Chen Yung-fa, David Goodman, Mobo Gao, Kathleen Hartford, William Hinton, Philip Huang, Chalmers Johnson, Pauline Keating, Mark Selden, and Ralph Thaxton.

23. For the post-1953 period, Anita Chan, Richard Madsen, and Jonathan Unger, *Chen Village under Mao and Deng*; Edward Friedman, Paul Pickowicz, and Mark Selden, *Chinese Village, Socialist State*; Huaiyin Li, *Village China under Socialism and Reform*; Jean C. Oi, *State and Peasant in Contemporary China*; Frank Dikötter, *Mao's Great Famine*; Yang Jisheng, *Tombstone*.

24. Vivienne Shue wrote an excellent pioneering study, but she had virtually no access to China's local archives. See her *Peasant China in Transition*.

highly influential and study of it can shed light on crucial themes such as CCP–peasant relations, the significance of land reform, and the importance of the founding years of the People's Republic of China.

The CCP–Peasant Relations

I began my research with one simple question: Given the CCP's reputed rise to power through mobilizing peasants, why did it ultimately fail so comprehensively to serve their interests? Chinese and Western scholars have expatiated tirelessly on how well the CCP knew peasants and how skillfully it mobilized them. But did it really excel in these two areas? What was the real nature of the CCP's relationship with the peasants? To better understand the party's rural policies in the 1950s, this volume sketches the CCP–peasant relationship within the context of the building of a modern state, and it contends that from the outset, the CCP failed to understand Chinese peasants.

James Scott has argued that the building of a "modern state" is a process of simplification, abstraction, and standardization. Social reality is chaotic, disorderly, and constantly changing, and no administrative system is capable of fully representing it. Thus, it is only through a heroic process of abstraction and simplification that the modern state could succeed in making society comprehensible and manageable. Simplification was the most basic tool of modern statecraft. Further, modern state officials have tendencies to bring the facts into line with their simplified views in order to construct a new society, a process that Scott names "the path from description to prescription."[25] The CCP was no exception. What made things worse was that the CCP developed its prescription for the ills of rural society even before it got around the studying and describing that society.

Chinese rural society had gone through dramatic changes since the 1840s, which Chinese intellectuals, generally living in cities, were often liable to ignore. In the 1920s, to be sure, some Chinese intellectuals, who were seeking to revive the nation and build a strong modern state, began incorporating the Chinese rural population in their grand plans for a new China thus set about trying to understand rural "reality." However, rural "reality" was not a fixed entity, but instead it was chaotic, was constantly changing, and varied from place to place. The "reality" was so complex that it could

---

25. James Scott, *Seeing Like a State*.

provide evidence that could be used to support any interpretation. Thus, for some Chinese intellectuals, their varied preconceptions guided them to "discover" different characteristics of the peasants and to prescribe widely varying solutions to rural problems. Chinese Communists were not exceptional in this respect. For example, although the young Mao Zedong dabbled in social Darwinism, liberalism, and anarchism, he soon was drawn to Lenin as a principal mentor and came to follow in his footsteps when approaching peasant issues. Mao was only one of many intellectuals who tended to view the "peasants" as the entities that the CCP *wanted* them to be (see Chapter 1).

The tension between the CCP's image of the peasantry and the reality on the ground was evident during such operations as grain collections, but before 1949, much of this tension was obscured by solidarity induced by constant warfare against a common enemy. One aspect of this tension in early twentieth-century China was the peasants' resistance to the state and state agencies, often for good reasons.[26] During the revolutionary years, the CCP openly positioned itself as an ally of the peasants in their conflicts with the state and gave party organizers considerable flexibility in accommodating peasants' concrete demands at the local level and in finding grounds for common interests with them.[27]

By contrast, when the CCP came to rule China after 1949, party leaders themselves became the state seeking to extract resources from the peasants, and probably adapted to this new role too easily and too quickly. The peasants, however, continued, although mostly passively, to resist the government's efforts to extract their resources. Particularly, tensions over grain grew acute after 1949 as the CCP's demands for grain to feed the urban sector surged, to the point that the party was no longer willing to offer much in return to the peasants. The gulf between the CCP's expectations of peasant enthusiasm for revolutionary sacrifice and the reality in the countryside

---

26. For a good summary of peasants' resistance to government reforms and rural rebels against modernity in late Qing and early Republic era, see Roxann Prazniak, *Of Camel Kings and Other Things*; Lucien Bianco, *Wretched Rebels*; and Lucien Bianco, *Peasants without the Party*.

27. Hartford convincingly shows that, again and again during the revolution, party organizers found that the issue uniting a local community was opposition to the state authorities, primarily over state or quasi-state extraction of produce from the countryside. Kathleen Hartford, "Fits and Starts," 166.

where farmers attempted to keep their surpluses, together with the frustrations in grain collection, set the stage for the CCP's decision to embrace Stalinist collectivization in the early 1950s (see Chapters 2, 3, and 6).

Despite this hardening of attitudes in the party–peasant relationship, the peasants should not be viewed as mere victims of policies formulated at the highest levels of power, and it should not be assumed that there was a simple and clear distinction between the party and the peasants. Groups of peasants or individuals on the receiving end of state policy often joined with political officials in ways that blurred the dichotomy between the party and the peasants. In what follows, I demonstrate the complexity of the relationship between the two groups—sometimes oppositional, sometimes symbiotic. In reality, the peasants constituted a diverse social force—made up of individuals who perceived their interests differently, who made different calculations of life strategies, and who sought to adapt directives from the center in different ways. In Chapters 4 and 5 I examine the fluctuations in the Mutual Aid and Cooperation movement between 1951 and 1953, showing how peasants turned the policy to their advantage and sought to pursue individual profit. However, the peasants' reactions in turn propelled the party to strengthen its control, to strip the peasants of their capacity to adapt the system to their own ends.

Simplifications are necessary for modern states, and gaps between the states' perceptions of the reality and the facts on the ground are intrinsic. Problems arise when the states can no longer neglect the gaps and are compelled to try to "fix" them. In observing the facts, Chinese Communists already had in their minds a vision of what the facts *should* be. Inspired by the socialist ideals of order and planning, they tried to make the facts conform to their imagined ideal type. This is a process from which tragedies often result.[28] This book shows how the CCP cadres stubbornly imposed socialist programs to get peasants organized, even after repeated failures. Blaming peasants' selfishness for the failures, the cadres responded by formulating more rigid programs with increasing socialist features, including remolding minds. In fact, an interesting—and neglected—aspect of modern China is the degree to which the state was reluctantly pulled into the troublesome and expensive micromanagement of society in ways that it did not intend.

---

28. Jacob Eyferth, *Eating Rice from Bamboo Roots*, 3.

Land and Land Reform

From the 1920s, Chinese Communists instituted land reform as the primary tool for mobilizing the peasants. Land reform remained the CCP's central rural policy until 1951. Constrained by censorship, even to the present day, Chinese scholars have overwhelmingly endorsed land reform as the right path to lift the peasants out of poverty. Some well-known works by non-Chinese scholars have also depicted Chinese peasants as embracing land reform.[29] But if we focus on the correlation between land reform and agricultural production, a sobering truth emerges: land reform was far from being an elixir producing rural prosperity.

The Communists assumed that the unequal distribution of land was the main cause of rural poverty. In a widely repeated formula, Mao Zedong asserted that landlords and rich peasants, together accounting for only 8 percent of rural households, owned 70–80 percent of the land.[30] In the absence of any national land survey before 1949, it is not clear how Mao arrived at these statistics, but the figure later became official dogma. Many scholars, in hindsight and with reliable evidence, have charged Mao with exaggerating the concentration of land ownership.[31] Having overestimated the extent of the inequality, the CCP assumed that there would be adequate land for all peasants once the extensive holdings of landlords and rich peasants had been redistributed.[32] This was no doubt far from the truth. The major problem for Chinese peasants was not uneven land distribution, but an extremely low land/population ratio: "The simple truth was that there did not exist sufficient resources to create prosperous proprietor–farmers in nearly 100 percent proportion to the total peasant population."[33] Tanaka estimates that in North China, if all land owned by landlords and rich peasants had been redistributed, only about two-thirds of poor peasant families would have achieved self-sufficiency, which required a minimum of five mu per capita.[34]

---

29. These include William Hinton, *Fanshen,* and Isobel Crook and David Crook, *Mass Movement in a Chinese Village.*

30. *Selected Works of Mao Tse-tung,* Vol. 4, 164.

31. For a historiographic review of research on this subject, see Liu Kexiang, "20 shiji 30 niandai."

32. Tanaka Kyoko, "Mao and Liu in 1947 Land Reform."

33. Ibid.

34. 1 mu = 1/6 acre.

Equal land distribution in itself was no solution. Tanaka argues that one reason why land reform became increasingly radical between 1946 and 1948 was that the party overestimated the land owned by landlords and rich peasants and kept pressing them to give up additional land that they did not own.[35]

My own case study in Shanxi Province supports Tanaka's findings. There, the level of land concentration fell far below Mao's estimate. Historically, farmers with no land of their own were extremely rare in Shanxi; most farmers were small landowners. Rural surveys in the 1930s revealed that owner–farmers comprised 57.67 percent of rural households; only 11.36 percent of rural households were tenants.[36] Between 1946 and 1948, land reform was carried out and the available land was almost equally redistributed among local peasants. After the land reform, on average, a middle-ranking peasant owned 3.5 mu of land, a poor peasant owned 3.3 mu, and a former landlord or rich peasant owned about 3 mu. For example, a survey of Yaozizhen village in Shanxi Province following land reform showed that the average output was 3.6 dan per capita[37]—an amount that barely allowed peasants to make ends meet.[38] Following the reform, many peasants could not subsist merely on the agricultural output of their land; income from sidelines became crucial to their survival. Land reform alone could not solve the problem of land shortage in China. Moreover, as I discuss in Chapter 1, as far as the material security of the peasants was concerned, there was no absolute correlation between land ownership and well-being.

At the time in the late Republic, a few Chinese scholars were acutely conscious of the flaws inherent in land reform. For example, Dong Shijin, the leading agronomist in China, who had received his PhD in agricultural economics from Cornell University in 1925 and was dubbed "the no. 1 in Chinese agriculture," was profoundly uneasy with land reform. In December 1949, he wrote to Mao Zedong, admonishing him not to carry out land

---

35. Tanaka Kyoko, "Mao and Liu in 1947 Land Reform."

36. Shanxi sheng difang zhi bangongshi, *Shanxi tongzhi*, 86.

37. *Dan* is the basic unit of weight used in pre-modern China. The value of 1 dan varied widely according to the locations, ranging from 80 catties, 100 catties, 120 catties or 150 catties. In this book, without specification, 1 dan = 150 catties = 167 pounds.

38. "Changzhi diweiqu jieshu tugai qingkuang" (The outcome of Changzhi prefecture's completion of land reform), Jincheng Municipal Archive (JMA), 1949. 004.2.

reform. In the letter, Dong argued that land was not a means of production: by itself, land could not produce grain. Land was not simply a natural resource, but an artificial construct—fertile land was the product of intense human labor, uncultivated land was almost worthless. Because land was not simply a natural product, its value and fertility could be impaired by neglect or maltreatment.[39]

Dong went further, pointing out that unlike in Russia, China's land system was far from "feudal" and that land ownership was not the primary means of exploitation; in fact, taking land from its rightful owners violated the principles of law and order. If the CCP continued the practice of land reform, Dong warned, negative consequences would follow. In the short term, landowners demoralized by the prospect of land redistribution would stop investing in and improving their holdings, resulting in a loss of fertility. Following the land reform, he argued, each peasant would own only a small parcel of land. Because small farmers' productivity levels were generally inferior to those of the large land owners, small holding did not result in more productivity; if everyone owned tiny pockets of land, then land yields would certainly fall. Speaking candidly, Dong added that because landlords and rich peasants formed China's social elite and helped society advance, they should be protected and encouraged. All poor peasants aspired to become rich peasants and landlords; they were not morally superior to the rich. Giving poor peasants a tiny plot was not the best way of helping them: they would become attached to a piece of land that would prove to be too small to support their families. When pressured by the CCP to pay agricultural taxes, resentment would quickly spring up and spread. In sum, if Chinese peasants, good and bad farmers alike, were all to be given the same amount of land, land fertility would decline over the long term.[40] So concerned was Dong over the issue that he dispatched hundreds of copies of his letter to other CCP leaders and intellectuals; however, they all disappeared like so many drops in the ocean. In 1950, Dong Shijin published a book in Hong Kong vehemently criticizing the party's land reform policy.[41] In 1951, he left China for the United States, where he served as an agricultural advisor to the State Department.

Dong's concerns were only too prescient, as I spell out in Chapter 3.

---

39. Dong Shijin, "Dong Shijin zhixin Mao Zedong tan tugai."
40. Ibid.
41. Dong Shijin, *Lun gongchandang de tudi gaige.*

However, the CCP was little concerned with heeding dissenting voices. The party found it all too convenient to overlook the fact that agricultural production is a complex business that involves not only land but also the contributions made by human expertise and labor, financial credits, livestock, farming tools, and supplies of fertilizer and seeds.[42] Where a family business is involved, additional factors such as the number of workers available, various sidelines, personal qualities like diligence, initiative, and the ability to read, and the element of luck all count toward economic success.[43] Land by itself does not produce rice, wheat, or cotton; it produces only weeds. Hence the redistribution of land alone did not guarantee higher production. On the contrary, land reform broke some important links in the agricultural production chain and disrupted the established farming cycle. The party failed to understand that redistribution tends to undermine rather than boost agricultural production, at least in the short term. In a broad sense, it not only misunderstood the relationship between productivity and the land, but also misunderstood the human relationship with the land. The common mentality that views humans as alienated from the natural world and nature as a resource to be exploited was further amplified by the Maoist ideology of a "war against nature," as Shapiro labels it. [44] As part of nature, the land was there to be conquered. Thus, the party had underestimated the complex repercussions of the land reform.

In the revolutionary years, the Chinese Communists acquired their revenue from confiscations, that is, from the redistribution of existing agricultural output rather than from increased yields. At this stage, the CCP apparently gave little thought to the correlation between land reform and agricultural productivity (see Chapter 1). But after 1949, the CCP had to

---

42. Steven Levine, *Anvil of Victory*, 177–216.

43. Moshe Lewin, *Russian Peasants and Soviet Power*, 44.

44. Judith Shapiro, *Mao's War against Nature*, 5. Mao Zedong, in 1917, wrote a short poem that could be understood either as "To fight together with heaven, it is great! To fight together with earth, it is great! To fight together with men, it is great!" or "To fight against heaven, it is great! To fight against earth, it is great! To fight against men, it is great!" Later the original verses were shortened and the latter interpretation prevailed. In retrospect, indeed Mao's life experience has conformed to the latter interpretation. Mao Zedong, "Self-encouragement: To Fight" (1917), available online http://www.bangnishouji.com/html/201510/219727.html, accessed November 10, 2015.

face a rural dilemma created by land redistribution. Once land was distributed more evenly, the party anticipated a static countryside, a situation that in reality could not last. Land reform divided land into smaller strips and produced numerous smallholdings, contradicting the then popular theory advocating large-scale production in agriculture.[45] It eliminated the households that produced most of the marketable surplus (landlords and rich peasants); at the same time, it created numerous households oriented to subsistence. As a result, it jeopardized food supply to the market, a consequence that the CCP never foresaw and was ill prepared to manage when it came to power in 1949 (see Chapter 3).

Reexamination of the "Good Years"

The *Resolution* depicts the period from 1949 to 1952 as the "good years" of Mao's China. According to this interpretation, all went well in China until 1953 when Mao Zedong, driven by a rigid ideology, launched a series of dramatic socialist transformation campaigns. In my view, this explanation represents a severe distortion of the CCP's painstaking transformation of its members from revolutionaries to rulers. The founding years of the PRC were a time of chaos, uncertainty, and fluidity. CCP leaders constantly asked themselves why they should adopt one kind of policy and not another. While their long-term goal was to build a wealthy and powerful socialist China, definitive knowledge of the first step to be taken eluded them. The only unchallengeable authority in the party, Mao Zedong, did not articulate his vision—probably because he was unable to formulate it for himself. Meanwhile, the other party leaders discussed, debated, and clashed over a variety of issues.[46]

The CCP was never a uniform bloc. There were tensions between cadres from the "white" (Guomindang-dominated) areas and those from "red" (Communist base) areas, and there were long-held prejudices between na-

---

45. Miao Xinyu, "Jianguo qian 30 nian."

46. Scholars have noted the CCP's difficult shift in its center of gravity from the village to the city and focused on the party's political consolidation in urban centers. Ezra Vogel, *Canton under Communism*; Kenneth Lieberthal, *Revolution and Tradition in Tientsin, 1949–1952*; James Gao, *Communist Takeover of Hangzhou*; Jeremy Brown, *City Versus Countryside*.

tive cadres and outsiders, for example. The situation was particularly tense in the founding years of the People's Republic, when the CCP was in the process of transforming from a decentralized wartime political system to a centralized hierarchical administration. Powerful figures at all levels sought to define their new political positions and fought with one another to demarcate their zones of influence; the Central Committee of the party in Beijing struggled to establish its authority with respect to national issues and to extend its control down to the local level. Hierarchies were in a continual process of being reconfigured (see Chapter 2).

Before 1949, the CCP's political system was marked by local initiatives and a lack of political accountability for failure.[47] For most of this time, the Chinese Communists worked from geographically unconnected base areas. Relations between center and peripheries were decidedly informal. Decentralized initiatives were often encouraged, or at least allowed. At the same time, local leaders often failed to take responsibility for their mistakes on the economic front. As a result of these various factors, local officials had strong incentives to launch experiments, especially involving more progressive programs. If a program succeeded, it would significantly bolster its promoters' political careers; if it failed, self-criticism would suffice. Until 1949, this rough-and-ready system seemed to work. Local initiatives fit well with regional variations and a decentralized political system.[48] Even when they failed, the damage was confined to a single region.

In 1949, the CCP was in the process of working out a centralized bureaucratic hierarchy. Two opposing pressures were at work. On the one hand, local officials continued their practice of taking local initiatives and experimenting with new policies, hoping to contribute to the new China as well as advance their own careers. On the other hand, Beijing was seeking tighter political integration by relying on centralized command and ideological control in its management of the provinces. The CCP leaders in Beijing opted to implement most, if not all, policies at the national level. Once a local initiative was adopted by Beijing, it likely would be forcefully applied across China, often in dogmatic uniformity; the "one-knife-cuts-all" approach was pursued regardless of regional variations and local practices.

Given this general approach, individual party operatives, even those of

---

47. Sebastian Heilmann and Elizabeth Perry, "Embracing Uncertainty," 24.
48. Jae Ho Chung, "Central–Local Dynamics," 300.

relatively low ranks, could on occasion have a significant impact on the nation. This reality is not well understood in much of the scholarly literature. Without denying Mao's dominant role, my concern in this book is to explore the roles of others who occupied lower rungs on the ladder of power. One such story is told in Chapter 3. Between 1950 and 1951, Lai Ruoyu, the governor of Shanxi Province, proved so adept at manipulating local initiatives that he ultimately succeeded in introducing his agricultural producers' cooperatives across China. In the process, Lai's faction in the party consolidated its control over Shanxi. As the epilogue expounds, Lai's career raises a crucial question about the political system created by Mao: What kind of bureaucracy was it?

Underlying Lai Ruoyu's socialist program were the practical difficulties the CCP faced in running countryside. Chapter 3 tells the story of how lower-ranked CCP cadres, frustrated by post–land reform reality, exhausted by day-to-day management of peasants, and fueled by their personal ambitions and local interests, demanded Stalinist-style collectivization. Only through their eyes can we see what collectivization meant to China. For scholars with the benefit of hindsight, collectivization represented the most repressive aspect of the Soviet model, which robbed the people of life and joy. But for many party cadres, the Stalinist model offered a solution to the problems involved in running the newly established China, not merely in the rural sector. Only when we appreciate these concerns can we ask the next question: Why in 1953 did Mao insist on introducing a full range of socialist transformation programs? Was it because, following the good years, China was ready for a transition, or, quite the opposite, because things did not go according to plan and Soviet models came to the rescue? This last question suggests a new perspective for approaching the founding years of the PRC.

Methods and Sources

In Mao's China, what or who decided the people's fate? This question has generated much debate. The "top-down" approach has portrayed an overwhelmingly powerful party hierarchy that closely monitored how people lived. By contrast, in recent years microstudies of particular Chinese villages and counties have adopted a "bottom-up" approach, emphasizing Chinese people's capacity to adapt to and even to influence policies imposed from above.[49] In this book, I examine previously overlooked agents working between these two extremes: government cadres of intermediate rank. Government cadres at the provincial, prefectural and county levels not only carried out orders from the center, but also interpreted or represented the people's responses, sometimes even taking the initiative to manipulate the communications between the center and the people. Only when we take this vital third layer into account can we observe the mechanism of Communist China from the top down, from the bottom up, and from government agents in between. We shall analyze this mechanism particularly in regard to the development of China's agricultural cooperativization movement. Viewing Communist China through the eyes of its cadres, we will come to a better understanding of how the regime worked and how it departed from the blueprint created by the party elite.[50] James Hughes reaches the same conclusion regarding Stalinist collectivization: "Policies were not always vertically channeled 'from above' in pure totalitarian fashion but often emerged from a complex bureaucratic interaction between the central, regional and local tiers of government."[51]

This book is based on extensive written sources, ranging from archival materials, local census returns, internally circulated reports to newspapers, and published documents. A significant proportion of these are party documents. Although I share other scholars' skepticism regarding the utility of party documents, I believe that if we read them against one another, we can extract a wealth of information from them.

While access to the Central Archives in Beijing remains a prerogative for a few party scholars, local archives have become increasingly accessible in recent years. I had the good fortune to be admitted to a number of archives in Shanxi Province, including the Shanxi Provincial Archive, Jincheng Municipal Archive (which contains documents from former Changzhi prefecture), Changzhi Municipal Archive, and Wuxiang County Archive. I discovered that investigative reports were regularly written on particular vil-

---

49. Anita Chan, Richard Madsen, and Jonathan Unger, *Chen Village under Mao and Deng*; Edward Friedman, Paul Pickowicz and Mark Selden, *Chinese Village, Socialist State*; Mobo Gao, *Gao Village*; Huaiyin Li, *Village China under Socialism and Reform*; Huang Shu-min, *Spiral Road*.

50. For a similar case, see Gail Kligman and Katherine Verdery, *Peasants under Siege*, 151.

51. James Hughes, *Stalinism in a Russian Province*, 207.

lages and counties and were submitted to the prefecture. Prefectural officials often drew statistics selectively from these reports, drafted simplified (and sometimes distorted) versions, and submitted them to the provincial cadres. Provincial officials emended them further and forwarded the edited reports to the North China Bureau, and sometimes directly to Beijing. At each layer of editing, some inconvenient aspects were deleted while other agendas were added. One example of such filtering and falsifying is presented in detail in Chapter 3. Although in a given case we lack the evidence to show which version was the closest to reality, an experienced eye can discern what had been deleted and what had been added through the process of channeling. This process reveals the issues that concerned the party's leaders, what they saw as problems and what they did not. These local archives reflect the architecture of the party apparatus. The reports are themselves hierarchical in character; by drafting or editing them, competing groups promoted their own interests and refined their agendas. Communications back and forth expose traces of the complex links that held China's enormous bureaucracy together.[52]

In my particular case, because Shanxi provincial leaders consistently defied their superiors at the North China Bureau, the latter regularly dispatched work teams to Shanxi. These teams submitted their reports, which likely reflected a different "reality," the one molded by the North China Bureau's agenda. Many of these reports highlighted mistakes and mismanagement in Shanxi. Combining reports from Shanxi and from the North China Bureau allows us to draw conclusions that may approximate the rural situation.

Some of these archival materials are valuable for what they inadvertently reveal, for example, the records of party committee meetings in Shanxi, which show evidence of internal disputes and competing factions. Certainly, some archival sources should not be taken at face value. For example, agricultural output figures were routinely massaged to satisfy the targeted audience of officials, who, in turn, were willingly deceived because the data reported would serve their interests. What were the limits of such falsification and the risks shouldered by these report writers? For the period under investigation, 1949–1952, it seems that there was a divide between possible, if not real, and illusionary numbers, a gap that would gradually

---

52. For a recent assessment of the value of official archives in socialist countries, see Kligman and Verdery, *Peasants under Siege*, 17.

fade and ultimately evaporate in 1958 when cadres were taught, "The size of your stomach will determine the size of your harvest." This implied that the land's output depended on one's determination of how high it could go and that nothing was impossible.

One important source is the restricted-access publication *Internal References* (*Neibu cankao*), which is still compiled in China today. The series publishes reports from low- to high-ranking party leaders. Its function is to regularly report ordinary people's mood, situations, and reactions to specific party policies. Issues are supposed to be circulated strictly internally and are allegedly uncensored. Many Chinese commentators believe that the issues prior to 1955 were more reliable, and that after 1956, they began to conform to party propaganda and declined in value.[53] Partly on the basis of reading these reports, party leaders, Mao Zedong included, responded to problems and complaints, and modified policies accordingly. Mao Zedong occasionally annotated the reports. This set of sources gives us a privileged window through which to observe what the CCP leaders knew.

This book also draws information from oral history. In the late 1980s, the journal *Documents on China's Agricultural Cooperativization* (*Zhongguo nongye hezuoshi ziliao*) sponsored a series of interviews with hand-picked peasants.[54] In recent years, Chinese scholars have managed to interview a number of high-ranking party members who served in Shanxi Province in the early 1950s. The interview of Han Chunde, a member of CCP's Shanxi provincial committee between 1949 and 1953, offers invaluable insights of the internal feuds in Shanxi. The interview was released, following Han's instructions, only after his death.[55]

The major problem with the sources is not in the censored documents, but rather in the documents' uncritical conformity to the categories that the CCP created. Thus the sources, whatever their content, fall under the

---

53. This is confirmed by Xiaojia Hou's conversations with Zhang Baijia in 2002 and Yang Kuisong in 2009; both are prominent party historians working in China.

54. *Zhongguo nongye hezuoshi ziliao*, Beijing, nos. 1–10.

55. Ren Fuxing's interviews with Han Chunde, March 9 and March 12, 2003, Beijing, available online http://difangwenge.org/read.php?tid=1549, accessed March 2, 2012. Han Chunde (1913–2000) was a Communist leader in Shanxi Province. In 1949, he served as the mayor of Taiyuan, the capital of Shanxi Province. Between 1949 and 1953, he was a member of CCP's Shanxi provincial committee, the leading circle of Shanxi. He left Shanxi in 1953.

shadow of preexisting master narratives. For example, the CCP uses the word *nongmin* (translated as "peasants" in this book) to refer to the rural population excluding landlords. It seems that peasants and landlords together occupy the whole Chinese countryside. The word "peasants" fails to account for many different status groups in the Chinese countryside. In reports, the CCP further divides peasants into categories such as "poor," "middle," and "rich," which at best reflect the households' economic holdings at one point in the past (when the party determined their class status), but obscure features like education, family affiliations, and the structure of the household. Although peasants' reactions and adaptive strategies are not determined solely by their class background, their class background is such an integral part of their objective identities, that it appears pervasively relevant in peasants' decision-making and actions. On paper, peasants appear extremely conscious of their class status while their actual social status and subjective identities often remain vague. If there were a way of avoiding the terms used by the party officials at the time, we might avoid the bias inherent in these master narratives. But the inconvenient truth is that if we disregard these terms, there would be little left, since we cannot escape the social structure that these terms reflect. Here I face the dilemma of seeking to make my subject comprehensible while being forced to use the terminology of the times—but always with awareness that it is problematic and is itself the reflection of a particular set of agendas.

So how did the CCP come to understand, or misunderstand, Chinese peasants?

1

Coming to Understand Peasants

The poor peasants, especially the portion who are utterly destitute, are the most revolutionary group.

—Mao Zedong (1927)[1]

The peasants actually have a lot of the landlords' mentality ... [Mao] did what he wanted to anyhow, and did not bother with careful research.

—local CCP cadres' comments on Mao's policy on the poor peasants (early 1940s)[2]

What we (the CCP) are doing and what we are saying are both remote from the masses. What the masses know and what the masses want are completely different from what we think of them as knowing and wanting. Today even cadres of peasant origin are talking the Party rhetoric.

—Zhang Wentian (1942)[3]

Realities: The Demise of an Old Story

In the long history of China, two broad historical processes dominated the first half of the twentieth century: the intrusion of capitalism and the building of a modern state. Together they transformed Chinese society and

1. Mao Zedong, "Report on the Peasant Movement in Hunan," 429–464.
2. David Goodman, *Social and Political Change in Revolutionary China*, 265.
3. Zhang Wentian xuanji zhuanjizu, *Zhang Wentian jinshan diaocha wenji*, 291.

placed the people at the mercy of the market and the increasingly intrusive state.[4] The peasants were no exceptions to these trends.

Scholars have disagreed about the nature of economic changes in rural society since the Opium War (1839–1842). Chinese Communist historians concur that the countryside experienced bankruptcy and that imperialism was to blame. Western scholars hold more diverse views. The moral economy school, represented by Eric Wolf, Robert Marks, and Ralph Thaxton, acknowledges the rural decline, but does not blame imperialism, instead attributing it to capitalist expansion and the building of a modern state, which destroyed China's traditional rural community and devastated the lives of the peasants.[5] A second group of Western scholars attributes the decline in China's rural economy to domestic factors. For example, R.H. Tawney lists the heavy tax burden, warlordism, population pressures, and uneconomic landholdings as causes. James Thomson attributes China's rural crisis to population pressures and ecological deterioration.[6] A third school of Western scholarship argues that the rural economy was stagnating rather than declining. This school is represented by Philip Huang, whose theory of "involutionary growth" describes a situation of economic growth without development. He attributes this phenomenon in rural China mainly to population pressures and a lack of technological advancement.[7] In contrast, a fourth group of scholars argues that following the Opium War, the rural economy indeed experienced development and commercialization and prospered until the 1920s, when China was consumed by civil war.[8]

Scholars in these various schools have based their studies on different bodies of research and adopted incommensurable standards. They established different theoretical models, paradigms, and assumptions in investigating Chinese peasants.[9] With no reliable statistics available at the national

---

4. Prasenjit Duara, *Culture, Power and the State.*

5. Eric Wolf, *Peasant Wars of the Twentieth Century*; Robert Marks, *Rural Revolution in South China*; Ralph Thaxton, *Salt of the Earth.*

6. James Thomson, *While China Faced West.*

7. Philip Huang, *Peasant Economy and Social Change in North China.*

8. Ramon Myers, "Agrarian System"; Thomas Rawski, *Economic Growth in Prewar China.*

9. For examination of the empirical and theoretical arguments contained in controversies in understanding Chinese peasants and peasant China, see Daniel Little, *Understanding Peasant China.*

level, the debate will no doubt continue without consensus emerging. However, scholars agree that Chinese peasants were subject to substantial changes that linked them more closely than ever to the market. Even in the North China plain, also called by some in this period the "hinterland," which was considered more self-reliant, farmers engaged in markets in complex ways.[10] For example, the leading crop in the North China plain was wheat, but the main staple for peasants was millet. Peasants chose to sell fine wheat for higher prices in the market, while purchasing cheaper millet for their own consumption. Cotton farmers sold much of their cotton in markets, purchased cheap machine-spun yarn from markets, wove cloth, and put their native cloth on markets again.[11] Often a small group of wealthy households, using the production of tenants and/or hired laborers, supplied half or more of the surplus marketed by the villages in a given area.[12] By the turn of the twentieth century, Chinese peasants had managed to adapt to rapid population growth and land shortages through rationalizing production, crop specialization, commercialization, and the export of labor.[13] A new agrarian system based on the market had emerged, but it was fragile, complex, and highly interdependent in character, exposing peasants to fluctuations in the market that occurred even beyond China. As Chinese peasants planted more cash crops and industrial crops that generated higher returns, domestic food production stagnated. Annually between the late 1920s and 1937, China imported grain from the world market, ranging between 0.4 billion catties and 4 billion catties.[14] The ideal of a closed, self-sufficient rural community was an illusion and was radically out of touch with reality.[15] However, many Chinese intellectuals, including Mao Zedong, retained a belief in this comforting myth.

Chinese peasants were eking out a precarious existence, a situation co-

10. Kenneth Pomeranz, *Making of A Hinterland*.

11. Cong Hanxiang, *Jindai ji lu yu xiangcun*.

12. Roman Myers, "Agrarian System," 254–256.

13. Surveys taken during the 1920s and 1930s reported that Chinese rural families sold a very high proportion of what they produced. For example, in 1937, John Buck found that roughly 50 percent of family income came from market sales. John Buck, *Land Utilization in China*.

14. Zhao Fasheng ed., *Dangdai liangshi gongzuo shiliao*, 33.

15. Philip Kuhn, *Origins of the Modern Chinese State*, 112; William Skinner, "Regional Urbanization in Nineteenth-Century China."

incident with the internal decay in rural society. In Ming and early Qing dynasties, governments levied taxes, corvées, and military conscription on the peasantry. However, in most other respects, the governments' writ stopped at the village gates. To govern the countryside, the state cooperated with local gentry, which—roughly speaking—acted as the mediators between the state and the peasants.[16] They were not government agents, had no power to levy taxes, and were forbidden from raising private armies. However, in the middle of the nineteenth century this system was seriously undermined by the Taiping Rebellion (1850–1864).[17] Anxious to secure help to quash the rebellion, the Qing government urged local elites to form militias and allowed them to levy taxes to finance their forces.[18] When the rebellion ended, local elites continued to manage local services; in so doing, they inevitably came into conflict with officialdom for control of resources and local authority. As a result, their willingness to stand up to the government on behalf of "their" peasants diminished.[19] Prasenjit Duara applies a different model, but draws a similar conclusion. He uses the brokerage model, as opposed to the gentry–society model, to analyze the way in which the imperial state in China dealt with rural communities. He categorizes two types of state brokers: entrepreneurial and protective. The former group viewed their jobs in terms of entrepreneurial categories such as clerks and runners at all levels of the subbureaucracy; the latter was drawn from the local community and sought to protect the interests of the community against the demands of the state and the entrepreneurial brokers. On the basis of his model, Duara observes the expansion of entrepreneurial brokers and the decline of protective brokers during the early twentieth century.[20]

During the Taiping Rebellion, fearing for their own safety, numerous wealthy families left their home villages for nearby towns. Many never returned. The outflow continued in the late nineteenth and early twentieth centuries. Higher standards of living, a greater variety of entertainment, and

---

16. Prasenjit Duara, *Culture, Power and the State*, 180.

17. The Taiping Rebellion was a military and social movement that, under its leader Hong Xiuquan, sought to overthrow the Qing and establish a "Heavenly Kingdom of Great Peace" in China. Jonathan Spence, *Search for Modern China*, 63.

18. Philip Kuhn, *Rebellion and Its Enemies in Late Imperial China*.

19. Mary Rankin, *Elite Activism and Political Transformation in China*.

20. Prasenjit Duara, *Culture, Power and the State: Rural North China*.

better educational opportunities lured more and more well-off rural families into the towns and cities. The number of absentee landlords rose. The impact of this wholesale desertion by the elite classes from their native villages was far-reaching. Now out of touch, these families could no longer sponsor the welfare programs they had traditionally supported; when disaster struck their former communities, they could no longer provide financial aid, even in the form of usury, to help give local families a new start. As a result, the villages became less resilient, a problem compounded by the collapse of the rural education system, which was traditionally tied to the civil service examinations.[21] When the Qing government abolished the examinations in 1905, the old rural education system fell apart. Offering courses ranging from the Chinese classics to science, modern schools required much greater investment and employed more staff. Few villages could afford them. More often than not, modern schools were built in towns and cities, drawing promising students away from the countryside; few returned to their home villages. Ironically, those who came back often chose to challenge the traditional rural system rather than support it. Many of these newly educated returnees became the earliest members of the Communist movement.[22]

For China's peasants, the creation of a modern state exacerbated the deterioration of their daily life. The process began with a series of reforms undertaken by the Qing dynasty in the late 1800s and continued uninterrupted throughout the twentieth century. The building of a modern state in China resembled the process undergone in early modern Europe, which included bureaucratization and rationalization, the drive to increase revenues for both military and civilian purposes, and the state's efforts to form alliances with new elites. This process was accompanied by the state's penetration into many facets of daily life and its extraction of resources. To finance a rapidly expanding administration, defense organizations, and modern schools, old taxes were increased and new ones levied, often in the form of surcharges. Bianco estimates that in the nineteenth century land taxes were between 2 and 4 percent of total land yield, with the exception of the

---

21. The purpose of rural education was to train students to pass the civil service examinations; the tutors were usually scholars who had passed the first level of these exams, but had failed to proceed further.

22. Lucien Bianco, *Peasants without the Party*, 44.

rich eastern part of the lower Yangzi River, where fiscal burdens were traditionally heavier. From around 1905, land taxes rose sharply.[23] An even bigger burden for peasants was the new surcharges. After 1914, localities were officially permitted to levy a surcharge on many taxes. These rapidly became one of the most arbitrary exactions levied and almost impossible to supervise. To give an idea of the scale of these exactions, Duara found that in 1934, five million yuan in revenue collected by all the counties of Hebei Province came from surcharges, compared with the provincial revenue of six million yuan raised from the land tax. These statistics are simply the figures that were recorded; further tax collection evaded official record-keeping.[24]

Peasants' traditional guardians, the gentry, withdrew from village life or took up new interests.[25] Fewer respectable gentry were willing to serve as village heads, and those who did so often saw the office as a means of feathering their own nests. They based their power on sources outside the traditional nexus, sometimes relying on brute strength and physical intimidation; but more often they derived their power from their links with county and subcounty administrations.[26] They tended to side with the state to extract even more from the peasants rather than making attempts to protect the local community. Thus new village headmen were often the local bullies—the authorities the peasants resented most. Official extortion in connection with tax collection was the most common reason for peasant riots. Bianco identifies two main periods of peasant uprisings, 1906–1911 and 1926–1936, both coinciding with major government reforms. The first period witnessed the Qing's new policies that attempted to rebuild local administration, survey land, and raise taxes; the second was the era when the Guomindang government came to power and introduced similar policies.[27]

In brief, from the mid–nineteenth century Chinese rural society underwent a series of dramatic socioeconomic and political changes. These

---

23. Ibid., 91.

24. Prasenjit Duara, *Culture, Power and the State,* 65–79.

25. Chang Chung-li, *Chinese Gentry*; Philip Kuhn, *Rebellion and Its Enemies in Late Imperial China*; Mary Rankin, *Elite Activism and Political Transformation in China.*

26. Prasenjit Duara, *Culture, Power and the State,* 223.

27. Lucien Bianco, *Wretched Rebels,* 91–110.

changes reached a crisis point in the 1920s, when surging taxes outstripped crop prices increases and the market turned against the peasants.[28] During the worldwide economic depression, prices for cash crops fell more rapidly than grain prices. It became harder for peasants to afford grain from the market, but many were too poor to allocate resources of land and labor to alternatives.[29] Constant warfare nurtured more predators, who competed to drain even more resources from peasants. The decade of the 1920s was truly a watershed. Shen Congwen, China's leading pastoral novelist of the time and a man with no political affiliations, visited his native village in 1934, after an absence of eighteen years. He found that "everything is different." He wrote, "On the surface it appears that everything has progressed tremendously, but following a careful examination, you will find a tendency to decadence in the transition. The most obvious thing is that the integrity, simplicity and beauty of humanity has almost completely disappeared." He concluded that "excessive taxes and levies and opium have sunk the peasants into destitution and laziness."[30]

In desperation, increasing numbers of peasants took to joining the army as a career path to support themselves and their families. In a survey of one regiment in North China in the 1920s, of more than 5,000 soldiers, 87.3 percent were from rural areas and 68 percent sent money back home to support their families. The most striking statistic is that 21.3 percent were only sons. For a family to send their single son to the army was nearly unheard of in Chinese tradition, but now that taboo had been broken, it was a sure sign of the desperation experienced by many rural families.[31] Meanwhile, peasant soldiers engaged in constant warfare became skilled in the use of modern weapons and more aware of the larger world outside their villages. When an army was disbanded or defeated, demobilized soldiers returned to their home villages bearing arms. Some competed for local leadership; others came to see crime as a way of life. It was not uncommon for peasants to farm their lands during the growing season and resort to robbery to make ends meet during the off-season.

From the 1920s to the 1940s, observers frequently recorded the break-

---

28. Lucien Bianco, *Peasants without the Party*, 91.
29. Roman Myers, "Agrarian System," 260–264.
30. Xiaorong Han, *Chinese Discourses on the Peasant, 1900–1949*, 38.
31. Zhang Ming, *Xiangcun shehui quanli*.

down of law and order, the disruption of transportation, and recurring famines in rural China. This was the time when many urban intellectuals turned their attention to peasant issues. Studies of rural China proliferated. Harry Lamley estimates that between 1926 and 1936, as many as 691 private or state-sponsored groups turned their attention to reform of the countryside; liberal intellectuals Liang Shuming and Yan Yangchu were among the most prominent of these intellectuals.[32] Many projects aimed at promoting mass education, economic cooperation, popular participation, agricultural technology, household industries, and the construction of public works. However, few produced lasting positive results.

Chinese Peasants in Perceptions

At the beginning of the twentieth century, Chinese intellectuals of virtually all schools perceived Chinese peasants as backward. Most of them referred to the peasants in the third person as "they."[33] Chen Duxiu, the cofounder of the CCP, and Sun Yat-sen, the founder of the Guomindang, were alike in criticizing Chinese peasants for their ignorance and seeming indifference to politics. Li Dazhao, One of the earliest Marxists in China and another cofounder of the CCP, in 1917 described the countryside as a dark and uneducated world. Yan Yangchu, a Western-trained liberal who later became a symbol of the mass education movement in China, also stressed the ignorance of the peasants in his writings. Similar attitudes are found in contemporary perceptions of the Boxer Rebellion (1899–1900), which arose among poor peasants and was widely perceived as a product of xenophobia, superstition and barbarism.[34]

The tone began to change in the 1920s, especially among those who were closely associated with politics. Revolutionary intellectuals began to

---

32. Harry J. Lamley, "Liang Shu-ming, Rural Reconstruction and Rural Work Discussion Society, 1933–1935," *Chung Chi Journal* vol. 8, no. 2, May 1969, 60; Charles W. Hayford, *To the People: James Yen and Village China*.

33. Xiaorong Han, *Chinese Discourses on the Peasant*.

34. Jonathan Spence, *The Search for Modern China*, A48; Xiaorong Han, *Chinese Discourses on the Peasant*. For an international perspective on Boxers, see Paul Cohen, *History in Three Keys: The Boxers as Event, Experience, and Myth*; Joseph Esherick, *The Origins of the Boxer Uprising*.

write favorably about peasant rebels throughout China's history. In 1924, the Communists reassessed the Boxer Rebellion and concluded that it was the solemn and stirring prelude to the Chinese national revolution. In the same year, Sun Yat-sen asserted that Chinese peasants needed to be educated about their national duties and rights as a preliminary to joining the revolution.[35] So important was the peasantry now considered that, in 1925, the United Front, the alliance between the Guomindang and the CCP, dispatched personnel to the countryside to infiltrate and reorganize a peasant secret society known as the Red Spears.

Soviet factors had played a crucial role in the reversal in attitudes toward the peasants. In May 1923, Moscow cabled the CCP stating that "the issue of the peasants [is] at the center of all our policies," and instructed the Chinese revolutionaries "to carry out peasant land revolution against the remnants of feudalism."[36] In response, the CCP's third Congress (June 1923) passed the "Resolution on the Peasant Question," which called on the party "to gather together small peasants, sharecroppers, and farm laborers to resist the imperialists who control China, to overthrow the warlords and corrupt officials, and to resist the local criminals and immoral elite, so as to protect the interests of the peasants and to promote the national revolutionary movement."[37] While much was said, little was done until 1925.

Right at the time, many Chinese intellectuals were adjusting their perception of their own role in society in tune with the times. Up until the May Fourth movement (1919),[38] the concept of the intellectual (*zhishi fenzi*), albeit a modern term, had been traced back to the Confucian designation of the scholar class, existing alongside peasants, artisans, and merchants. This traditional social division sat uneasily with the Marxist definition of the ownership of the means of production. In the 1920s, following Soviet success and influenced by Lenin's writings, a Marxist–Leninist analysis of the intellectual class was introduced to China. Drawing on Lenin, Chen Duxiu stated that intellectuals did not constitute an independent social class. Chi-

---

35. Xiaorong Han, *Chinese Discourses on the Peasant.*

36. Jung Chang and Jon Hallidays, *Mao: The Unknown Story,* 39.

37. Stuart R. Schram and Nancy Hodes, eds., *Mao's Road to Power,* vol. 2, 164.

38. The May Fourth movement began with the student demonstrations that took place in Tiananmen Square on May 4, 1919, heralding a period of anti-establishment agitation and intellectual ferment. Jonathan Spence, *Search for Modern China,* A59.

nese Communist Party leaders had to identify themselves with the working class or the peasant class to meet Lenin's standard.[39] Prompted by Chen's statement, increasing numbers of Chinese intellectuals came to consider themselves as representatives of these groups, at least rhetorically. Many began to address the peasants as "we" rather than as "they."[40]

Meanwhile, the deterioration of living conditions and growing violence in the countryside in the 1920s shocked Chinese intellectuals and demonstrated peasants' potential for resurrection.[41] Some intellectuals argued that the poorer China became, the more revolutionaries there would be and the earlier the revolution would succeed. It became fashionable for intellectuals and students with rural origins to return to their home villages to work alongside the peasants. Peng Pai, Liu Dongxuan, and Yun Daiying were among these pioneers. However, few imagined their destiny lay in farming, but rather saw themselves as having a calling to organize the peasants in support of their missions.[42] They looked to the countryside to learn about rural people and, more specifically, to explore effective ways of mobilizing peasants. They conducted field research in various regions of China. Based on their fieldwork, they claimed to have discovered the "reality" of peasant life and thus prescribed their own solutions. However, the rural "reality" varied from place to place, according to climate, landholding practices, ecological features, local culture, and sources of alternative employment. Given the fact that a vast nation like China encompassed not a single static rural reality, but many changing conditions, intellectuals' perceptions of Chinese peasants in the 1920s and 1930s were determined more by ideology than facts. In other words, their varied beliefs and commitments led them to "discover" different characteristics of the peasantry and thus prescribe different solutions.[43]

Precisely at this time, Marxist writings, especially Lenin's works, reached China and were sought after by Chinese Communists. Right after 1917, Lenin's work was translated and introduced to China. In the early 1920s, the journal *New Youth* published many of Lenin's writings. In 1924, when Lenin

---

39. Eddy U, "Reification of the Chinese Intellectual: on the Origins of the CCP Concept of Zhishifenzi," *Modern China* 35 (2009): 604–631.

40. Xiaorong Han, *Chinese Discourses on the Peasant*, 71.

41. Harry J. Lamley, "Liang Shu-ming," 60; Charles W. Hayford, *To the People*.

42. Xiaorong Han, *Chinese Discourses on the Peasant*, 121.

43. Ibid., 171.

passed away, a collection of his work in his memoir was published in Beijing. In 1925, on Lenin's first death anniversary, *New Youth* published a special volume entitled "The Call of Lenin" (*Liening hao*). Xie Wenjin, based on Lenin's salient article "To the Rural Poor," published the article "Lenin and Peasants" to introduce Lenin's views on the peasants. This article is considered one of the CCP's most important works on peasants in the early years. Lenin's views on the peasants thus left a profound impression on the CCP's understanding of the Chinese peasantry and would mold its future rural policies.[44]

Lenin asserted that the origins of rural poverty lay in unequal land distribution, which produced rival classes: landlords, rich peasants, middle-ranking peasants, and poor peasants. He foresaw further polarization and class crystallization in rural Russia and anticipated that conflict among these various social classes would dominate rural society. Under these conditions, class consciousness would breed all the more rapidly.[45] Following a Marxist analysis of capitalist organizations, Lenin assumed that the peasants acted consistently to maximize their gains by rationalizing production. He believed that all peasants would work hard and produce more if they possessed adequate farming equipment. Beneath this rationale lay the idea of "the sanctity of labor" that was formulated after the October Revolution.[46]

Lenin's views have been strongly challenged by research on the Russian peasant economy. As early as 1907 Sombart noted high vertical mobility as a major determinant of a low degree of "class consciousness" and of limited "class antagonism" in the political sphere.[47] Alexander Chayanov, probably Russia's finest agrarian economist of the early twentieth century, convincingly showed that the peasant economy cannot be understood in the terms employed by a discipline that originated in the study of the capitalist economy. Russian peasants produced primarily for family consumption and sought to attain a balance between producing surpluses and personal satisfaction. As for the cause of rural poverty, Chayanov emphasized the high

---

44. On how Lenin's work was introduced in China, see Ding Shijun, "Liening zhuzuo zai Zhongguo de chuban he chuanbo."

45. Esther Kingston-Mann, *Lenin and the Problem of Marxist Peasant Revolution*.

46. Xiaorong Han, *Chinese Discourses on the Peasant*, 141.

47. Teodor Shanin, "Socio-Economic Mobility and the Rural History of Russia 1905-30."

ratio of consumers to laborers in the household as the fundamental factor. [48] Decades later, Teodor Shanin reaffirmed the multidirectional and cyclical mobility of peasants.[49] In sum, scholars have questioned the suitability of applying a logic drawn from manufacturing to agriculture, and challenged the belief that the economic returns of mechanization were necessarily higher than those derived from family farming.[50]

The outcome Lenin predicted did not occur in Russia. The discrepancies between the complex realities of Russian rural life and Lenin's own description of that reality would constitute the crux of the Bolsheviks' difficult relationship with the peasants after 1917. As one contemporary opponent of Lenin commented, "what the peasants really wanted would come as an unpleasant surprise to Russia's revolutionary optimists."[51] This hard reality, however, was withheld from the Chinese communists.

Chinese Communists seem to have inherited Lenin's basic presumptions: the correlation between poverty and landlessness, class polarization and class consciousness, and the sanctity of labor. Chinese Communists believed that class struggle existed in the countryside and could be mobilized by the promise of land reform. In China, these presumptions failed to reflect the complexity of the rural world, just as the intellectuals' plans failed to account for the peasants themselves.

In China, land concentration varied in different regions. Regardless of the degree of concentration, there was no absolute connection between family wealth and land ownership. Peasants who owned land did not necessarily live better or feel safer than tenants.[52] The custom of partible inheritance, or the division of the land equally among male inheritors, was practiced by virtually all households in China, large or small, wealthy or poor, in the north or the south.[53] A family's land was typically divided into small strips, scattered throughout the village. With an equal chance of inheritance among sons, Chinese society was quite mobile, with movement common

---

48. Naniel Thorner, Basile Kerblay, and R. Smith, eds., *A.V. Chayanov on the Theory of Peasant Economy.*

49. Teodor Shanin, *The Awkward Class* (Oxford: Oxford University Press, 1972).

50. James Scott, *Seeing Like a State: How Certain Schemes to Improve the Human Condition Have Failed,* 165.

51. Esther Kingston-Mann, *Lenin and the Problem of Marxist Peasant,* 160.

52. John Buck, *Land Utilization in China,* 37.

53. Roman Myers, "Agrarian System," 244.

both up and down. As the old Chinese saying put it, albeit it simplistically, "Nobody stays rich for three generations; nobody stays poor for three generations."

Evidence of class consciousness among the peasantry was scarce in China when the twentieth century began. Chinese scholar Tang Zhiqing points out that there were no fixed social classes or castes in China. All social groups were constantly in flux. While many peasants went into bankruptcy as the result of natural disasters or personal misfortune, others made their fortune through good luck and/or sheer hard work. The rural poor viewed village life in similar ways to landlords, and indeed aspired to the latter's role and social status. Poor peasants were potential landlords.[54]

At the same time, peasants did not necessarily enjoy hard work: if they worked hard it was likely because it was necessary for survival.[55] When this pressure was relaxed, a significant proportion chose to work less hard. The CCP also believed that the peasants were open to the idea of continuously investing in production and applying new technologies to increase production. It would soon discover the disappointing truth on this score, as I discuss in some detail in Chapter 3. The gulf between the Chinese Communists' perceptions of Chinese peasants and the reality in the countryside was daunting. A good case in example is Mao Zedong, who emphasized his deep affiliation with the countryside and for decades had claimed the ultimate authority of "knowing peasants."

Mao Zedong Approaching Peasants, 1920–1927[56]

Well known for his down-to-earth qualities, Mao Zedong was born and raised in a peasant family. However, regardless of appearances, Mao did not identify himself as a farmer and never aspired to be one. Despite being the son of a successful peasant-turned-landlord, in the years that followed, Mao undertook one field investigation after another in an attempt to "understand" the rural situation. As a teenager, in common with many educated

---

54. Tang Zhiqing, *Jindai Shandong nongcun shehui jingji yanjiu*, 384–614.
55. Xiaorong Han, *Chinese Discourses on the Peasant*, 141.
56. The quotations in this section lacking individual citations are from the "Report on the Peasant Movement in Hunan" (February 1927), in *Mao's Road to Power*, vol. 2, 429–464.

young people, Mao considered peasants to represent the most backward and benighted part of Chinese society.[57] After joining the CCP, from 1921 to 1923, Mao was mainly concerned with urban issues and paid little attention to the peasants, whose political demands, he thought, "are simply for honest officials and a good emperor."[58] He was frank in his privileging of urban revolutionaries: "Thirty million [rural people] are too scattered. ... It would be too late to wait for thirty million people to wake up ... the responsibility has inevitably fallen on the shoulders of our 300,000 citizens of Changsha."[59] For years he ignored the Comintern's directions to forge an alliance with the peasants, as did most other Chinese Communists. Mao lacked faith in peasants' revolutionary potential, believing that peasant revolts were capable of producing a new emperor but never a new system.[60] Up to 1925, in his known writings and conversations Mao made only sporadic references to the peasantry.

A sea change soon came, however. In December 1924 Mao left Shanghai for his home village in Hunan. In the following months, he witnessed a great deal of peasant unrest triggered by the Northern Expedition, a military campaign, undertaken by an alliance of Guomindang and CCP forces under the leadership of Chiang Kai-shek, to free China from the warlords and unify it under a single government. Chiang established his Nationalist government in Nanjing following the expedition.[61] When Mao returned to politics from this vacation, his chief concern switched to the peasants. He organized peasant associations and night schools; more importantly, he began to envisage a place for the peasants in his blueprint for a future China.

As late as in 1926, Mao encountered Lenin's work. As a frequent contributor to *New Youth*, Mao must have read Lenin's works that were published in the journal. Records show that in June 1926 Mao was making references to Lenin's writings.[62] Mao particularly held high regard for the article "Lenin and Peasants." In 1926, he included this article in his collec-

---

57. Philip Short, *Mao: A Life*, 152.

58. Mao Zedong, "Hunan under the Provincial Constitution" (July 1, 1923), in *Mao's Road to Power*, vol. 2, 171; also see Nick Knight, *Rethinking Mao*, 73.

59. Mao Zedong, "Appeal to the 300,000 Citizens of Changsha in Favor of Self-Rule for Hunan," in *Mao's Road to Power*, vol. 1, 572.

60. Philip Short, *Mao: A Life*, 152.

61. Jonathan Spence, *Search for Modern China*, A60.

62. Chen Jin, *Mao Zedong dushu biji*, 261.

tion of writings on peasants as he lectured for peasants in Guangzhou. In the year to come, Mao would learn how he could incorporate the peasants into his theory of revolution, as Lenin had done, and could inject into this group a degree of class consciousness that they had rarely possessed. It also marked Mao's growing from a youth who was interested in politics into a career politician devoted to building a strong China.

As Mao became a politician, he became adept at presenting a carefully selected portion of reality as the whole truth and simplifying complex relationships in order to offer ready solutions to problems. His perceptions of the peasants followed a similar track; it had little to do with who peasants were or the particular problems the peasants had identified for themselves, but a great deal to do with how they could fit into Mao's plans for a new China. In 1927, Mao released his masterwork on the peasants, the "Report on the Peasant Movement in Hunan" (Hunan Report).[63]

Indeed, this report was a landmark. Past analyses of the report have focused on its theorization of the significance of the peasants to the Chinese revolution and its undisguised eulogy of the poor and their violence.[64] This chapter points out some other features.

In 1926, Mao used ownership of land, in accordance with classical Marxism, to divide the peasants into eight subgroups: big landlords, small landlords, owner–peasants, semi–owner-peasants, sharecroppers, poor peasants, farm laborers and rural artisans, and vagrants.[65] However, in the Hunan Report, Mao demonized ownership of land: "If he has land, he must be a bully, and all gentry are evil." Mao excluded landlords from the peasant class, placing them in opposition to the peasants and to the Chinese revolution. He then used living conditions as a secondary classification tool, dividing the remaining peasants into three categories: rich, middle, and poor. Rich peasants were those who had surplus money and grain; middle peasants lacked surplus money or rice, were not in debt, and were in a position to assure themselves of clothing, food, and shelter every year; poor peasants

---

63. The quotations in this section lacking individual citations are from the "Report on the Peasant Movement in Hunan" (February 1927), in *Mao's Road to Power*, vol. 2, 429–464.

64. Stuart R. Schram, *Thought of Mao Tse-Tung.*

65. Mao Zedong, "An Analysis of the Various Classes among the Chinese Peasantry and Their Attitudes towards the Revolution" (January 1926), in *Mao's Road to Power*, vol. 2, 303.

were wholly or partially dispossessed. One year earlier, in January 1926, Mao had excluded vagrants from the group of revolutionary poor peasants, at a time when he was still deciding what he was looking for in a vanguard group.[66] But in this report, he saw an opportunity to make use of vagrants' potential. As he put it:

> The only kinds of people in the countryside who have always put up the bitterest fight are the poor peasants. As for organization, it is they who are organizing things there, and as for revolution, it is they who are making revolution there. They alone are the deadly enemies of the local tyrants and evil gentry, and they strike them without the slightest hesitation. They alone are capable of carrying out the work of destruction.

Now for the first time Mao had clarified what he sought: those who "alone are capable of carrying out the work of destruction." In terms of revolutionary potential, Mao ranked the poor peasants above all other groups: "They did whatever they liked and turned everything upside down; they had created a kind of terror in the countryside." Because they had nothing to lose, they would challenge the status quo with little hesitation. Mao confidently announced that "the poor peasants, especially the portion who are utterly destitute, are the most revolutionary group." It seems that he equated the potential for insurrection of these impoverished peasants with their awareness of the necessity for revolution. With very little statistical evidence behind him, Mao asserted that the class background of a peasant would determine his reaction to the revolution. In his opinion, rich peasants would remain inactive throughout the course of the revolution, middle-ranking peasants would vacillate in their support, and only the poor peasants would throw their weight wholeheartedly behind the revolution. The Hunan Report unreservedly praised the actions of this last group. The lasting legacy of the report in the annals of modern China is Mao's declaration that poor peasants are—and indeed, are compelled to be—the most reliable ally of the CCP. This assertion was honored throughout the revolutionary years and during the PRC under Mao, regardless of its distance from reality.

---

66. Mao Zedong, "An Analysis of the Various Classes among the Chinese Peasantry and Their Attitudes towards the Revolution" (January 1926), in *Mao's Road to Power*, 308.

Mao's key assertion is problematic on a number of levels. The degree of class awareness Chinese peasants had remains a question. Poor peasants often thought in similar ways to rich peasants and, indeed, aspired to their status. They did not want to change the system, but rather to change their positions in the system. Because the economic circumstances of the peasants were in constant flux, so were their class affiliations. How could the CCP accommodate such variables?

Most strikingly, even if the rural population could be divided into classes, their official class designations would not necessarily determine their reactions to the revolution. Bianco finds that poor peasants did not always respond more positively to revolutionary appeals than their wealthier counterparts. Factors other than class affiliation, such as the generational divide and marital status, often determined political loyalties.[67] Coming from a family of a small landlord, Mao Zedong himself is a case in point. The CCP itself provides further examples: many of its early members came from families of landlords and rich peasants. It was not long before CCP cadres came to realize that peasants, especially poor peasants, did not actually behave as Mao had prescribed in the Hunan Report. For example, in the 1940s, a number of CCP cadres indicated that they had found Mao's emphasis on poor peasants overly optimistic. As one cadre said, "The peasants actually have a lot of the landlords' mentality. It is hard to use education simply mechanically." Another cadre bluntly suggested that Mao's investigation of the peasants had been less than thorough: "[Mao] did what he wanted to anyhow, and did not bother with careful research."[68] Despite these misgivings, once the CCP had established itself in a particular area, it devised programs in favor of poor peasants in accordance with Mao's stated views and provided poor peasants with special training and opportunities for political advancement.[69] The party was not ready to adjust its perception of poor peasants; instead, it decided to adjust the peasants to conform to its perceptions.

In the Hunan Report, Mao described several cases in which peasants targeted and attacked what he described as "local tyrants and evil gentry." But who were these villains? A close reading of the report reveals that the chief targets of unrest were local quasi–government agents. Mao asserted that the peasants were aiming to overthrow feudal rule and smash the *tu*

---

67. Lucien Bianco, *Peasants without the Party*, 237.

68. David Goodman, *Social and Political Change in Revolutionary China*, 265.

69. Lucien Bianco, *Peasants without the Party*, 237.

and *tuan*. The *tu* and *tuan* in fact referred to newly established subcounty administrative divisions and were the product of the modern government's efforts to extend its influence into the countryside. According to Mao, "The peasants were not so much concerned with the president of the Republic, the provincial military governor or the country magistrate; their real 'bosses' were these rural monarchs." Several local bullies that Mao listed as deserving of execution were heads of the defense corps in the towns. Is it possible that peasants were rising not against the landlords, but against the intrusion of the state? Nevertheless, constrained by his ideological blinkers, Mao chose to interpret what he saw as an example of class struggle by the local peasantry against the landlord class.

The peasants' economic claims exposed the real nature of these insurrections. Peasants were experiencing the negative impact of the market and, in response, were attempting to limit and control their interactions with the various actors in the market. Although Mao used the phrase "Hitting the Landlords Economically" in the report as the title for the section on the peasants' economic demands, the peasants' demands had less to do with landlords than with the market, especially the market for grain. The peasants' first call was for a prohibition on attempts to corner the market and export grain out of the local area. They demanded a ban on distilling and sugar-making, as well as a veto on exorbitant feasts and limitations on the number of pigs, chickens, and ducks that a family could raise because the animals also consumed grain. At the same time, the peasants wanted to limit trade with the towns. While they demanded a freeze on rents and land deposits and a ban on canceling tenancies, they did not challenge landlords' ownership of land. In this sense, they were more reformists than revolutionaries.

Last, but not least, the Hunan Report set a precedent for conducting rural investigations that would yield major conclusions providing the basis for political action. By conducting field research, Mao was able to accumulate information and, more importantly, to invest himself with the authority to claim a firsthand understanding of Chinese peasants. Mao carefully crafted the image of someone who spoke on behalf of the peasants. As a way of silencing his opponents, he often asserted, "He who has not made an investigation has no right to speak."[70] However, this approach contained a

---

70. Mao Zedong, "Circular of the General Political Department on Investing the Situation regarding Land and Population" (April 2, 1931), in *Mao's Road to Power*, vol. 4, 55.

considerable number of methodological flaws. Mao's preferred method was to investigate a few areas in depth.[71] His investigations usually lasted from a week to a few months, during which he collected information mainly by attending peasant meetings organized by local CCP cadres. The breadth and depth of his knowledge was bound by his limited sources and by the questions he asked. Mao always initiated his investigations with some specific purpose in mind. The Hunan Report is an excellent example of his use of investigations of specific localities to build up support for his position within the party. Mao wrote this report to convince his fellow Communists of the rising tide of revolution, a revolt that would be spearheaded by the poorest peasants. The tone was euphoric; the objective of the Hunan Report was to "talk up the peasant movement in the face of resistance from within the leadership ranks of his own party, not to allude to the failings of the peasants of which he was already aware."[72] This intention predisposed Mao to interpret the turbulence caused by the Northern Expedition as a shining example of the revolutionary potential of the peasants.[73] Not to mention that local conditions varied so dramatically in China that this approach contained obvious drawbacks.

The method of investigation appeared to be part of a bottom-up process, but could be easily manipulated by CCP officials for their own ends, thus becoming in fact a top-down imposition.[74] This model of social investigation based on an examination of "typical cases" persisted through the Mao era. It was not until the 1980s that Chinese scholars began to discuss the subjective bias inherent in this research methodology and accept that a reliance on "representative" research subjects would represent the views of only a select minority of respondents.[75]

This report was Mao's announcement that he was henceforth designating the peasants, especially the poorest, as the major destructive force of China's Communist revolution—sweeping away the old order so that the new could be put in place. It reflected his discovery of the contemporary collective power of the peasants, as well as the readjustment of his personal views about them.

---

71. Philip Short, *Mao: A Life*, 304.
72. Nick Knight, *Rethinking Mao: Explorations in Mao Zedong*, 78.
73. John Fairbank and Albert Feuerwerker, *Cambridge History of China*, 301–306.
74. Sebastian Heilmann, "Policy-Making through Experimentation," 62–73.
75. Patricia Thornton, "Retrofitting the Steel Frame," 251.

Mao's brief experience in the Hunan countryside would accompany him all his life and lay the groundwork for his diagnosis of the problems faced by China's rural masses.[76] To a large degree, from this point forward, Mao developed a stereotype of what he imagined a Chinese peasant should be, based on what he saw during his time in Hunan. He became increasingly adept at simplifying China's rural realities and depicting peasants in ways that fitted his plans for national revolution. After years of honing his thoughts on the matter, Mao fell victim to belief in the illusions he had created. In a broader sense, this was a development deeply rooted in the origins and communal ideology of the revolution, which accentuated the inherent tendency of human beings to simplify experience.[77]

The Hunan Report itself had little to say about land reform. After the CCP consulted with Soviet agents, a land policy was agreed on. In line with a long tradition of equalizing land holding and Republican calls for "land to the tiller," the party proposed to redistribute the holdings of large landlords, government-owned land, public land, and abandoned land to landless peasants and peasants in need.[78] Mao became a member of the party's Land Committee and asserted that as "the peasants will not support the revolution until its final victory unless they are given land. ... [o]ur party has resolved to support the peasants in their struggle for land, and will never cease to do so until the land problem has been completely solved."[79] Underlying the land reform program were the CCP's aspirations for raising and supporting its own army. The year 1927 witnessed escalating skirmishes between the Guomindang and the CCP. Before long, the Guomindang–CCP alliance broke down completely and the Guomindang ruthlessly purged their erstwhile ally. In August 1927, the CCP launched an armed struggle against the Guomindang. Over the next two decades, the building of a Communist army became the core of Mao's revolutionary strategy. Reflecting endemic warfare during this period, Mao noted in 1927 that "political power is obtained from the barrel of a gun."[80]

---

76. Philip Short, *Mao: A Life*, 174.

77. Ci Jiwei, *Dialectic of the Chinese Revolution*," 72.

78. Mao Zedong, "Draft Resolution on Solving the Land Question" (April 1927), in *Mao's Road to Power*, vol. 2, 502–503.

79. Mao Zedong, "Declaration to the Peasants" (March 16, 1927), in *Mao's Road to Power*, vol. 2, 472–475.

80. Stuart R. Schram, "Introduction," in *Mao's Road to Power*, vol. 3, xxi.

Chairman Mao Leading Peasant Soldiers, 1928–1934

After a series of failed attempts to occupy Guomindang-controlled cities, Mao switched to the strategy of "going up to the mountains." In October 1927, Mao Zedong led his forces to Jinggangshan, a remote mountainous area along the provincial border between Hunan and Jiangxi. There, he began to build the Red Army and established a base. This period marks the first step toward Mao's emergence as the leader of a peasant-based revolution. To win over the majority of peasants—those with few resources—Mao seized on the tool of land redistribution: confiscate land belonging to the enemy class and redistribute it among poorer peasants. Originally the enemy class was landlords, but it soon expanded to include rich peasants and even middle, land-owning peasants.[81] Land redistribution was designed to benefit the poorer peasants but it was also a means of funding the revolution, as any cash that was seized went to support the army.[82]

The CCP believed that once peasants owned the land, they would work harder and produce surplus to support the Communist cause. However, the party was often disappointed by what really happened. While the peasants were pleased to receive new allocations of land, they were reluctant to give anything back. For example, in 1930, Western Jiangxi underwent three rounds of land redistribution during which many well-off peasants abandoned their land and fled the district. Each peasant in Donggu village received a minimum of 16 dan of rice (1 dan was equivalent to 80 catties there)—hardly an incentive to undertake additional work. The recipients reasoned, "I have received several dan of rice in the distribution; it is enough to eat, and I don't want to farm the public land."[83] As a result, a great deal of productive land went unused.

Mao was acutely aware of the potential harmful effects of land redistribution polices on agricultural production. He did not hesitate to admit that

---

81. Mao Zedong, "Land Law" (February 7, 1930), in *Mao's Road to Power*, vol. 3, 256.

82. In party documents, this aspect of land reform was carefully circumvented, with only sporadic references to it. Mao Zedong, "Carry Out a Broad and Thoroughgoing Land Investigation Movement" (June 1, 1933), in *Mao's Road to Power*, vol. 4, 394–397.

83. Mao Zedong, "The Situation Regarding Land Redistribution in Western Jiangxi" (November 12 and 15, 1930), in *Mao's Road to Power*, vol. 3, 673–679.

"'developing production' is not the number one criterion of our present tactics. It is 'winning over the masses' that is the number one criterion of our present tactics."[84] One reason Mao was able to disregard rural production was the Red Army's reliance on expropriation as a way of maintaining essential supplies. The disruptions to rural production could be accommodated, at least in the short term.

Between 1927 and 1931, Mao served as the leader of a Red Army that was under constant threat of annihilation. His hostility toward rich peasants and owner–peasants continued unabated, which was certainly reinforced by the Soviet trend of dekulakization. From this time, Mao's antipathy toward the wealthy became widespread and would last for decades—many of his speeches during this period were reproduced and widely disseminated in the 1940s. Although Mao did not have a long-term plan for the peasant economy, he did show an interest in Stalin's collectivization model, which he regarded as the wave of the future for Chinese peasants.

In 1931, Mao's Red Army settled down in Ruijin, Jiangxi Province, and founded the Central Soviet Base Area, staying there until 1934. The CCP continued to draw most of its revenue from expropriation. As long as it could expand the territory, it could access fresh sources of supply; thus rural productivity was not an urgent concern. Taxes accounted for a trivial portion of the CCP's total income.[85] In 1932, the Guomindang launched another encirclement campaign against the Communists, using the blockhouse strategy, which emphasized a slow, methodical advance, with all units on a given front advancing a short distance in tandem so that none was left isolated and exposed, then fortifying each newly acquired patch of territory.[86] To enable it to concentrate on the fighting, the CCP relieved the Red Army of its duties of revenue collection.[87] The inflow of external funds dried up and it was not long before the base areas faced a revenue crisis. To deal with it, the party was forced to expropriate funds from within, starting with local landlords and rich peasants. The party imposed fines on land-

84. Mao Zedong, "Conclusion of the Joint Conference and Announcement of the Establishment of the Front Committee" (February 16, 1930), in *Mao's Road to Power*, vol. 3, 268–271.

85. Zhongguo nongmin fudanshi bianji weiyuan hui, *Zhongguo nongmin fudanshi* (The history of Chinese peasants' burden), 72.

86. See Stuart R. Schram, "Introduction," in *Mao's Road to Power*, vol. 4, lxxi.

87. Chen Yung-fa, "Civil War, Mao Zedong and Land Revolution," 9–19.

lords, collected "donations" from wealthy peasants, and even conscripted the latter into forced labor brigades.[88] The better-off peasants either fled the area or simply had no more to give. The party then turned to the rest of the rural population for revenue.[89] In 1933, the party launched a new campaign to reassess each person's class status with the purpose of finding "hidden" landlords and rich peasants, whose land would be distributed and whose grain and cash could be used to support the army. The campaign resulted in a windfall of money and property for the party.[90] The CCP's financial needs were temporarily met, "but the costs in terms of loss of popular support and social upheaval almost certainly outweighed what was gained."[91] That summer, famine hit parts of the area, and armed brigands infiltrated.

Under these circumstances, Mao Zedong, then serving as the chairman of the Chinese Soviet Republic, no longer the commander of the Red Army, admitted the party's past errors in neglecting economic affairs and sought to find new economic solutions.[92] He put forward an agenda centering on the government's control over trade and the distribution of strategic supplies. Facing a labor shortage caused by large-scale Red Army recruitment and other workers having fled the region, Mao's solution was straightforward: "adjusting the use of labor power in an organized way and encouraging women to participate in production."[93] He urged the formation of mutual aid teams and plowing teams that would pull laborers together and form them into new units. Thus, Mao had learned another important lesson in governance: rearrange the workforce to conform to the needs of the government. Yet Mao had little time to implement these plans. In 1934, the CCP

---

88. Mao Zedong, "Conscript the Rich Peasants and Organize Forced Labor Brigades" (November 25, 1932), in *Mao's Road to Power*, vol. 4, 327.

89. Stuart R. Schram, "Introduction to Vol. 3," in *Mao's Road to Power*, vol. 3, lxxiii.

90. Mao Zedong, "Carry Out a Broad and Thoroughgoing Land Investigation Movement" (June 1, 1933), in *Mao's Road to Power*, vol. 4, 394–397.

91. Stuart R. Schram, "Introduction to Vol. 4," in *Mao's Road to Power*, vol. 4, lxix.

92. Mao Zedong, "Smashing the Fifth 'Encirclement and Suppression' and the Tasks of Economic Construction" (August 12, 1933), in *Mao's Road to Power*, vol. 4, 479–490.

93. Mao Zedong, "Report of the Central Executive Committee and the Council of People's Commissars of the Chinese Soviet Republic to the Second National Soviet Congress" (January 1934), in *Mao's Road to Power*, vol. 4, 656–713.

launched the legendary Long March to escape the Guomindang encircle-ment. Chinese scholar Zhang Ming points out that the Red Army left the Ruijin base area not merely as a result of military defeat, but because of internal economic collapse. Unable to expand and continue extracting resources from outside its base areas, the Red Army rapidly exhausted its limited internal resources.[94]

During this wartime period of governance, Mao accumulated knowledge and experience of centralized planning, direct government intervention, and the state's ability to organize the forces of production that includes laborers and tools. He realized the necessity of implementing central control over grain, trade, manufacturing, and even the peasantry. After years immersed in a wartime economy, Mao and many of his colleagues were easily tempted to take shortcuts that would allow them to control the economy by direct state intervention. It is hardly surprising that they would be receptive to straightforward yet extremely simplified methods of managing the peasants such as Soviet-style collectivization.

Yan'an: Dilemma on Taxes

Having endured the Long March, Mao and his army arrived in the border regions of Shannxi and Gansu provinces in October 1935 and established the Shann–Gan–Ning border region government centered in Yan'an.[95] There the CCP put in place programs of land confiscation and redistribution. The fact that a small number of absentee landlords held a disproportionately large share of the land in the region made land redistribution relatively easy and profitable for poor families.[96] In Yan'an, the party continued the practice, which "depended almost completely on fines, confiscations and the extralegal method of 'attacking local gentry' for revenue and left the 'emancipated peasants' largely to themselves."[97]

---

94. Information from Xiaojia Hou's conversation with Zhang Ming in Hong Kong, October 2005, and in Beijing, September 2007.

95. Mark Selden, *Yenan Way in Revolutionary China.*

96. For the peculiar land conditions in Yan'an, see Pauline B. Keating, *Two Revolutions,* 72.

97. Chen Yung-fa, "The Blooming Poppy under the Red Sun," 265.

The Xi'an Incident in December 1936 paved the way for the second united front between the CCP and the Guomindang.[98] As a result of the negotiations, the CCP agreed to halt confiscating landlords' property and implementing land reform. In exchange, the Guomindang promised the Communists generous financial subsidies.[99] In 1939, 89.66 percent of the CCP's government revenue came from the Guomindang subsidy.[100] Because of this new income stream, for a few years, the CCP showed little interest in levying taxes. In 1937, the party requested 14,000 dan of grain, which accounted for only 1.28 percent of the peasants' total output.[101] Although radical land reform was not carried out in Yan'an, its place was effectively taken by "revolution by installment"[102] or "silent revolution."[103] Rents were reduced and landlords and wealthy peasants opted to sell their extra land, which was often purchased by poor and middle-ranking peasants. In the space of a few years, middle-ranking peasants came to form the majority of the rural population in the area.

In the late 1930s, as the Guomindang engaged in a series of ill-fated battles with the Japanese, resulting in their retreat to the southwest, the CCP succeeded in establishing its influence in much of the northern Chinese countryside, behind the Japanese lines, or, more precisely, in the interstices of the Japanese control of cities and railways. In 1937, the CCP claimed to have 40,000 members and 80,000 full-time soldiers; by early 1940, membership had grown twentyfold to nearly 800,000, and its armed wing totaled approximately 500,000. The Communists' rapid expansion alarmed Chiang Kai-shek, and relations between the CCP and the Guomindang once again began to sour. In January 1941 three thousand troops of the New Fourth Army, a Communist guerrilla force, were killed by Guomindang forces in an ambush as a result of having defied Chiang's warning not to cross the

---

98. Warlord Zhang Xueliang kidnapped Chiang Kai-shek to get him to agree to a united Chinese effort against the Japanese. Negotiations between the Guomindang and the CCP resulted in Chiang's release.

99. Gu Longsheng, *Mao Zedong jingji nianpu*, 98.

100. Huang Zhenglin, *Shann–Gan–Ning bianqu shehui jingji shi*, 189.

101. Ibid., 197–199.

102. Tetsuya Kataoka, *Resistance and Revolution in China*.

103. Edward Friedman, Paul Pickowicz and Mark Selden, *Chinese Village, Socialist State*.

Table 1. The CCP's Grain Levies in Shann–Gan–Ning, 1937–1945[104]

	Cultivated land (mu)	Total agricultural output (dan)	Planned grain levy (dan)	Actual grain collected (dan)	Percentage of collected grain tax against output
1937	8,626,006	1,116,381	10,000	14,197	1.27
1938	9,894,483	1,211,192	10,000	15,955	1.32
1939	10,07,6000	1,754,285	50,000	52,251	2.89
1940	11,742,082	1,526,471	90,000	97,354	6.38
1941	12,132,169	1,455,860	200,000	201,617	13.85
1942	12,413,582	1,483,683	160,000	165,369	11.14
1942	13,387,213	1,812,215	180,000	184,123	10.16
1944	13,387,213	1,817,221	160,000	160,000	7.83
1945	14,256,114	1,600,000	124,000	124,000	7.75

Yangzi River. Triggered by this incident, the Guomindang cut off its subsidy and imposed an economic embargo on the Communists. At the same time, the new Japanese commander in northern China launched a series of savage mopping-up operations—the infamous "three-all" (kill all, burn all, and loot all) campaigns, administering a major setback to the Red Army.[104]

Facing blockades from both the Guomindang and the Japanese army, the CCP was forced to fall back on its internal resources. Its budget fell sharply into the red.[105] In 1940, the CCP revised its taxation system and decided to levy taxes on 80 percent of the population in the areas under its control.[106] The party increased requisitions of grain from 90,000 dan in 1940 to more than 200,000 dan in 1941—fourteen times the amount taken in 1937, as Table 1 indicates. Panic over grain supplies in 1941 prompted the CCP to collect grain by any means and from whomever had a surplus. Local CCP administrations also imposed additional cash or grain levies to fund schools, cadre training, and construction projects. War service duties were

104. Stuart R. Schram, "Introduction," *Mao's Road to power*, vol. 7, liii–lxiii.
105. David Apter and Tony Saich, *Revolutionary Discourse in Mao's Republic*, 218.
106. Pauline B. Keating, *Two Revolutions*, 148.

reaching their limits; according to one survey taken in 1941, local laborers each performed an average of 115 to 130 days of corvée work.[107]

Angry residents turned against the Communists, sometimes resulting in open rebellion. For instance, in December 1939, the Shann–Gan–Ning government assigned Huan County a quota of 8,500 dan in grain tax, and local cadres were planning to collect even more. In response, a revolt broke out in January 1940. Peasants from seventeen townships rebelled and 2,500 self-defense personnel joined the revolt.[108] When a rumor spread that the 1942 quota would be in excess of 200,000 dan, the peasants became convinced that the more they produced the more tax they would have to pay. They turned to other forms of resistance: in the winter of 1941, they sold their oxen and donkeys and let their farms run down. Total agricultural production dropped, while unit yields fell even more sharply. Many peasants left the Shann–Gan–Ning base areas. A widely circulated story told how, during a storm, a CCP cadre was struck by lightning and killed. Hearing the news, local peasants prayed for lightning to strike Chairman Mao.[110]

The rural economy was on the verge of collapse. Having to rely on internal resources rather than external income, it became crucial for the CCP to boost agricultural production.[111] In 1941 the CCP sent an investigation team, led by the head of its propaganda department, Zhang Wentian, to explore "ways of increasing agricultural production and improving the peasants' livelihood."[112]

A respected Marxist theoretician, Zhang Wentian had the unusual experience of having studied abroad, first in Japan, then in the United States, and in the Soviet Union. As early as 1922, he had read Lenin's work on his New Economic Policy (NEP) and became convinced of the merits of capitalism in making the transition from feudalism to socialism.[113] Between 1941 and 1942, spending almost a year in the countryside, Zhang devoted himself to examining rural conditions—much more thoroughly than Mao Zedong

107. Ibid., 149.
108. Huang Zhenglin, *Shann–Gan–Ning bianqu shehui jingji shi*, 201.
109. Wu Yong, "1941 nian Shann–Gan–Ning bianqu jiuguo," 59.
110. Jin Chongji and Chen Qun, *Chen Yun zhuan.*
111. Huang Zhenglin, *Shann–Gan–Ning bianqu shehui jingji shi*, 241.
112. Zhang Peisen, *Zhang Wentian nianpu*, vol. 2, 665.
113. Zhang Peisen, "Zhang Wentian he liening de xin jingji zhengce."

ever did. From the outset, Zhang was shocked to discover, "What we [the CCP] are doing and what we are saying is remote from the masses. What the masses know and what the masses want are completely different from what we think of them as knowing and wanting. Today even cadres of peasant origin [who should know better] are talking the party rhetoric."[114]

Because Marxism was based on the concept of class, Zhang considered it crucial to understand the complex relationships between the classes in the countryside. He acknowledged that the CCP's past debates on agriculture had rarely been based on reality: the party simply knew too little about the peasants. Zhang implied that the party's understanding of landlords and wealthy peasants had been based on oversimplified assumptions that ignored the complicated rural situation. Zhang sharply criticized these assumptions, arguing that the "subjectivism" to which they were prone may have made his CCP comrades sleep better at night and made their life more comfortable, but it failed to advance their understanding of the situation on the ground.[115]

The investigation convinced Zhang Wentian of the complexity of the rural economy; he realized that lack of land was not the sole cause of rural poverty. Early in his probe, he asserted that middle-ranking peasants were the mainstay of the rural economy.[116] And toward the end of his study, he came to appreciate the crucial contribution that rich peasants made to rural prosperity. Zhang asserted that this group's contribution to the economy would ultimately benefit society at large. After reexamining the CCP's former financial practices, he could only condemn them: "It is a mistake to try and improve people's livelihoods by redistributing other people's wealth; it is better to do so by increasing production and increasing social wealth."[117]

This year-long investigation constituted a rare attempt by a high-ranking CCP official to understand the complexities of the rural economy. Sadly, on returning to Yan'an, Zhang Wentian became a major target of the Yan'an Rectification movement initiated by Mao.[118] Zhang was immediately re-

---

114. Zhang Wentian xuanji zhuanjizu, *Zhang Wentian jinshann diaocha wenji*, 291.

115. Ibid., 292–293.

116. Zhang Peisen, *Zhang Wentian nianpu*, 671.

117. Ibid., 693.

118. In 1942 Mao Zedong launched a campaign aimed at strengthening the dominant role of his ideology in the CCP. Major targets included Wang Ming and Zhang Wentian.

quired to engage in continuous acts of self-criticism, and was never given the chance to work on economic issues in Yan'an, despite his thorough investigation. Although Zhang Wentian had come to understand the gulf between what the CCP knew of the rural world and the real situation, his voice was effectively suppressed. Zhang's prescription for overcoming economic hardship, based on his firsthand observations of the rural situation, was for the party to work closely with middle-ranking and wealthy peasants and to provide economic incentives to encourage new forms of capitalism and commercial development in rural China. However, this prescription did not fit with the narrative of the rural world created by Mao Zedong, one that recognized class exploitation and the need to diminish it and to shift resources to the fledgling socialist state. Zhang's reports were suppressed and remained unpublished until 1989.

Mao Zedong would not have been impressed with Zhang's observations, if he even bothered to read them. Mao was also searching for a way of raising agricultural productivity, but one very different from Zhang's more genuinely investigation-based proposals. Mostly built on Soviet writings and his earlier experience in Ruijin, Mao advocated a straightforward solution: reorganize the labor force.[119] As peasants fled or resisted the party's increasing demands by slackening their work rate, it became imperative to exert control over them. Mao believed that everyone, including the elderly, women, and "lazy" peasants, should be participating in rural production. He believed that "a huge inspirational effort was needed to persuade peasants to keep all farmland in production."[120] Mao advocated the formation of mutual aid teams throughout the entire base area, which would then allow the party to "persuade" the peasants to plant the kinds of crops it required and ensure that they returned to their full work capacity. In addition, mutual aid teams could better coordinate wartime services.[121] Mao's years of intensive study of Soviet literature in Yan'an were now to be put to use. Inspired by the Soviet experience, Mao would endow his mutual aid teams with a special significance.

---

119. Huang Zhenglin, *Shann–Gan–Ning bianqu shehui jingji shi*, 260–261.

120. Pauline B. Keating, *Two Revolutions*, 155.

121. Huang Zhenglin, *Shann–Gan–Ning bianqu shehui jingji shi*, 293–300.

Elixir of *Short Course* and the Fetishism of "Get Organized"

After arriving in Yan'an, among his other duties Mao found the time to read Marxist writings. Although he had proven his skills as a military leader during the Long March, some of his rivals in the party continued to denigrate him as a mere guerrilla commander who knew little about Marxist theory. Mao was determined to demonstrate his mastery of communist ideology. He first worked on the Marxist classics as presented by the influential Soviet scholars Mitin and Shirokov, and also read the works of Chinese Marxist philosophers Li Da and Ai Siqi. In the summer of 1937, Mao was sufficiently well informed to deliver a series of lectures on dialectical materialism.[122] However, when it came to the Marxist classics, Mao was unable to compete with his rivals in the party, particularly the "returned student faction" (*liusupai*) who had spent years training in the Soviet Union. As a result, Mao turned his back on the Marxist classics and sought a new approach to ideology.[123]

Mao discovered two theoretical positions to assist him in his task. The first was the concept of the Sinification of Marxism: "[T]hat is to say, making certain that in all its manifestations it is imbued with Chinese characteristics; using it according to Chinese peculiarities ... becomes a problem that must be understood and solved by the whole party without delay."[124] Mao attacked those of his comrades who "studied Marxism–Leninism not to meet the needs of revolutionary practice, but purely for the sake of study," as well as those who were unable to "apply the viewpoint and method of Marx, Engels, Lenin and Stalin to the concrete study of China's present conditions."[125] From the Yan'an Rectification movement of 1942 to the Seventh Party Congress of 1945, this concept played a central role in the glorification of Mao Zedong as a leader who had made brilliant theoretical contributions to the communist movement. In the end, Mao's colleague Liu Shaoqi praised Mao Zedong thought as "an admirable model of the nationalization of

---

122. Stuart R. Schram, "Introduction," in *Mao's Road to power*, vol. 6, xxx–xxxii.

123. Gao Hua, "Zai dao yu shi zhijian."

124. Mao Zedong, "On the New Stage" (Oct. 1938), in *Mao's Road to Power*, vol. 4, 539.

125. Mao Zedong, "Reform Our Study" (May 1941), in *Mao's Road to Power*, vol. 7, 749.

Marxism," describing it as "the highest expression of the wisdom of the Chinese nation, and its highest theoretical achievement."[126]

The second vehicle that Mao used to gain a reputation as a Marxist theorist was the Soviet textbook, *The History of the Communist Party of the Soviet Union (Bolsheviks), Short Course.* Published in the Soviet Union in 1938, the *Short Course* was no ordinary textbook. It was composed under Stalin's direction and later Stalin even claimed part of authorship of the work, a claim readily accepted by Chinese communists.[127] By narrating and, where considered necessary, fabricating Bolshevik history, the book reinterpreted Marxist theory, legitimized Stalin's leadership, and told the story of how the Bolsheviks had successfully constructed socialism in the Soviet Union. Stalin promoted the book in the Communist world as the official history of the Soviet Union and pressed it on the leadership of other Communist movements.[128] Chinese Communists living in Moscow swiftly translated the book into Chinese and dispatched copies to Yan'an. For the next two decades, the book served as a "crash course" in the training of CCP cadres. Li Wenhan, who taught the *Short Course* in Yan'an, recalled that in the 1930s and 1940s party leaders learned about Marxism and Leninism from the text.[129]

Mao Zedong himself was particularly fond of the *Short Course*. He called it "the encyclopedia of Marxism" and listed it as essential reading for high-ranking cadres, a privileged status that it held until 1955.[130] As Mao asserted,

> In studying Marxism–Leninism, we should use the *History of the Communist Party of the Soviet Union (Bolsheviks), Short Course* as the principal material. It is the best synthesis and summary of the world communist movement of the past hundred years, a model of the integration of theory and practice, and so far the only comprehensive model in the entire world.[131]

---

126. Stuart R. Schram, "Introduction," in *Mao's Road to Power*, vol. 6, liv.

127. Li Hua-yu, *Mao and the Economic Stalinization of China*, 96.

128. Ibid., 96–97.

129. Ibid., 98.

130. Chen Jin, *Mao Zedong dushu biji*, 304–307.

131. Mao Zedong, "Reform Our Study," in *Selected Works of Mao Tse-tung*, vol. 3, 17–26.

This book provided Mao with a new narrative to accompany the study of Marxist theory and allowed him an alternative method of acquiring legitimacy as an original thinker. Inspired by the *Short Course*, Mao ordered the preparation and publication of a documentary work, *From the Sixth Congress—The CCP's Internal Secret Documents*, which was intended to reconstruct the party's past so as to both legitimize Mao's leadership and to lay the groundwork for his role as a leading theorist.[132] The *Short Course* also provided Mao with a blueprint for China's transition to socialism. Benjamin Schwartz notes that Mao uncritically accepted the image of "socialism" as described in this text. Li Hua-yu goes further, arguing that Mao closely followed the steps outlined by Stalin in the *Short Course* and after 1949 created a Stalinist economic structure as set out in the text.[133] Certainly, in the early 1940s, when Mao was overwhelmed by the economic crisis in Yan'an and was seeking a practical method of reorganizing the peasants, the *Short Course* provided him with an ideal formula that could link the creation of mutual aid teams with a viable socialist future.

The *Short Course* informed Mao that Lenin "regarded co-operative societies in general, and agricultural cooperative societies in particular, as a means of transition—a means within the reach and understanding of the peasant millions—from small, individual farming to large-scale producing associations, or collective farms."[134] The book went on to demonstrate the effectiveness and popularity of collective farms among Soviet peasants. Deeply impressed by this shining example of Soviet success, in 1943 Mao Zedong delineated the socialist future for Chinese peasants along very similar lines:

> Among the peasant masses a system of individual economy has prevailed for thousands of years, with each family or household forming a productive unit. This scattered, individual form of production is the economic foundation of feudal rule and keeps the peasants in perpetual poverty. The only way to change it is gradual

---

132. Tony Saich, "Writing or Rewriting History?" 302.

133. Li Hua-yu, *Mao and the Economic Stalinization of China*, 95–96.

134. *Lian gong (bu) dangshi jianming jiaocheng*, 322. For the English translation, see *History of the Communist Party of the Soviet Union*, 261–262.

collectivization, and the only way to bring about collectivization, according to Lenin, is through cooperatives.[135]

Viewing collective labor as a progressive form of production and a superior way of "liberating" productive forces, Mao regarded individual peasant farming practices as backward. When Mao Zedong drew on the *Short Course* to establish his authority as an interpreter of Marxist theory, he was at the same time inoculating himself with its concepts. His writings readily absorbed the language and concepts of this work. There is one paragraph of the Chinese edition of the *Short Course* from which Mao seems to have drawn terminology and even imagery for his well-known declaration cited above:

> Scattered and disunited, each on his tiny, even dwarf individually run farm, destitute of anything like serviceable implements or traction, having no way of breaking up large tracts of virgin soil, without prospect of any improvement on their farms, crushed by poverty, isolated and left to their own devices, now the peasants had at last found a way out, a way to a better life, in the amalgamation of their small farms into cooperative undertakings, collective farms; in tractors, which are able to break up any 'hard ground,' any virgin soil.[136]

Armed with Stalinist theory and Stalinist language, Mao Zedong believed that he had found a way to liberate Chinese peasants. He now determined that not only would he allocate poor peasants land, but also teach them how to farm, skills that in the end would transform them into new kinds of laborers and lead them into the next stage of socialism. This new formula was also significant in that it solved the puzzle that Mao had long been wrestling with: how to justify the peasants as revolutionary agents in Marxist terms. By transforming them from small producers into collective workers, their revolutionary character would become self-evident. For the

---

135. Mao Zedong, "Get Organized," (November 19, 1943) in *Selected Works of Mao Tse-Tung*, vol. 3, 156.

136. *Lian gong (bu) dangshi jianming jiaocheng*, 365–366.

rest of his life, Mao Zedong adhered rigorously to this formula and sought to apply it time and again.

The liberation process began with mutual aid teams, an organizational form that was anything but new to Chinese peasants. There were many types of such associations all across China, although the majority of them were temporary and based on reciprocity.[137] In most parts of China, mutual aid teams were formed within kinship circles or among very poor families that lacked the equipment or draft animals to farm independently. But in the Yan'an area, as a result of the severe labor shortage and the scarcity of resources, mutual aid teams had spread beyond the poorest families. There such teams consisted of four or five peasants, ten at most. They were always short-term and informal: no leadership, no bookkeeping, and no collective ownership of property. Even the Communists acknowledged that it was very difficult to develop mutual aid teams into something on a larger scale.[138] Based on a careful study of villages in northern Shanxi Province, Keating concludes that "before 1943 the communists, in large part, failed to build durable, self-managing associations of villagers for the basic reason that peasants resisted being forced into groups they judged to be a nuisance and a waste of time."[139]

The fact that, traditionally, mutual aid teams were established on the basis of private ownership did not prevent Mao from portraying them as embodying progressive socialist features and as a necessary means to accomplish the transition to collective farming. In late 1943, Mao published an article entitled "On Cooperatives," in which he asserted that mutual aid teams would evolve into "a renewal of the production system, a revolution of relations among the people."[140] He made these high-sounding claims despite admitting that "at present they are only of a rudimentary type and must go through several stages of development before they can become cooperatives of the Soviet type known as collective farms."[141] Mao frequently used the term cooperative in conjunction with these groups, partly because Lenin had used it and partly because it was a very popular term in China in

137. Chen Yung-fa, *Making Revolution*, 215–219.
138. Pauline B. Keating, *Two Revolutions*, 52–53.
139. Ibid., 186.
140. Mao Zedong, "On Cooperatives."
141. Mao Zedong, "Get Organized."

the 1930s and 1940s.[142] It would become evident that "getting the peasants organized" meant organizing them into mutual aid teams, although at this point in 1943, Mao had not considered how to bridge the gap between mutual aid teams and collective farms.[143]

Mao's articles on mutual aid teams and collectivization were widely circulated. The idea that the *organization* of production was the determining factor in increasing productivity was universally disseminated, and the slogan "Get organized" was never questioned. Before long, the Mutual Aid movement was launched in all Communist base areas.

Generally speaking, the movement went through two stages.[144] In 1943, party officials encouraged peasants to form mutual aid teams by providing economic incentives such as agricultural loans and in most cases did not intervene in the management of the teams. The peasants, many solely interested in the incentives offered, were quick to form teams—at this stage, kin-based, seasonal farming teams were the great majority. At the same time, there is evidence that some local cadres simply invented figures that suggested a favorable outcome. For example, in Qingyang city, of the 417 mutual aid teams established on paper, 416 were bogus.[145]

In 1944, the Mutual Aid movement evolved into its next phase, when the party called on local CCP agents to actively intervene and monitor the movement.[146] The cadres strengthened their control over mutual aid teams and attempted to imbue the teams with more "progressive" features. These measures were taken in an attempt to prove that mutual aid teams "could increase productive forces several times over," and that by implementing them the peasants would lose their "private ownership mentality" and recognize that collective land management was a necessity.[147] The trust and goodwill on which traditional mutual aid teams were based were set aside. Instead, strong leadership, mostly provided by party members, was applied to manage these new economic relationships—now based on compulsion rather than voluntary association. Local cadres pressed wealthier families to

---

142. Miao Xinyu, *Jianguo qian 30 nian.*

143. Mao Zedong, "Qieshi zhixing shida zhengce," in *Mao Zedong wenji*, 70–71.

144. For an analysis of these two stages in Yanshu, see Pauline B. Keating, *Two Revolutions*, 205–240.

145. Shi Jingtang, *Zhongguo nongye hezuohua yundong shiliao*, 264.

146. "Bixu jishi jiuzheng laodong huzhu yundong zhong de quedian."

147. Pauline B. Keating, *Two Revolutions*, 225–226.

join the teams and provide livestock for them.[148] Reports on the management of large teams show a striking complexity in their organization. The cadres organized members' work routines, designing a variety of measures to monitor performance and distribute rewards, which were based on a work point system.[149] Yet Keating finds that, in reality, it was very rare for harvests to be divided up according to work points earned, as each family kept the crops grown on their own land.[150] Villagers fought over whose land would be cultivated first. When their demands were not met as they wished, some feigned illness, while others destroyed their tools and slaughtered their livestock to avoid joining a team. The story of Dongfengren village, in Xiyang County in central Shanxi Province, provides an excellent example of this dynamic at work.[151]

Wherever local cadres tried to enforce the practice, mutual aid teams were formed by coercion, which then quickly fell apart. Thousands of mutual aid teams were created in 1944; few remained in 1945.[152] There were documented cases of mutual aid teams that were successful over the long term. One often-mentioned case was the "Jia Baozhi land and transport cooperative" in Baijiagou village in Shanxi Province. Baijiagou village was almost destroyed in an attack by Japanese troops in 1943. In 1944, in the face of tremendous difficulties, four local party members recruited four poor peasants to form a land and distribution cooperative. Of the eight members, one organized war services for the whole team, six worked on land, and Jia Baozhi himself started a trading business. The cooperative was extremely successful and attracted more members. Jia Baozhi was later given a first-degree model laborer award. His cooperative continued to expand, especially in its sideline operations, which included a textile mill and a coal mine.[153] But overwhelmingly more failures were reported. Although no statistics survive to help us assess the success of mutual aid teams, in the 1950s

---

148. Ibid., 224.

149. Work points were awarded based on the quantity and quality of labor performed. Each point translated into an allocation of grain. Vivienne Shue, *Peasant China in Transition.*

150. Pauline B. Keating, *Two Revolutions,* 218–220.

151. Thi Minh-Hoang Ngo, "A Hybrid Revolutionary Process," 284–312.

152. "Huzhu zu zhong de jige wenti."

153. Ren Ziming and Zhao Mingze, "1944 nian Jia Baozhi chuangban tudi yunshu hezuoshe."

when the party attempted to demonstrate the long history of the practice, it could only find a couple of positive examples, such as the case of Jia Baozhi. When it came to explaining the reasons for the failure, one Shandong provincial head hit the nail on the head: "In the past, the peasants took care of their own land. Now when land is collectivized, peasants do not care about farming land as much as before. The larger the size of cooperative farms, the smaller proportion each peasant has and the less he cares about the land. As a result, this kind of collective farming often leads to a drop in production." Privately, he considered the campaign for collective farming to be a "naive idea that fails to fit the peasants' requirements, and won't work."[154]

Although the Get Organized campaign was not a great success, it continued to enjoy the support of rank and file party members, who understood that mutual aid teams were politically correct, and they had something to do with socialism. Most importantly, mutual aid teams were strongly endorsed by Chairman Mao. Mao Zedong was nurturing his personality cult in the mid-1940s, and few CCP cadres dared question his ideas. The high failure rate of mutual aid teams was attributed to the inadequacies of local leadership, fiscal mismanagement, and a lack of organization and discipline. Such failures were never linked to the theory on which the movement was based, nor to the persistence of peasant individualism. In any case, as far as the party was concerned, this later factor was not an insurmountable obstacle to the viability of mutual aid teams. It was possible to mediate the contradictions between self-interest and the interests of others; according to this line of thought, the party simply needed to guide the peasants.[155] Although this mentality prevailed at the time, and proved to be long-lasting, it was not held by everyone. In 1950, Zhang Wentian used the term "mutual aid fetishism" to describe the popular belief that these village associations could solve China's rural problems, an issue discussed more fully in later chapters.[156]

The Get Organized campaign, then, did not resonate with peasant culture, nor did it raise land yields and resolve the revenue crisis in Yan'an. What really rescued Yan'an's economy was probably the secret production and export of opium. In 1942, profits from opium production were said to account for 40.9 percent of revenues from the region; in 1945, a deficit in the

154. Ye Yangbing, *Zhongguo nongye hezuohua yundong yanjiu*, 151.
155. Pauline B. Keating, *Two Revolutions*, 22.
156. Zhang Peisen, *Zhang Wentian nianpu*, 904.

base area's finances was transformed into a profit. The "blooming poppy" had enabled the CCP border region to overcome its financial crisis where conventional means had failed.[157]

The success of the secret opium harvest was transmuted into the very public acclimation of the high "performance" of mass organizations. The former was elided from the history sanctioned by the CCP; the latter became a popular myth to take its place.

Conclusion

It has been a long and difficult journey for Chinese Communists to "understand" Chinese peasants. In the 1920s, Chinese intellectuals, Communists included, turned their attention to rural problems. Overwhelmingly, they subordinated the peasant issues to the national question, giving the creation of a strong China priority over better living conditions for the rural poor. Their understanding of the peasant class was shaped by the wider national context more than by the realities of the rural scene. More precisely, given the magnitude of regional differences in China, there were multiple rural realities to draw on. The Communists' ideological commitments ensured that they would read China's rural realities through the lens of class struggle and exploitation, a tendency evident in the thought of Mao Zedong.

Like many of his contemporaries, Mao valued the peasants as a vehicle for China's national revival more than as a group that justified attention and investment in their own right. Since the peasants were viewed as the *means* of the revolution, they were never considered the ends toward which economic policy should be shaped. When Mao chose to see rural people in a more objective light, he could find few virtues to praise. Inspired by the Soviet experience, he learned to see the peasants as what they could be— revolutionaries in the making. He simplified the complex reality of the rural situation.

During the 1930s and 1940s, the CCP encountered repeated problems in its attempts to encourage peasants to pay more taxes. Mao and many of his comrades learned some important lessons about governance during the Jiangxi Soviet (1931–1934) and the Yan'an period. As World War I had sig-

---

157. David Apter and Tony Saich, *Revolutionary Discourse in Mao's Republic*, 223; Chen Yung-fa, "The Blooming Poppy under the Red Sun."

nificantly affected Soviet approaches to governance,[158] the CCP's experience of wars helped shape its policies and practices following the war.[159] Having run a wartime government, the CCP had abundant experience of intervention in agricultural distribution, requisitioning, and rationing. It tended to overlook the holistic character of agricultural production, instead treating it like another theater of war. During the revolutionary era and after, military language was heavily used in slogans urging increased farm production: the party spoke of infiltration, fronts, enemies, sabotage, and battles. As in wartime, daring schemes and spontaneous acts went unpunished—indeed, they were encouraged. Moreover, following years of wartime experience, Mao assumed that the peasants would ultimately endorse whatever policies the party prescribed. Neither should the party fear committing errors and excesses, which would be remedied eventually. As Levine concludes, Mao and his supporters ignored the lessons of the civil war: "Whatever the adverse odds and no matter what the obstacles, revolutionary objectives could be reached by mobilizing the masses and mustering up sufficient will and determination."[160]

However, the circumstances surrounding the Communist regime were special, if not extraordinary. Government had a highly decentralized structure, in which most policies were decided by county-level authorities. The provincial level was almost irrelevant. While Mao cut his administrative teeth on managing the townships, this apprenticeship was not readily transferable to the enormously expanded environment of the People's Republic of China.[161] Establishing a system that linked central government with provincial and county structures in the previously scattered base areas, and maintaining the party hierarchy, would impose numerous conflicts of interest at the local level. The CCP's governing at the provincial level proved both problematic and manipulative, which is discussed in the remaining chapters.

---

158. Peter Holquist, "'Information is the Alpha and Omega of Our Work,'" 415–450.

159. Steven Levine, *Anvil of Victory*, 247.

160. Ibid., 248.

161. Jae Ho Chung, "Central–Local Dynamics," 299.

2
Debating Policies from Above

To be in opposition is one thing; to be in power is totally different.

—Apter and Saich[1]

Our policies reflect conditions very similar to those in the USSR
before the capitalist uprising in 1918 and the development of their
NEP policies, so their experience is worth considering.

—Liu Shaoqi[2]

On October 1, 1949, at the Tiananmen gate in Beijing, Mao Zedong declared the founding of the People's Republic of China (PRC). At one stroke,
the CCP became recognized as the dominant political force in China. From
this moment on, the CCP faced a daunting task in managing a country as
vast and diverse as China. Uncertain times were ahead as the party mopped
up the remaining Guomindang areas, oversaw the newly acquired regions,
shaped the state apparatus, and restored the collapsed economy. Important
decisions had to be made immediately to meet these new challenges. Although Mao Zedong had dreamed of painting "the freshest and most beau-
tiful" pictures on a blank sheet of paper,[3] China had never been a blank
sheet, and neither was the party itself. On the contrary, in 1949 the party

---

1. David Apter and Tony Saich, *Revolutionary Discourse in Mao's Republic*, 27.
2. Liu Shaoqi, "Guanyu xin Zhongguo de jingji jianshe fangzhen," in *Liu Shaoqi
lun xin Zhongguo jingji jianshe*.
3. Mao Zedong, "Introducing a Cooperative" (April 15, 1958).

resembled a blueprint streaked with permanent marks and wrinkles that could distort the architect's original vision.

Conflicting Agendas and Conflicts in the Party

At the Second Plenary Session of the CCP's Seventh Congress, held in March 1949, party leaders, with the presence of Soviet advisors, convened to envision China's future. Uncertainty enveloped the meeting, and party leaders debated which policies should be adopted over others. Broad consensus was quickly reached on the questions of industrialization and the ultimate goal of social transformation based on the Soviet model, but how these aims should be adjusted to Chinese conditions and the pace of the transition were matters for debate, especially as no one delegate possessed an exact knowledge of the first steps to be taken. The session contented itself with setting up new economic strategies for accommodating a mixed economy under the banner of New Democracy, a concept introduced several years before. Capitalism was seen as a force to be harnessed rather than thoroughly suppressed, and "All capitalist elements in the cities and countryside which are not harmful but beneficial to the national economy should be allowed to exist and expand." However, the delegates asserted, "The existence and expansion of capitalism in China will not be unrestricted and uncurbed as in the capitalist countries." On the contrary, "It will be restricted from several directions—in the scope of its operation and by tax policy, market prices and labor conditions." Anticipating resistance from the bourgeoisie, especially from the owners of large private enterprises, the Communists declared that "restriction versus opposition to restriction will be the main form of class struggle in the new democratic state." As for the agricultural sector, there was no doubt that "it is possible to lead the development of agriculture in the direction of modernization and collectivization," while "both at present and during a relatively long period of time in the future our agricultural and handicraft industry are and will remain dispersed and individualized in terms of the basic form." Mao then told the congress that "the view that they [the peasants] may be left to take their own course is wrong."[4]

The above statements contradicted each other, and thus left significant room for different interpretations. Suffice it to say that the session failed to

---

4. Zhu Yonghong, "Reflections on the Party's Policy," 51–59.

deliver a precise and clear agenda for the party members to follow. How did this situation arise? The contradictions were much more than simply rhetorical. They reflected the CCP's uncertainty over the prioritizing of policies, revealed its ambivalence about New Democracy, and were rooted in internal divisions in the configuration of the PRC.

Theoretically, the New Democracy policy was grounded in Lenin's New Economic Policy (NEP) of the early 1920s. In the late 1940s, when the CCP began to prepare itself for ruling China, it frequently consulted with Stalin on a wide range of issues. As Soviet archives reveal, the CCP had planned to establish a one-party socialist government. Stalin was not supportive of this concept. Breaking with his own ideas expressed in his writings from the 1920s and 1930s, Stalin preached gradualism and suggested that his Chinese comrades adopt a moderate approach to governing China. As he cabled Mao, "For the time being [there will be] no nationalization of all land and no abolition of private ownership of land will be effected, no confiscation of the property of the commercial and industrial bourgeoisie, from the petty up to the big bourgeoisie, no confiscation of the property of not only big landowners, but also of the middle and small ones living by hired labor."[5] Officially, the CCP accepted his suggestions. In February 1949, Liu Shaoqi reported to Anastas Mikoyan, Stalin's special agent who was visiting the CCP headquarters, that "the transition to socialism will be lengthy in terms of time, and harsh in terms of struggle … we shall have to wait ten to fifteen years for the full offensive against capitalist elements in our economy."[6]

Liu Shaoqi was the most prominent advocate for New Democracy in the years to come, on various occasions, both within the party and to a broader audience. For Liu, China's situation in 1948 resembled that of the Soviet Union during the NEP period: "Our policies reflect conditions very similar to those in the USSR before the capitalist uprising in 1918 and the development of their NEP policies, so their experience is worth considering."[7] Liu reiterated that China was still in the initial stages of New Democracy and that private ownership was to be protected and capitalism encouraged. Before moving to a fully socialist regimen, China needed to improve its econ-

---

5. Andrei Ledovsky, "Two cables from correspondence between Mao Zedong and Joseph Stalin," 95.

6. Andrei Ledovsky, "Mikoyan's Secret Mission to China," 86–87.

7. Liu Shaoqi, "Xin Zhongguo jingji de xingshi yu jingji jianshe fangzhen," in *Liu Shaoqi lun xin Zhongguo jingji jianshe,* 49.

omy, increase the wealth of its people, and strengthen the nation. However, not all the CCP cadres wholeheartedly embraced New Democracy. As Bo Yibo recalled, in 1949 only a limited number of CCP cadres were familiar with Lenin's NEP. Rather, many cadres were confused by the New Democracy policy and questioned the necessity and merits of tolerating capitalism.[8] Above all, although Mao Zedong had outlined the term "New Democracy" in an essay in 1940, he actually showed little interest at this time.

First and foremost, Mao had long identified capitalism with foreign imperialism and never fully appreciated the progressive side of capitalism. As a youth, he viewed capitalism simply as a form of oppression and exploitation, and he "often used 'capitalism' simply as a pejorative term for all types of exploitation and inequality."[9] Second, his knowledge of the economy had been shaped by his wartime experiences, where centralized control of resources had been the norm. To Mao, it seemed a simple and natural transition from a state-controlled war economy to a planned economy. Mao was eager to begin building a socialist China immediately. After all, this was a goal that the party had pursued for a decade, a mission that would fulfill his deepest desires, and an accomplishment that would place him and China at the summit of the Communist world. Stalin counseled him against this course and pressed him to accept New Democracy as an appropriate stage of development. Mao nurtured doubts about New Democracy, and he was not alone.

Many CCP cadres of peasant origin had devoted themselves to the Communist revolution out of desperation, few having received formal training in Marxism. They viewed the revolution primarily as a social revolt, and identified themselves with China's traditional slogans of social rebellion, such as "Level out the differences between the rich and the poor" (*jun pinfu*). This slogan had elements in common with the CCP's early programs for mobilizing the peasants—such as the equal distribution of land and property. Many participants in the Communist revolution hence equated the wholesale redistribution of land and property with socialism. The CCP was not blind to its peasant cadres' understanding of egalitarian socialism and labeled it unapprovingly as "absolute equalitarian Communism" or "agricultural socialism."[10] While such a mindset may have facilitated war mobi-

---

8. Bo Yibo, *Ruogan Zhongda juece yu shijian de huigu*, vol. 1, 65.

9. Maurice Meisner, *Mao Zedong*, 88.

10. Wang Haiguang, "Zhengzheng yu quanzheng."

lization, it certainly disrupted existing laws and the social status quo. When the CCP moved from its revolutionary phase to assuming power, it disapproved of the premature pursuit of equality. For example, on April 1, 1948, Mao stated that "such thinking (agricultural socialism) is reactionary, backward and retrogressive in nature. We must criticize it."[11]

On July 27, 1948, through the letters to the editor column of the Xinhua News Agency, the CCP publicized the drawbacks of agricultural socialism. Taken on its own, absolute equalitarianism carried out in a small-peasant economy would not increase productivity. On the contrary, it would impair social productivity. Having criticized agricultural socialism, the letter had nothing but praise for the New Democracy policy, which promised to protect private ownership. Only through the development of capitalism and modern industry, and following agricultural collectivization based on mechanization, could socialism be achieved.[12] It is noteworthy that the CCP chose a newspaper column to spread this message, rather than more formal channels—it is doubtful whether most rank and file members would have been aware of it. In the years to come, Liu Shaoqi would repeat a similar critique of agricultural socialism, phrased in increasingly strident tones. It is interesting to note that, following the appearance of this piece, Mao Zedong never spoke another word against agricultural socialism.[13]

During the revolutionary years, the understanding of socialism held by most grassroots cadres was rooted in egalitarianism. Those cadres, much like Mao Zedong, had adapted to the state-controlled economy during wartime and had become receptive the Soviet-style planned economy. They had learned to associate capitalism with evil. But in 1949, all of a sudden, in the name of New Democracy, socialism no longer meant equal distribution and capitalism was to be protected. They were no doubt confused by this swift reversal in policy.[14] Since the CCP had won the war, they asked, Why are we retreating instead of moving forward? The confusion would develop into mistrust when policy differences became intertwined with the power struggles and grassroots defiance of authority that had been nurtured in earlier decades.

---

11. Mao Zedong, "Speech at a Conference of Cadres in the Shansi–Suiyuan Liberated Area," in *Selected Works of Mao Tse-tung*, vol. iv, 227–240.

12. North China Bureau, *1948 nian yilai zhengce huibian*, 39–45.

13. Wang Haiguang, "Zhengzheng yu quanzheng."

14. Ibid.

The CCP's military revolution originated in a number of relatively independent base areas. Over time, multiple factions had developed. The two largest factions comprised cadres stationed in the "red" area bases and the Red Army on the one hand and those working in the "white" areas under enemy control on the other. The mistrust between the two groups went back to the late 1920s. By 1945 Mao Zedong was recognized as the chief representative of the red bases, while Liu Shaoqi was made spokesman for the white areas and became the heir apparent to Mao.[15] Since then, the seeds of conflict between Liu Shaoqi and a number of prominent generals had been planted.

These differences in leadership, this way or another, connected to the concerns of the common soldiers. There is an old Chinese saying, "Fight for the heavens together, and divide the heavens together." Most of the cadres from the revolutionary areas were of peasant origins and saw the Communist revolution in terms of a social rebellion. They shed their blood in anticipation of being rewarded for their part in the struggle, believing they had earned a share of the fruits of victory. They were brave fighters, yet usually barely literate. Prior to 1949, they mostly fought and worked in rural areas and had little understanding of the modern urban world. They scarcely qualified as bureaucrats to be entrusted with the management of cities and a modern economy. After 1949, their overwhelmingly rural backgrounds had become a liability and even an embarrassment for the new regime. General Huang Kecheng once commented frankly that peasant cadres who had worked only in rural areas were generally not suitable for city work.[16]

By contrast, many cadres from the white areas were educated and knowledgeable about the wider world; they had had years of experience living in cities. Not surprisingly, they were better suited to working in an urban environment and many quickly found a place in the new system. Many outstripped their peers from revolutionary areas, giving rise to resentment.[17] Liu Shaoqi, head of the Organizational Department of the CCP's Central Committee, which was charged with cadre promotions, did nothing to allay these feelings. Instead, he exacerbated them.

Between 1945 and 1950, Mao was engaged in the military campaign to

---

15. Central Committee of the CCP, *Guanyu jianguo yilai dang de ruogan lishi wenti de jueyi.*

16. Jeremy Brown, *City versus Countryside in Mao's China,* 20.

17. Wang Haiguang, "Zhengzheng yu quanzheng."

"liberate" China from Guomindang forces, leaving most party matters in the hands of Liu Shaoqi. In the late 1940s, Liu was the head of both the Organizational Department of the CCP and the North Bureau (*beifangju*), where the new capital, Beijing, would be located. When the CCP came to build its new central apparatus in the future capital, Liu overwhelmingly favored cadres from the North Bureau under his jurisdiction. For example, he promoted his confidants Peng Zhen and An Ziwen to replace him as joint heads of the Organizational Department. He supported the appointment of Bo Yibo, another member of Liu's inner circle, as head of the Financial Department of the Central CCP. All three men had worked under Liu in the North Bureau prior to 1949. Suddenly, they leaped into the inner circle of the party leadership.

At the same time, Liu maintained firm control over the North Bureau, putting his close associate Liu Lantao in charge. Grasping the chance to create a new political apparatus and to capitalize on the geographical advantage of propinquity to the capital, Liu Shaoqi placed his followers, nearly all of whom were from white areas, in key posts in Beijing, while the party's military leaders were scattered across China fighting a bloody civil war.[18] Liu's obvious favoritism irritated cadres from the revolutionary areas. In addition to feeling resentment over being excluded from the center of power, they also held doubts about the integrity of their white counterparts, many of whom had been jailed and later released by the Guomindang. Prior to 1949, cadres from revolutionary areas had felt superior because of their experience of battle, their unquestionable integrity, and their impeccable history of opposing the Guomindang. However, in 1949, this situation was reversed, especially in Beijing, and cadres from the revolutionary areas felt discriminated against. Even so prudent a general as Lin Biao expressed his concern that "it is very dangerous to us that cadres from white areas control the central CCP."[19] Nursing resentments, cadres from the revolutionary centers could not help being suspicious of Liu Shaoqi and New Democracy, which he so strongly endorsed.

In hindsight, the rift between the two factions was a powerful factor driving a series of political events after 1949. On many occasions this rivalry influenced the course of events and amplified existing tensions. In addition to their fierce mutual opposition, the two factions each harbored a number

---

18. Yang Kuisong, "Jianguo chuqi zhonggong ganbu renyong zhengce kaocha."
19. Ibid.

of internal splinter groups. For example, the revolutionary bases had comprised nineteen separate base areas during the Anti-Japanese war and the white areas were divided between the South Bureau (*nanfangju*) and the North Bureau. Competition and friction among these various groups was often fierce, as explained in Chapter 3.

How did Mao Zedong, China's new ruler, fit into this developing power structure? Mao was a politician who spent much more time studying Chinese history than reading the Marxist classics.[20] Mao saw his new role as resembling that of a founding emperor, rather than as a leader of a modern political party bound by rules and procedures. On taking office, he immediately sought to consolidate his own supremacy in the new system. He saw that the key to safeguarding his position lay in balancing conflicting power relationships. Mao needed to secure the balance of power between the party and the army, between the center and the periphery, and among his close subordinates. Learning from Chinese history, Mao understood that the most urgent challenge following the founding of a new regime, especially the one created through large-scale rebellions, was to curb the power of the army, as the founders of the Han and Ming dynasties had encountered.

In 1948, Mao was convinced that the CCP would defeat the Guomindang within a year, and he divided the People's Liberation Army into four field armies, each responsible for conquering a different part of China. As these forces accomplished their tasks between 1949 and 1950, they formed military regions where they wielded military and administrative power, forming another level of administration between central and provincial government. Growing out of the four military regions, together with the two former liberated regions in Northeast and North China, six grand bureaus were established: Northeast China Bureau, Northwest China Bureau, North China Bureau, Southwest China Bureau, Central–South China Bureau, and East China Bureau. The provinces were grouped into these bureaus as follows:

- Northeast China Bureau: Heilongjiang, Jilin, Rehe, Liaoning;
- Northwest China Bureau: Gansu, Ningxia, Shaanxi, Xinjiang, Qinghai;
- North China Bureau: Chahar, Hebei, Shanxi, Suiyuan;
- East China Bureau: Anhui, Fujian, Jiangsu, Shandong, Zhejiang;

---

20. Examination of Mao's reading notes and the personal library Mao kept in his bedroom confirms this view. Chen Jin, *Mao Zedong dushu biji*.

- Central–South China Bureau: Henan, Hunan, Hubei, Jiangxi, Guangxi, Guangdong;
- Southwest China Bureau: Guizhou, Xikang, Sichuan, and Yunnan.

These six grand bureaus covered all of China and were responsible for the administration of military, political, and economic affairs in their vast territories. They reported directly to the Central Committee of the CCP and supervised the provincial-level administrations below them. With the exception of the Northeast China Bureau, run by Gao Gang alone, each grand bureau had two leaders. Of the eleven grand bureau chiefs, nine were army commanders, a situation that deeply concerned Mao.[21] As a result of the tacit strategies Mao employed, within two years eight of these army commanders had either been transferred out of their original military regions or reappointed to posts that had little direct contact with the army.[22] Seven years later, all six grand bureaus were abolished.

When Mao was breaking down the power of the revolutionary army, it seems that he tacitly approved Liu Shaoqi's maneuver to disfavor military personnel. But as the army's power waned, Mao began to concern himself about his colleague, comrade Liu Shaoqi. In the space of a few years, Liu had built a power base at the center of the party, especially in the Organizational Department and in the economic sector. Although Liu frequently consulted with Mao on important issues and sought Mao's approval, the two men had very different agendas. Liu wholeheartedly endorsed New Democracy and even publicly encouraged capitalism from time to time. He did not hesitate to declare his preference for economic revival over building socialism. In one meeting with businessmen, he even urged capitalists to exploit the workers because it was good for the economy.[23] Not surprisingly, Liu's approach generated confusion, even anger, among other Communists. Mao, by contrast, did not spell out his own agenda. In the early 1950s, as Frederick Teiwes observes, "While reserving the right to insist on his own way in matters of prime concern, such as the Korean decision, Mao's general approach was to encourage broad discussion in order to reach a consensus."[24]

---

21. Only Rao Shushi of the East China Bureau and Bo Yibo of the North China Bureau were not army commanders.

22. Yang Kuisong, "Jianguo chuqi zhonggong ganbu renyong zhengce kaocha."

23. Zhao Jialiang and Zhang Xiaoyun, *Banjie mubei xia de wangshi*, 42–44.

24. Frederick C. Teiwes, *Politics at Mao's Court*, 17.

Although alarmed by Liu Shaoqi's rising authority and doubtful of the merits of New Democracy, Mao chose not to confront Liu Shaoqi immediately. However, the contrasting approaches of these two senior Communist leaders came to surface eventually and were reflected in their different attitudes to the peasant problems.

Controversies in Governing Peasants: Searching for Alternatives

Land reform had been the CCP's leading rural policy. As discussed in the introduction, however, land reform tends to impair rural productivity, not to improve it; and it disrupts the existing social order. Radical land reform in North China between 1946 and 1948 clearly demonstrated these facts to the CCP leaders, especially Liu Shaoqi.

The war against Japan ended in 1945, and civil war between the CCP and the Guomindang broke out the following year. Between 1946 and 1948, the party carried out radical land reform in areas that had been liberated, presumably to finance wartime mobilization.[25] Liu Shaoqi, Mao's top confidant at the time and a specialist on urban workers, was assigned the task of implementing land reform, despite his lack of experience in this area. Liu reprinted Mao's Hunan Report and had it distributed to every cadre as the official guide to the party's rural policies. He called on local cadres to eliminate the landlords and rich peasants. In justifying these moves, Liu asserted that "the opinion of 90 percent of the masses is the law, is our policy."[26] The peasants, especially poor peasants, were virtually promised that anything they did to landlords would go unpunished, an assurance that they diligently exploited. Poor peasants attacked, beat, and sometimes murdered landlords, wealthy peasants, and even villagers who happened to have a surplus. In some villages in Shanxi Province, for example, all the landlords were killed in a single night. In extreme cases, poor peasants even attacked local CCP cadres, some of whom took their own lives in response.[27]

Officially, this land reform was completed with great success. But in

25. Research on radical land reform in North China between 1946 and 1948 is discussed in Huang Daoxuan, "Mengyou yihuo qianzai duishou?"

26. Yang Kuisong, *Zhonghua renmin gongheguo jianguoshi yanjiu*, 45–46.

27. Ibid., 72.

reality it was responsible for hundreds of thousands of deaths in the countryside and provoked enormous disruption in rural production. Many peasants slaughtered their farm animals and abandoned their land. Middle-ranking peasants no doubt put less effort into farming; poor peasants, who had received allocations of land and other commodities, had little impetus to work harder. Moreover, convinced that the CCP would continue to provide their needs, many sold land, livestock, and other goods they had received, and spent the money on food and drink.[28] Although aware of the excesses and atrocities committed in its name, the CCP at first was willing to pay a high price to aid the wartime mobilization effort even at the cost of marginalizing rural productivity.[29] The lasting trauma generated by land reform among the Chinese peasantry, along with the new rural leadership it had created composed mainly of poor peasants, would handicap the party in its handling of rural matters after 1949—a story told in subsequent chapters.

During land reform, with 30–40 percent of male laborers (in some areas 60–80 percent) having joined the Red Army, mutual aid teams were formed as a solution to a pressing labor shortage. In these teams, the principles of voluntary participation and equal exchange were abandoned, and members were urged to be constantly at the team's disposal. In Shanxi Province, the slogan was "All peasants under heaven are one family." The mutual aid teams further shouldered a variety of administration duties. In sum, the party utilized mutual aid teams as administrative units, imposing them on the villagers and monitoring them directly. As a result, participation rates were unusually high. In Changzhi prefecture of Shanxi Province, for example, in 1947, 93 percent of laborers joined mutual aid teams.[30]

In 1948, violence in the countryside had escalated to such a degree that a group of high-ranking CCP officials sounded the alarm. Speaking out, Xi Zhongxun questioned the rationale behind granting poor peasants the power to lead land reform. He argued that, after years of CCP occupation of base areas (and the programs it had carried out in favor of poor peasants), if villagers remained impoverished it was either because of bad luck, laziness, or addiction to opium or gambling. Poor peasants were not respected by

---

28. Steven Levine, *Anvil of Victory*, 213–215.

29. Chen Yung-fa, "Reconsidering Yan'an, Again."

30. Shanxi sheng nongye hezuoshi bianji weiyuanhui, "Shanxi sheng zuzhi qilai de lishi qingkuang," 593–596.

others. Having them lead land reform was to entrust leadership to social misfits.[31]

Having few concerns about "leftist" mistakes and with a deep-rooted faith in the poor peasants, Mao Zedong saw these disturbances as a demonstration of the peasants' revolutionary spirit. But as the Red Army marched to victory, and the CCP began to consider its impending takeover of China, fomenting social disruption gave way to a desire for a peaceful and productive countryside. Eventually, in 1948, Mao decided that the time had come to rectify the excesses that had occurred during land reform.[32] The CCP News Agency began to repeatedly emphasize that improving agricultural production was a major priority for the party and called for protection to be given to farm animals.[33]

Liu Shaoqi shouldered the main responsibility for not curbing excesses in a timely fashion and he made a self-criticism. The year-long experience of "leading" peasants must have provided him with fresh understanding of peasants. In years to come, the CCP leaders would split over the best strategy for governing the peasantry. Liu Shaoqi, accompanied by Zhang Wentian, drawing inspiration from Lenin, came to propose an alternative to Mao's method of governing peasants.

Stalinist collectivization was not the sole socialist model for the peasantry. In 1923, Lenin had published his final important article, "On Cooperation," in which he stated, "If the whole of the peasantry were organized in cooperatives, we would be standing firmly with both feet on the soil of Socialism."[34] Yet he died in 1924, and had done little to further the idea. It was up to his followers to define the nature and role of socialist cooperatives. In the second half of the 1920s, heated debates broke out between Nikolai Bukharin and Stalin. Simply put, Bukharin believed that Lenin's ideas had referred to Supply and Marketing Cooperatives (SMC). As the name suggests, SMC emphasized good circulation, not production. Bukharin believed that peasants should be allowed to farm their own land privately. By organizing peasants in SMCs, the state could monitor small producers through commodity circulation and indirectly control them through

---

31. Yang Kuisong, *Zhonghua renmin gongheguo jianguoshi yanjiu*, 72.
32. Ibid., 98.
33. *Xinhuashe pinglun*, 346–358.
34. V.I. Lenin, "On Cooperation."

economic regulations.[35] By contrast, Stalin interpreted Lenin as referring to producers' cooperatives in which the state would organize small producers in collective production and directly administer their production process. The private sector would be eliminated.

The consensus among scholars today is that as Lenin said little in his article about producers' cooperatives, Bukharin's interpretation was closer to what Lenin envisaged.[36] Nonetheless, in the late 1920s, Bukharin was politically defeated by Stalin and his theories were erased from Soviet history. When the *Short Course* was compiled, Lenin's ideas were manipulated to conform to Stalin's own. Enthusiasts for the *Short Course*, such as Mao Zedong, no doubt believed that Lenin had originally advocated collectivization and knew little of Bukharin's interpretation. However, a few CCP comrades including Zhang Wentian and Liu Shaoqi, both of whom had studied in Moscow in the 1920s, did know of Bukharin's views. In fact, Zhang was known in the CCP for his knowledge of Bukharin.[37]

In the late 1940s, Zhang Wentian served as governor of Heilongjiang Province in Northeast China. His focus was on economic issues, and he suggested that the party shift its emphasis from fomenting class struggle to encouraging rural production. He criticized the party's actions in forcing peasants to join mutual aid teams. Instead, he promised to protect peasants' private property and advocated Supply and Marketing Cooperatives. Zhang was profoundly influenced by Lenin's concept of the "transition from capitalism to socialism" and the NEP.[38] Zhang also incorporated Bukharin's ideas into his own thinking, although he did not give Bukharin, then vilified as a traitor in the Soviet Union, any credit. Like Bukharin, Zhang asserted that SMCs were a crucial element in the transition to socialism:

> At present, SMCs in the countryside are the economic engine directing the economic activities of small producers, and the central linkage between agricultural production and consumption. Following land reform, they became the most important form of organization for peasants and small artisans. Without cooperatives, it would

---

35. Moshe Lewin, *Russian Peasants and Soviet Power.*

36. Li Hua-yu, *Mao and the Economic Stalinization of China*, 72.

37. In 1953, Zhang Wentian was asked to teach Li Weihan, then the head of the United Front Department, about the Bolshevik thinker. Li Weihan, *Huiyi yu yanjiu*, 744.

38. Li Hua-yu, *Mao and the Economic Stalinization of China.*

be impossible to organize thousands and thousands of small agricultural producers on an economic footing.[39]

In another piece, Zhang concluded that SMCs could not only facilitate the circulation of commodities between cities and the countryside, but could also connect the state-owned economy with small producers.[40] He wrote, "Today, we should be paying particular attention to consumer cooperatives which have the potential to connect the state-owned economy and the private economy."[41] However, Zhang Wentian's ideas directly conflicted with the plan devised by Gao Gang and were not put into practice in the northeast.

Zhang Wentian was not the only advocate of SMCs in high places—at almost the same time, Liu Shaoqi was writing a series of articles on the subject. Like Zhang Wentian, Liu Shaoqi understood the value of capitalism to China, arguing that the rush to eliminate capitalism was a leftist mistake: "You will have to invite it [capitalism] back even if you have already eliminated it."[42] Liu promised to preserve peasants' private property and planned to integrate China's economy through setting up a national marketing administration—the SMCs were to be the instrument to achieve this goal.[43] Liu pointed out that Lenin and Stalin had both emphasized the importance of cooperatives and stressed that the alliance between the cooperative movement and the state-owned economy would lead China toward socialism. The SMCs had a key role to play in this process:

> Obviously, without widespread SMCs as the bridge connecting small producers and the state-owned economy, the country, led by the proletariat, will be unable to direct hundreds of thousands of scattered

---

39. Zhang Wentian, *Zhang Wentian xuanji*, 402; Li Hua-yu, *Mao and the Economic Stalinization of China*, 73–74.

40. Zhang Peisen, *Zhang Wentian nianpu.*

41. Zhang Wentian, "Guanyu dongbei jingji goucheng ji," 32–33.

42. Liu Shaoqi, "Guangyu xin minzhu zhuyi jianshe wenti" (On the construction of New Democracy) (September 1948), in *Liu Shaoqi lun xin Zhongguo jingji jianshe.*

43. Liu Shaoqi, "Lun xin minzhu zhuyi shiqi de jingji yu hezuoshe" (On the economy of the New Democratic period and the cooperatives), in *Liu Shaoqi lun xin Zhongguo jingji jianshe.*

small producers, and the construction of a national economy along the lines of New Democracy will not proceed smoothly.[44]

Here Liu Shaoqi proposed SMCs as the means of assuring that large numbers of peasant farmers would produce in accordance with proletarian demands. A close reading of Liu's writings on cooperatives in this period reveals that his language was not derived from the *Short Course*, but rather from Lenin's work on the NEP. Liu Shaoqi showed little interest in forming mutual aid teams and, when speaking or writing about cooperatives, he often did not include mutual aid teams. When at a Politburo meeting in September 1948 Liu suggested organizing cooperatives across China, he referred only to SMCs. (The record shows that Mao Zedong then interrupted Liu, stating that mutual aid teams were also a form of cooperative.)[45]

Liu's proposals seemed convincing. Even Chairman Mao admitted that "Comrade Liu Shaoqi has done some impressive research on this (cooperative) issue."[46] As part of New Democracy policy, Liu urged that "the transfer of agriculture onto socialist lines be envisaged only on condition that agriculture has been provided an industrial base."[47] Mao seemed to agree; as he told Mikoyan, "We have given land to the peasants, but we have not given them the commodities they need and which we do not have. If we do not develop industry, we shall not be able to supply the peasants with commodities."[48] Officially, Liu Shaoqi's plan to encourage the private rural economy and give priority to increasing rural production over collectivization was adopted. It was announced that SMCs were to be established on a national scale.

It is particularly noteworthy that the two advocates of the SMC model,

---

44. Liu Shaoqi, "Dui 'guanyu dongbei jingji goucheng ji jingji jianshe jiben fangzhen de tigang' de ruogan xiugai" (Several amendments to 'Outline of the basic guidelines for economic reconstruction and organization of the economy in the northeast region'), in *Liu Shaoqi lun xin Zhongguo jingji jianshe*.

45. Liu Shaoqi, "Xin minzhu zhuyi jingji jianshe wenti" (Problems in constructing the New Democratic economy), in *Liu Shaoqi lun xin Zhongguo jingji jianshe*.

46. Mao Zedong, "Muqian de xingshi he dang zai 1949 nian de renwu" (The current situation and the mission of the Party in 1949) (January 8, 1949), in *Mao Zedong wenji*, vol. 5, 229–236.

47. Andrei Ledovsky, "Mikoyan's Secret Mission to China," 86–87.

48. Ibid., 87.

Zhang Wentian and Liu Shaoqi, had both been educated in the Soviet Union in the 1920s and were leading Marxist theoreticians in China. As we have seen, Zhang Wentian had conducted a year-long investigation in the early 1940s, and Liu had learned a great deal about Chinese peasants through his experience in charge of land reform between 1946 and 1948. By coincidence or not, the two comrades, on the eve of the founding of the PRC, both rejected an immediate transition to Stalinist collectivization and advocated SMCs for Chinese farmers. How did it come about that the two Chinese Communists who probably knew most about Marxism and the Soviet Union, and had recently worked closely with Chinese peasants, rediscovered Bukharin's views at this critical moment? Did they both foresee the adverse effects of reduplicating the Stalinist collectivization model in China? Did they see its drawbacks on Chinese soil? Unfortunately, neither man has left any inkling of his doubts about the Stalinist model.

For his part, Mao was not entirely convinced of the merits of New Democracy or of the SMC. Quite the contrary, he warned against letting the peasants take their own course.[49] Increasingly, Mao became concerned about the power Liu Shaoqi had accumulated and Liu's deviation from Mao's party line. A master at balancing conflicting interests and strengths, Mao recruited supporters whose ideas were more in tune with his own and who could stand up to Liu Shaoqi. Among this group, Gao Gang, a member of the Politburo and chairman of the Northeast China Bureau, stood out.

Gao Gang Facing up to Liu Shaoqi

The Northeast China Bureau administered China's northeastern provinces (known to some as Manchuria), a vast region bordering the Soviet Union. Manchuria was a territory with a frontier economy. It had an abundance of land and lower population pressures than most of China, with approximately 6 mu of cultivated land per person, more than twice the rate in the Chinese heartland. Japan occupied Manchuria between 1931 and 1945 and

---

49. Mao Zedong, "Zai Zhongguo gongchangdang di qi jie zhongyang weiyuan hui di er ci quan ti huiyi shang de baogao" (Report to the Second Plenary Session of The Seventh Central Committee of the Communist Party of China), in *Selected Works of Mao Zedong*, vol. 4.

turned it into the most industrialized region of China. After the defeat of Japan in 1945, the CCP, with Soviet assistance, took over much of the land. It was in Manchuria, particularly in Harbin, the most important city in the region, that the CCP learned its first lessons in administering cities. There the CCP was taught that the most urgent task was to *feed* the urban residents under its jurisdiction. There, the CCP cadres were instructed that the chief criterion to judge their performance was their ability to fulfill the tax quota. Harbin municipality established a Grain Regulation Committee that abolished the free grain market and replaced it with a rationing system, soon extended to include coal and charcoal.[50] Many of the CCP officials who managed Manchuria's economy before 1949 assumed high-ranking positions in the economic sector in Beijing after 1949; they included such prominent figures as Chen Yun and Li Fuchun, who would adeptly transfer the lessons they had learned in Manchuria to China as a whole, as discussed in Chapter 6.

By 1947, the CCP had imposed land reform in Manchuria, confiscating and redistributing all lands belonging to landlords and the surplus land of wealthy peasants. It was not a smooth process; the CCP sent fifteen thousand cadres into the countryside to make the revolution happen.[51] In the short term, land reform severely undermined agricultural production. The middle-ranking peasants reduced their efforts in the fields to the minimum. Some poor peasants sold off the property they had received during land reform and devoted the income to food and drink, content to await the next redistribution round without needing to work. In 1948, in Manchuria as in North China, the CCP halted its program of radical land reform.

The CCP, anxious to keep the cities fed, made demands on the peasants for increased production of grain, fodder, livestock, and labor power. It encouraged peasant farmers to form mutual aid teams to make best use of the labor power and to lay the foundations for the future socialist agricultural system. However, when teams were formed by farmers, the better-off peasants likely took charge of the teams and often took advantage of their poorer members. Whether or not to intervene in support of poor farmers was not an easy decision. If the party intervened, it violated the principle of voluntary participation; if it failed to do so, the mutual aid teams would end up

---

50. Steven Levine, *Anvil of Victory*, 196.
51. Ibid., 207.

being run along the very class lines it was committed to oppose.[52] (A similar dilemma would arise in Shanxi Province, as discussed in the following chapters.) The CCP commander in Manchuria, Gao Gang, chose to intervene. His support for the mutual aid teams became intertwined with his political struggle with Liu Shaoqi.

Gao Gang was a military veteran, having had an outstanding career in the Red Army, fighting first in Northwest China and later in Northeast China. By 1949, he was regarded as the "king of the Northwest" (*dongbei wang*) and was a rising star in the party. A few years younger than Liu Shaoqi, Gao's discontent with Liu dated back to 1947, when Liu chose to support his confidant Peng Zhen over Gao Gang in disputes over land reform. Being a cadre from the revolutionary areas was a further reason for Gao to distance himself from Liu Shaoqi, the leader of cadres from white areas. In Gao's words, "Liu did not support us, and we did not defer to him very much at all."[53] After the CCP took over the northeast, further conflict broke out between the two. As an exponent of the immediate socialist transformation of agriculture and industry, Gao advocated following the Stalinist model as presented in the *Short Course*. In Manchuria, Gao Gang used the slogan, "Building a model of Soviet socialism." After Gao had failed to support the New Democracy policy in party meetings, Liu Shaoqi openly reproached him for his "leftist" error.[54]

For his part, Gao Gang rejected this charge. In addition to his authority in Manchuria, Gao was also known for his close ties with his Soviet counterparts, due in part to geographical proximity. He had nurtured a particularly close relationship with Ivan Kovalev, Stalin's special envoy to the CCP between 1948 and 1950. Kovalev referred to Gao Gang as a "true comrade" and "an exceptional man." Andrei Ledovsky, who served as Soviet consul-general in Mukden from 1950 to 1952, also admired Gao and remembered him as an orthodox pro-Soviet Communist who was sympathetic to the Soviet model of economic planning.[55] Gao Gang did not let these valuable contacts go to waste. Details of top-level CCP meetings reached Stalin through Kovalev. Kovalev, perhaps inspired by Gao Gang, hinted in one report that differences in the economic blueprints supported by various CCP

---

52. Ibid., 192.

53. Zhao Jialiang and Zhang Xiaoyun, *Banjie mubei xia de wangshi*, 42–44.

54. Ibid.

55. Paul Wingrove, "Mao's Conversations with the Soviet Ambassador."

leaders were signs of an internal political struggle. Kovalev claimed that pro-American and anti-Soviet sentiments were rife in the CCP; Liu Shaoqi and Bo Yibo were among the leaders he mentioned as allegedly harboring pro-American sentiment.[56] While his true intentions remain unclear, Stalin later passed on Kovalev's report to Mao. Although Mao's personal reaction to the report is also a matter of conjecture, between 1950 and 1953 Mao did not question Gao Gang about his connections with the Soviet Union. When after Stalin's death Khrushchev and Malenkov secretly arrested the KGB director Lavrentiy Beria in June 1953, Mao sent Gao Gang to Moscow to take part in an emergency hearing.[57] This episode illustrated Mao's faith in Gao Gang; had he nurtured any suspicions of Gao's inappropriate links with the Soviet Union, Mao would not have assigned Gao this extremely sensitive mission. Regardless of how Mao read Stalin's motivations, Kovalev's report must also have alerted Mao to the political risks of appearing to encourage pro-American sentiment in China. After all, as we now know from Soviet archives, in 1950 Stalin was very wary of the possibility of a rapprochement between China and the United States.[58] Thus differences on economic policy had become tied to sensitive political questions and could potentially be seen as an ideological issue. The stakes had risen.

In 1949, Gao Gang accompanied Liu Shaoqi on a visit to the Soviet Union. After Gao Gang returned to China, he spoke openly about Stalin's discontent with Liu Shaoqi and Stalin's favoring of Gao himself.[59] In February 1950, Gao Gang wrote to Mao Zedong about a speech Liu had given in Tianjin in 1949. Gao accused Liu of suggesting that China was headed down the road of capitalism, not socialism.[60] Gao warned Mao that these views had generated negative reactions, both in the CCP and in the international Communist community. Indeed, New Democracy had itself generated suspicion among members of the international Communist community. One example of this disquiet emanated from Velio Spano, a prominent figure in

---

56. "Ivan Kovalev's report to Stalin," 88–92.

57. Zhao Jialiang and Zhang Xiaoyun, *Banjie mubei xia de wangshi*, 61.

58. Thomas Christensen, *Useful Adversaries*, 140–147.

59. Zhao Jialiang and Zhang Xiaoyun, *Banjie mubei xia de wangshi*, 56.

60. Liu Shaoqi made the statement in a specific context, but Gao Gang took the comment out of the context, in a misleading way. Sadly, this is how Liu's statement was circulated. Zhao Jialiang and Zhang Xiaoyun, *Banjie mubei xia de wangshi*.

the Italian Communist Party who had traveled extensively in China. Spano was the first international reporter who reached China after the liberation and was highly valued by the CCP. Mao Zedong and Liu Shaoqi invited Spano to a banquet and Spano requested a confidential meeting with the Soviet chargé d'affaires in Beijing, P.A. Shibaev. He wanted to talk with Shibaev not as a Soviet diplomat, but as a member of the Bolshevik Communist Party. Spano told Shibaev that "blindness to the danger of capitalism swiftly regenerating itself and the underrating of the working class were typical shortcomings of the majority of the top functionaries in China he had talked with."[61] As the CCP valued its reputation in the international Communist movement, it was important for it to retain its ideological credentials.

In the midst of these international tensions, Gao Gang continued to pursue close ties to the Soviet Union. During his visit to the Soviet Union he visited collective farms. After he returned to China, he committed himself to achieving the transition to collectivization by calling on the peasants to "get organized" and to "actively develop [agriculture] toward [modernization and] collectivization"—both slogans promoted by Mao in the mid-1940s.[62] Gao Gang implied that putting off collectivization on the pretext that suitable machinery was lacking was an ideological error. He also urged the mutual aid teams to compete with individual farmers. On January 4, 1950, the *Northeast Daily*, Manchuria's leading newspaper, published Gao Gang's speech calling for the upgrading of mutual aid teams and promising them financial privileges. While the article did not explicitly state that private farmers would be handicapped in any way, the implications were obvious that they would be.[63]

Not surprisingly, Liu Shaoqi was not pleased by these developments. On January 23, 1950, he told An Ziwen, the head of the Organizational Department in Beijing, that mutual aid teams in Northeast China were based on a run-down and impoverished private economy and did not constitute fertile ground for socialism. Liu simply did not believe it was possible for mutual aid teams to develop into viable collective farms and considered that launch-

---

61. Arlen Meliksetov, "'New Democracy' and China's search for socio-economic development routes," 80.

62. Shi Jingtang, ed., *Zhongguo nongye hezuohua yundong shiliao*, 1020–1026.

63. Bo Yibo, *Ruogan zhongda juece yu shijian de huigu*, 204.

ing collectivization prematurely was an opportunist error of the "left."[64] It is alleged that when Gao Gang showed a record of this conversation to Mao Zedong, Mao was not pleased.[65]

In addition to his internal critiques of Gao Gang, Liu Shaoqi also sought to communicate his concerns to his Soviet comrades. In January 1950, Liu Shaoqi did an interview with O.I. Chechetkina, a *Pravda* correspondent. In the interview, Liu focused on peasant issues, explaining to Chechetkina: "Wealthy farmers will help productivity increase and will supply towns with goods. ... The new wealthy farmers are only beginning to appear and should not be curbed. ... If we try ordering capitalism to stop, it will get us nowhere. On the contrary, we shall make things worse by [doing] that, because millions of peasants will turn against our regime."[66] Chechetkina dutifully sent the report back to Moscow, but there is no record of the Soviet response.[67] Again, on August 26, 1950, Liu told Soviet Ambassador N.V. Roshchin, "We are most grateful to Comrade Stalin for his timely advice about improving relations with private capital, both urban and rural, [and] about the treatment of wealthy farmers."[68] As Arlen Meliksetov notes, the political backing of Stalin was of tremendous importance to Liu Shaoqi.[69]

As we have seen, many of the CCP rank and file supported an immediate transition to socialism. They asked questions like, Since our goal is agricultural collectivization, why don't we carry it out today? Articles published in the *Northeast Daily* emphasized the need to advance the mutual aid teams and to give a variety of incentives and advantages to mutual aid teams at the cost of individual peasants. Numerous mutual aid teams were formed in Manchuria and a number of incidents involving coercion and discrimination against private farmers were reported.[70] Yet Gao Gang received no

---

64. Liu Shaoqi, *Liu Shaoqi lun xin Zhongguo jianshe*, 153–155.

65. Bo Yibo, *Ruogan zhongda juece yu shijian de huigu*, 207.

66. Arlen Meliksetov, "'New Democracy' and China's search for socio-economic development routes," 79–80.

67. Chechetkina's report is housed in the Foreign Policy Archives of the Russian Federation.

68. Foreign Policy Archives of the Russian Federation, folio 0100, list 43, portfolio 10, folder 302, 178. Quoted from Arlen Meliksetov, "'New Democracy' and China's search for socio-economic development routes," 80.

69. Ibid.

70. Bo Yibo, *Ruogan zhongda juece yu shijian de huigu*, 204–209.

reprimand. On the contrary, Zhang Wentian, a critic of Gao Gang's peasant policies, was transferred out of Manchuria, becoming the Chinese delegate to the United Nations—an assignment he learned of through a news broadcast. Having worked on economic reconstruction in Manchuria for years, Zhang accepted his new post with reluctance. In the years to come he made several appeals to return to the economic sector, but received no response.[71] In the end, it was Gao Gang's economic plans that prevailed in Manchuria.

Gao Gang portrayed himself as an orthodox pro-Soviet Communist and justified his policy of "getting the peasants organized" on the grounds that it was based on Stalin's essay, "On Several Problems of Leninism."[72] It is doubtful that faith in Stalin's theories alone drove Gao Gang to confront Liu Shaoqi; political ambition was more likely the motivation. Mao had tacitly let comrade Gao Gang become aware of his discontent with Liu Shaoqi. As Gao recalled, Mao had a litany of complaints about Liu: Liu had offered Mao little assistance after 1949, Liu could take no credit in building the base areas, he was not respected by the army, and he had "often wavered." Most seriously, Mao alleged that Liu had attempted to reduce him to a mere figurehead in the party.[73]

The rift between Liu and Mao gave Gao Gang the chance to curry favor with Mao. At the same time, the influence of Soviet collectivization theory should not be overlooked in this dispute. By 1949, CCP cadres were familiar with collectivization, at least on paper, thanks to Mao's advocacy in the mid-1940s. Any plan that differed from it would readily generate suspicion and confusion. Gao Gang played the Soviet card to attack Liu Shaoqi on ideological grounds. What is puzzling is that at the time, as Li Hua-yu shows, Stalin himself was advising the CCP to accommodate a mixed economy and Liu Shaoqi was diligently following Stalin's suggestions. However, at the same time, Gao Gang was using Stalin's early writings to attack Liu and was supported by Soviet comrades who would have been in a position to know Stalin's current attitude. The role that Stalin himself played in the affair is yet to be fully determined. We should be aware of the complexity of Stalinism. As Thomas Bernstein argues, there would be more than one Stalinism, for

71. Zhang Peisen, *Zhang Wentian nianpu*, 900–903.
72. Liu Jianping, "Nongye hezuohua juece."
73. Zhao Jialiang and Zhang Xiaoyun, *Banjie mubei xia de wangshi*.

example, revolutionary Stalinism and bureaucratic and middle-class Stalinism, which may explain the changes.[74]

The feud between Gao Gang and Liu Shaoqi was deeply rooted in the conflicts between cadres from the revolutionary bases and cadres from the white areas, although it appeared in the form of disagreement in policies. Gao Gang was not the only Chinese leader who questioned Liu Shaoqi's rural policies. As the Korean War broke out in June 1950, Gao shifted his focus from economic reconstruction to war logistics, allowing him to consolidate his links with top army generals. Another of the CCP's local leaders, Lai Ruoyu from Shanxi, took up the fight against Liu Shaoqi over peasant issues, as I explore in the next chapter.

---

74. Thomas Bernstein, "Introduction." Given that Gao Gang was labeled a "counterrevolutionary" and he committed suicide in 1954 after losing his political struggle against Liu Shaoqi, documents and records relating to Gao Gang are extremely scarce in Chinese sources. Ledovsky's bibliography of Gao Gang (in Russian) has not been translated into either Chinese or English. A.M. Ledovsky, *Delo Gao Gang–Rao Shushi*.

3

Collectivizing from Below

Shanxi is not a good place, too many factions. It does not look easy to stay there or stay long.

—Gao Kelin[1]

Here we have two principles: first, what the masses actually need rather than what we fancy they need; and second, what the masses are willing and determined to do rather than what we are determined to do on their behalf.

—Mao Zedong[2]

The so-called [momentum] from the masses simply amounted to following the masses, rather than leading them. The right way was to collect the various opinions of the people, investigate them and form a common viewpoint, then to propagate it and explain it to the masses, so making it the opinion of the masses.

—Lai Ruoyu[3]

---

1. Gao Kelin was appointed by Beijing as the first secretary of Shanxi party branch in July 1952. He only served the post for six months, then he went back to Beijing and refused to return to Shanxi. Ren Fuxing's interviews with Han Chunde, March 9 and March 12, 2003, Beijing.
2. Mao Zedong, *Selected Works of Mao Tse-tung*, vol. 4, 227.
3. *Shanxi Daily*, July 1, 1951.

Politics of Power in Shanxi Province

At the provincial level, leaders were appointed by Beijing, but the process was far from transparent. Striking a balance was crucial—balancing cadres from the revolutionary areas against those from white areas, outsiders versus locals, powerful individuals and the cliques formed around them, and so on. As Chinese historian Yang Kuisong argues, from Beijing's point of view the ideal candidates for the post of first party secretary at the provincial level were returned natives: people who had been born and raised in the province, had built their revolutionary careers elsewhere, and then returned home to act locally. As a native, one would be expected to have an understanding of local peculiarities; on the other hand, having been absent for long periods, one would most likely not have established strong local networks that could act at cross-purposes to central policy.

Although such arrangements would best serve Beijing's interests, in practice it was difficult to maintain this kind of balance. Generally speaking, in the newly liberated regions, cadres from the liberation army, often outsiders, dominated the top positions and political conflicts frequently broke out between these newcomers and local party members who had emerged from underground. A similar principle and situation held for prefecture and county party secretaries. Until the 1970s, in the newly liberated regions party posts above the county level were mostly held by outsiders to the area concerned, while branches of the government below the county level were dominated by natives of the areas in which they served.[4] It is not surprising that these provincial and prefectural leaders, many of whom were outsiders, learned about the local situation largely through reports generated from below and that much was lost in the channeling process. This may help explain the disconnection between leaders in the provinces and those in local positions during Mao's era—a communication failure responsible for a number of otherwise avoidable human catastrophes.

In the older liberated regions, the composition of the party leadership was more complex; here a larger proportion of provincial leaders were local revolutionaries. But a longer history of Communist control in these areas also generated personal and institutional problems. For example, before 1949, there were dozens of revolutionary base areas, large and small, dotting

---

4. Yang Kuisong, "Jianguo chuqi zhonggong ganbu renyong zhengce kaocha," 3–38.

the North China landscape, often lying along provincial borders. A single base area might include parts of three or even four provinces, and one province might have accommodated three or four base areas on its territory. Each base area had its own apparatus and personnel, duplicating neighboring territories. Consequently, when the base areas were abolished and reorganized into provinces and prefectures, chaos ensued. Old enmities resurfaced, while new problems sprang up. Shanxi Province provides a good illustration of this situation.

Shanxi Province is located in North China, lying to the east of Yan'an. It was on the front lines of the conflict with Japan from 1937 to 1945. Many Communists in Shanxi saw the province as central to the CCP revolution. Three border regions, Shanxi–Hebei–Shandong–Henan (*Jinjiluyu*) to the east, Shanxi–Cha'ha'er–Hebei (*Jinchaji*) to the northwest, and Shanxi–Suiyuan (*Jinsui*) to the southeast, were established and brought under the leadership of the North Bureau (*beifangju*) of the CCP. The Shanxi–Hebei–Shandong–Henan border region was further divided into three base areas: Taihang, Taiyue, and Tainan, each with a separate party apparatus. Of the three, Taihang base area in southeast Shanxi was the largest and most important, forming the long-term field headquarters of the CCP's Eighth Route Army and the headquarters of the North Bureau.[5]

From the mid-1930s, Communist forces stationed in many different border regions and base areas contested power first with Japan, and later with the Guomindang. At the same time, conflicts developed from within, although few details of these internal power struggles were revealed to outsiders. Prior to 1949, multiple party organizations with parallel structures operated in Shanxi, making for a very complex situation when the CCP came to make decisions about leadership in 1949. Communist cadres from different border regions and base areas competed to secure positions in the new system. Naturally, some succeeded at the expense of others. During the process, patronage networks, as well as personal grudges, were nurtured. According to a local proverb, "[Shanxi is under] Taihang's domination, party members from Taiyue are doing well, the cadres from Jinchaji are all right, but the cadres from Jinsui are crawling on the ground."[6] This local say-

---

5. David Goodman, *Social and Political Change in Revolutionary China*.

6. Ren Fuxing's interviews with Han Chunde, March 9 and March 12, 2003, Beijing.

ing succinctly encapsulated the outcome of internal competition in the province.

Many cadres from the Shanxi base areas—as the former site of the North Bureau where Liu Shaoqi held such firm control—were promoted to posts in Beijing. It seems that Liu Shaoqi especially favored cadres from the Taiyue base area. An Ziwen and Bo Yibo, who had both worked for many years in Taiyue, were sent to the new capital. Liu Lantao had also worked in Taiyue before being appointed third party secretary of the North Bureau, which directly supervised Shanxi Province. At the same time, cadres from the Taihang base area, headed by Lai Ruoyu, found they had less influence than their former comrades from the Taiyue base area.

Lai Ruoyu was a Shanxi native. From 1938 he had worked in Taihang, and was later promoted to party secretary of the Taihang base area. In 1949, he was appointed to assist the People's Liberation Army take over Taiyuan, the capital of Shanxi Province. Once this had been achieved, Lai became the de facto administrator of Shanxi. Not surprisingly, he looked after his colleagues from the Taihang base area, and cadres from Taihang comprised a significant part of the Shanxi provincial leadership. Because of his long-term service and prominent position in the province, Lai anticipated that he would become first party secretary in Shanxi. However, when the Shanxi provincial government was formally established in September 1949, Beijing appointed Cheng Zihua to serve as first party secretary, with Lai Ruoyu as vice-secretary. Cheng Zihua was a high-ranking veteran and a Shanxi native, but he had been away fighting outside the province for a number of years. This made him the kind of returned native that Beijing was looking for.

The reason often given for Lai Ruoyu being passed over was that the CCP Central Committee in Beijing considered him to be too junior for the post. Given the rapid elevation of An Ziwen and Bo Yibo from the Taiyue base area, this explanation is not entirely convincing. The role played by Liu Shaoqi in the decision is not clear, either. Judging by Lai Ruoyu's defiance of Liu's orders in 1950, he was unlikely to have been under Liu's patronage, and it is unlikely that Liu would have endorsed Lai's candidacy in 1949. The tone in which Lai Ruoyu addressed Liu Lantao, his direct supervisor in the North Bureau and Liu Shaoqi's confidant, further suggests that the two men did not get along. The evidence shows that Liu Lantao made continual efforts to get rid of Lai Ruoyu, right up until Lai's death in the late 1950s.

Along with positioning themselves in the new system, provincial leaders sought to put Shanxi on the new political map of China. During the revolutionary years Shanxi was one of the central areas for the Communist revolution. But as the CCP extended its control, the political center moved eastward from Yan'an to Beijing. Shanxi began to lose its allure. How did the provincial leaders deal with this change, especially where the peasantry was concerned? Peasant issues were central to the local political landscape until 1949, when Mao declared, "The center of gravity of the party's work has shifted from the village to the city."[7] Many of the former base areas were distant from the cities, and cadres such as Lai Ruoyu now needed to deal with the consequences of their decline in political importance.

On the eve of the founding of the PRC, Chinese Communists, from Mao to grassroots party supporters, experienced a mix of anxiety, aspiration, and ambition. For Lai Ruoyu, it was a time of intense frustration. Cheng Zihua had come from nowhere and taken the position to which Lai aspired. Lai's former comrades from the Taiyue base area now ranked higher than he did, and his adversary Liu Lantao was now his superior. Lai Ruoyu and his colleagues had tasted the bitterness of being abandoned in the boondocks. How could they revive their lost glory, gain the attention of the party leadership, and move up through the ranks in the new system? To achieve these goals, Lai Ruoyu fell back on an old practice—creating model experiments.

When Cheng Zihua arrived in Shanxi in early 1950, Lai could hardly disguise his discontent. Lai defended his negative attitude to Cheng by claiming that he had "some disagreements of principle with him."[8] One of these disagreements concerned the state's dealings with the peasants. Following the lead of Zhang Wentian and Liu Shaoqi, Cheng Zihua endorsed the official policy of creating SMCs to build a bridge between farmers and the state.[9] Lai Ruoyu, however, favored a transition to collectivization by way of mutual aid teams—the approach advocated by Gao Gang.

Lai Ruoyu already had concerns about the relationship between the CCP and the peasants. He had worked in the Taihang base area for a decade. Like other base areas in North China, Taihang underwent radical

---

7. Mao Zedong, "Report to the Second Plenary Session of the Seventh Central Committee of the Communist Party of China," in *Selected Works of Mao Tse-tung*, vol. iv, 363.

8. Ren Fuxing's interviews with Han Chunde, March 9 and March 12, 2003, Beijing.

9. Yang Deshou, ed., *Zhongguo hezuoshe jingji sixiang yanjiu*, 174.

land reform in 1947 and was one of the first areas to complete the program. Following land reform, the middle-ranking peasants became the majority and the landlords were eliminated as a class. Consequently, from the peasants' point of view, they had accomplished their revolutionary goals and had no idea of the next step. Well aware of these problems, Lai Ruoyu warned his colleagues that implementing land reform was an easy task compared to leading peasants forward to the next stage. He believed that it was crucial that the party lead the peasants on to full-fledged socialism.[10] In a speech he gave in September 1949, Lai implied that if the party left the peasants to their own devices, they would be unlikely to move toward the CCP's grand goal of "modernization and collectivization."[11]

In September, 1949, Lai instructed his confidant, Wang Qian—who had also begun his career in the Taihang base area and was about to assume the position of party secretary of Changzhi prefecture—to instigate an investigation into social conditions in Changzhi and suggest how the party might take its work to the next level. Lai underlined the importance of this exercise to Wang Qian: "You can ask other comrades to take on other duties—you must take this task very seriously and find the right answers."[12] Although Lai did not explain his purpose further, Wang Qian was well aware of the kind of answers for which Lai was hoping. In the spring and winter of 1950, Wang Qian launched two major investigations in several villages in Changzhi prefecture. In the summer of 1950, as a follow-up to Wang Qian's investigation that spring, the Agricultural Department of Shanxi Province conducted a microstudy of the rural economy in six villages in Wuxiang County of Changzhi prefecture. Numerous reports were produced ranging from village to provincial level. When combined with other internal documents, these reports confirmed Lai's earlier concerns by showing that from the state's perspective, the post–land reform experience for peasants in Shanxi had failed to live up to expectations.

---

10. Liu Guiren, *Lai Ruoyu zhuan*, 88.

11. Lai Ruoyu, "Zai shengwei kuoda huiyi shang de jianghua" (Speech to the enlarged provincial conference) (September 1, 1949), SPA, 00.29.1.

12. Wang Qian, "Weishenme yao shiban nongye shengchan hezuoshe," 656.

Post–Land Reform Rural Predicament

During the revolutionary years, Changzhi prefecture was a key part of the Taihang base area. By the spring of 1949, 96.3 percent of the villages in the prefecture had completed land reform. Taking Yaozizhen village in Tunliu County as an example, of its eighty-eight households, the average land-holding was 4.1 mu per person, and the average output of grain per capita was 3.6 dan. (Former landlords and rich peasants up till now had only owned an average of 2.29 mu per person.[13]) According to official records, following land reform overall agricultural production had improved and the total output of two-thirds of the villages in Tunliu County exceeded prewar levels.[14] However, today, aid organizations and economists generally define self-sufficiency as equivalent to between 45 and 51.1 catties of unhusked grain per month, or 600 catties per year.[15] The peasants themselves considered 700 catties of unhusked grain per year as the minimal standard for subsistence.[16] On paper, the farmers of Tunliu fell below this level. The secret to their survival was income from sideline work and from clandestine landholdings. Despite this, between 1949 and 1951 party documents have insisted that peasant livelihoods had improved overall.

Nevertheless, from the point of view of the state, the situation was not so encouraging. Liu Shaoqi's plan to establish SMCs was not working as intended. Although these SMCs had been established at various levels from provinces to villages, they were operating as conventional commercial outlets and played a minimal role in connecting peasant farmers with the urban centers—not to mention their intended function of regulating the peasant economy.[17]

---

13. "Jin dongnan diwei youguan nongye shengchan de zongjie he tugai qing-kuang" (Summary of agricultural production and land reform in southeast Shanxi Province) (1949), JMA, 004.2.

14. The report acknowledges that existing data on prewar production was inaccurate. "Changzhi diwei 1949 nian yilai nongye shengchan zongjie" (Summary of agricultural production in Changzhi prefecture since 1949) (Dec. 10, 1949), JMA, 1.1.4.

15. Jean C. Oi, *State and Peasant in Contemporary China*, 47. The CCP's standard was much lower during this period: around 400 catties per year was considered the minimal income.

16. Gao Wangling, *Renmin gongshe shiqi Zhongguo nongmin fanxingwei tiaocha*, 38.

17. "Bo Yibo guanyu diyici hezuo huiyi de baogao" (Bo Yibo's report on the first

What concerned Shanxi leaders most was the rural cadres. The radical land reforms of 1946–1948 carried out in the older liberated areas of North China, together with the rectification of cadres between late 1947 and early 1948, had reconfigured rural power structures. Here, land reform overwhelmingly favored "the poor and hired tillers" of the soil.[18] Middle-ranking peasants were hit hard. Prior to 1947, in many of the older liberated regions, middle-ranking peasants—and occasionally wealthy ones—had assumed the post of village head, often through local elections. In part this was because middle peasants were better educated, could provide meals to supervisors and visitors, and knew how to circumvent orders from above. But following land reform, this situation was reversed. The rectification program of 1947 made class background the dominant criterion for cadres; many village heads of middle-peasant origins were considered compromised and were pushed aside.[19] In the Taihang base area, nearly all the established village cadres were relieved of their duties,[20] and 1,800 out of 8,000 cadres were disciplined—one-third were expelled or put on probation.[21] In their place, poor peasants, who had been prominent in the political struggle and had profited from land reform, rose to power. Most of the new rural cadres were poorly educated and limited in their goals. They were not particularly good farmers, and they enjoyed little moral authority, as Xi Zhongxun acknowledged.[22] Their authority relied heavily on their ability to fight the "class enemy" and win party support. Moreover, to prevent nepotism, the rectification movement relocated cadres above county level. Thus, cadres often knew little about conditions in the places where they exercised their authority and had little in common with the local peasants.[23]

With land reform completed and the new China at last taking shape, a large number of local cadres found themselves without a role. Within each province, the administrative ladder climbed from the village at the bottom to township (*xiang*), district (*qu*), county, prefecture, and province. Offi-

national congress of cooperative workers) (July 1950), SPA, files on cooperation, vol. 50.

18. Chen Yung-fa, "Civil War, Mao Zedong and Land Revolution," 11–29.
19. Huang Daoxuan, "Mengyou yihuo qianzai duishou?"
20. "Gei Huabeiju zuzhibu de gongzuo baogao," 511–518.
21. Ibid.
22. Yang Kuisong, *Zhonghua renmin gongheguo jianguoshi yanjiu*, 72.
23. "Gei Huabeiju zuzhibu de gongzuo baogao."

cially, only cadres of township level and above were categorized as state employees and received salaries from the government payroll, leaving village cadres without official financial support. When the civil war was over, many village cadres believed that their mission was accomplished and that they should return to working for themselves. Working for the party was increasingly considered a burden. They had failed to deal with the new problems posed by the peasants, they did not want to be constrained by party regulations, and, more importantly, they no longer saw any benefit in serving the party. As one village cadre put it: "There are no more fat profits to be had from the revolution, so why should we suffer any further? Serving the people is not as appealing as working on my own land."[24] For example, during the land reform process in Suyu village in Wuxiang County, sixty-eight CCP members and thirty-six activists put their name to a document stating that "only the CCP can save China." By contrast, in 1951, there were only twenty-two CCP members in the village, half of whom did not participate at all in party affairs, many asserting that they would live a happier life without the CCP.[25]

Afraid of being forced to relocate south to help with the liberation and fearful of being drafted into the army, some cadres even renounced their party membership. One party branch in Xianghuan County, Changzhi prefecture, went so far as to declare its own dissolution: "We have participated in the fighting against the Japanese and against Chiang Kai-shek. Now that the land has been redistributed, and Japan and Chiang have been defeated, our mission is over. Therefore our branch has been dissolved."[26] Wang Qian was acutely concerned by such an incident, which he regarded as extremely disturbing and dangerous for the party.[27] To motivate village cadres, prefectural leaders organized training classes to inform rural cadres about the new directions that the revolution was taking, especially ways of improving agricultural production and learning from the Soviet Union. In response, many village cadres showed a renewal of interest: "Now there is something in the future to aspire to."[28]

---

24. Ibid.

25. "Zhengzhi diaocha baogao" (Political investigation report) (June 22, 1951), JMA, 1.1.48.

26. Wang Qian, "Weishenme yao shiban nongye shengchan hezuoshe," 657.

27. Ibid., 655–658.

28. "Gei Huabeiju zuzhibu de gongzuo baogao."

Guiding the peasants was another area of disappointment for party bosses. Following the war, the CCP set out a new mission for its rural cadres: guide peasant farmers to produce more. Many village cadres did not fully understand this assignment. They complained that the peasants already knew how to farm their land and required no guidance from the party. Or, more practically, that they lacked party directives spelling out how they were to accomplish their mission—in stark contrast to the era of land reform when the cadres had been swamped by directives, which had in effect sapped their initiative.[29] Hence, instructing the cadres in how to guide peasant farmers in boosting agricultural production became an "urgent and large issue that had to be addressed."[30] As each farming season (spring, summer, and fall) came around, the Shanxi provincial government prompted its local agents to take the lead in agricultural production. County authorities sent work teams into the villages to check up on the rural cadres.[31]

Nor did the attitudes adopted by peasant farmers please the party. The CCP had believed that once peasants obtained their own land, they would be willing to purchase better tools, apply new technologies, and invest in their holdings. However, in most cases, post–land reform peasants, especially those of middle rank, were reluctant to work harder or invest in production. Unit yields had not significantly improved. There were several reasons for this situation. First, the land reforms of 1946–1948 were still fresh in the collective memory and peasants feared that their newly acquired property would in turn be "socialized" (equally redistributed) in the near future. Thus, they lacked the motivation to increase production; it was enough to simply meet a family's basic needs. The lesson they had learned from the past was, "If your output increases one-tenth, your burden will increase ten times."[32] (The CCP's tax policies between 1949 and 1952 indeed laid a disproportionate burden on the better-off peasants, as I discuss in

---

29. "Shanxi sheng chunji shengchan jiancha baogao" (Report on an investigation into the spring plowing in Shanxi Province) (March 31, 1950), SPA, C55.1002.64.

30. Ibid.

31. John Burns defines work teams as "cadres organized at one level of the government or party to go down temporarily to lower levels in order to investigate and report on conditions there, supervise the implementation of policy and solve problems as they arise on the spot." In addition, Jean C. Oi stresses the role of work teams in the administration and regulation of economic policy. Jean C. Oi, *State and Peasant in Contemporary China*, 92.

32. "Shanxi sheng chunji shengchan jiancha baogao."

Chapter 6.) Acknowledging the peasants' reluctance, the CCP put forward slogans such as "Work harder to accumulate family wealth." These slogans did little to meet their concerns; rather they aroused suspicion and confusion within the party.

In addition to farmers' fears of being "socialized," there was something deeply rooted in peasant culture that prevented them from adopting new technologies. Based on his research on Southeast Asian rural societies, James Scott argues that peasants prefer to avoid economic disaster rather than take risks to maximize their average income.[33] Many peasants resist innovation because adopting new strategies might entail abandoning familiar systems that involve minimal risks. In the case of China, following land reform family holdings were fairly small and households contained fewer members.[34] A family with fewer laborers and smaller plots regarded itself as vulnerable and became risk-averse; a common catchphrase was "Safety first." Increasing production was not a high priority for these families.[35] Although it is unknown if the CCP was aware of this aspect of peasant psychology, the CCP understood that few peasants could afford the cost of new farming tools. For his part, Wang Qian quickly realized that state agents and activists could organize peasant farmers to buy tools collectively. The question now became how to achieve this preliminary goal.

After receiving allocations of land and being free of the burden of forced rents, large numbers of peasant farmers probably experienced improved living conditions. Middle-ranking peasants were now the dominant group in the countryside. Nonetheless, from the point of view of the state, the changes that had taken place in the rural areas did not directly benefit other sectors of the nation. The availability of grain on the market experienced a steep decline. Prior to land reform, it was not uncommon for a small group of wealthy households, namely landlords and rich peasants, to supply at least half of the entire surplus marketed by a given village.[36] Wuxiang County revealed that although prewar landlords and rich peasants made up 5.99

33. James C. Scott, *Moral Economy of the Peasant.*

34. During the land reform process, extended families usually divided into smaller units to keep the land area per family smaller and thus avoid members being labeled as landlords or rich peasants.

35. James C. Scott, *Moral Economy of the Peasant*, 19.

36. John Fairbank and Albert Feuerwerker, *Cambridge History of China*, vol. 13, 254–255.

percent of the rural population, they provided 28.9 percent of total output. Middle-ranking peasants, on the other hand, probably produced only enough food for themselves. In 1948, following land reform, 86 percent of the rural population in Wuxiang County consisted of middle-ranking peasants, who produced approximately 86 percent of total output. Comparing 1949 production level to prewar yields, although peasant farmers as a whole produced 9.1 percent more grain, the amount of surplus grain sold on the market had dropped dramatically. Before the war, the annual total of grain sent to market from the six villages stood at 2,154 dan, in 1950 it dropped to 702 dan.[37] Peasant farmers were unwilling to sell their surplus grain; they preferred to eat better and live better, or simply build up their supplies.[38] A 1992 study showed that, on average, peasant consumption of grain increased from 370 catties per capita in 1949 to 440 catties in 1952.[39] Alarmed by this trend, the CCP, especially those charged with drawing up the budget, became increasingly concerned with securing a generous share of the peasants' surplus grain.

In the wake of land reform, not all peasants found that their lives had improved. One of Wang Qian's reports on the six villages in Wuxiang revealed that prior to land reform the settlements contained 329 poor peasant families. As a result of the 1946–1948 land redistribution, 88 percent had become middle-ranking or upper-middle peasants. However, two years later, nineteen households had fallen back into the "poor" category. The causes were diverse. Five households were affected by the deaths of laborers or livestock, four declined as a result of "laziness," three because of mismanagement of sideline work, and two because of an increase in family size. Conditions for former wealthy peasants and landlords, now members of ostracized groups, were worse.[40] Changzhi prefectural officials were now keenly aware that factors other than the lack of land—natural disasters, fluctuations in manpower, marriage, indolence, even excessive indulgence—could all lead

37. "Wuxiang liuge cun jingji diaocha" (An investigation of the economic base of six villages in Wuxiang) (August 7, 1950), JMA, 024.11.

38. "Wuxiang liuge cun nongye shengchan zhong zuzhi huzhu de kaocha baogao" (An investigation into the organization of mutual aid teams for agricultural production in six villages of Wuxiang) (August 7, 1950), SPA, C77.04.0002.

39. Jin Guantao and Liu Qingfeng, "Zhongguo gongchangdang weishenme fangqi xin minzhu zhuyi," 17.

40. "Changzhi diqu wuge cun tugai shengchan zhong jieji bianhua de diaocha."

to poverty. This fluid social situation lent weight to the theories of Shannin and Chayanov on the multidirectional mobility characteristic of the peasantry, as mentioned in Chapter 1. However, the Chinese investigators were not interested in conducting academic studies and seeking out causes—rather, they wanted solutions.[41]

Peasants did not hesitate to sell their land as the result of financial difficulties or when seeking opportunities outside farming. A report on one village showed that thirty-five households were in the process of selling their land and four had already sold. A small number of peasants went bankrupt or were unable to make enough to feed their families. While many communities faced real hardship, the traditional relief system had been dismantled and there was as yet nothing to take its place. The party was unwilling to assume full responsibility for feeding the needy, partly because of a lack of financial resources. A new system was needed to support the casualties of land reform and feed the hungry.

Traditionally, peasant farmers not only decided how much of their produce they would sell on the market, but they also chose the kinds of crops to be planted. Growing conditions varied across different regions. For example, in Sichuan Province in southwest China, if soil conditions permitted, farmers preferred to plant cash crops that were much more profitable than grain. Castor-oil plants and tobacco were popular choices. By contrast, in the poorer Changzhi prefecture, many peasants opted to plant grain to feed their families and avoid taking economic risks. Farmers' preference for food crops in Changzhi might relate to their decade-long war experience, when the market was unstable and self-sufficiency was crucial. It was not uncommon for these planting regimes to conflict with the state's plans, especially as the state could change their plans at any time, leaving the farmers committed to raising their current crops. For example, in Changzhi, the Shanxi provincial government in 1950 directed the growing of cotton and other cash crops, but in late 1951 and 1952 grain became government's priority and farmers were discouraged from planting cash crops. Finding a way to keep planting practices in line with the needs of the state was a constant challenge for provincial leaders.

Another problem encountered by cadres of all levels was how to work out a concrete production plan. Within the framework of the kind of centrally planned economy the CCP intended to create in the early 1950s, ad-

---

41. Ibid.

ministrators at each level of the system were required to make a plan and act accordingly. Agriculture was no exception. From central party leaders down to village heads, each was tasked with compiling an annual production plan. Each spring, local CCP cadres expended enormous amounts of time and effort in devising production plans. Peasant farmers were reluctant, if not downright unwilling, to make such decisions; after all, with weather unknown, who could predict future yield? Pressed too hard, peasants and rural cadres fabricated plans and rarely followed them. Rather, they treated such schemes with contempt.[42] In sum, for all practical purposes, private family farming was inconsistent with a centralized national economy.

On top of this, the party encountered an entirely new phenomenon in the countryside: surplus labor. The CCP had nearly always operated under conditions of labor shortages; mutual aid teams had first been organized during wartime to deal with this very problem. Women had been encouraged to step out of their homes and work in the fields. When the civil war ended, the situation reversed itself. Conscripts were relieved of military service, and women and landlords continued to work on the land, resulting in a decline of landholdings per active farmer. Underemployment was widely reported across the nation. To make matters worse, in 1950 large numbers of soldiers were scheduled to be demobilized in the near future. The problem of absorbing this surplus labor force into rural society challenged regional leaders.

Even as the new China came into being, the CCP faced an uphill battle in the countryside. Many rural cadres failed to see a bright socialist future on the immediate horizon and had few aspirations to serve the party. Even the keener ones were still dependent on detailed directives from their superiors. Farmers showed little enthusiasm about increasing production; they consumed more and provided less to the market. The poor remained poor, with some becoming destitute. Some Communist leaders believed that class polarization was on the rise. "Lazy" peasants remained inactive and had no hesitation about selling the land they had received following land reform. The party found it had little control over local farming regimes. All these were new and unanticipated phenomena and needed to be fixed. As had happened in the Soviet Union in the mid-1920s, although it was de-

---

42. Peasants' contempt and rural cadres' struggles in drafting production plans are mentioned in many documents cited in this chapter.

cided that the existing structures must be changed, it took some time before the appropriate means of implementing these decisions were found.[43]

Shanxi Leaders' Solution: Upgrading Mutual Aid Teams

Wang Qian and other Shanxi leaders were not pleased by what they found on assuming their new roles, and were therefore uncomfortable with leaving the peasants to their own devices. Tao Lujia, director of the Propaganda Department in Shanxi, who had visited the USSR and knew about its veterans' organizations in the countryside, suggested that militia be used to "lead" the peasants. Wang Qian dismissed the idea on the grounds that the militia was a political and military organization. When Tao Lujia then suggested SMCs as a suitable vehicle, Wang Qian once again disagreed, for several reasons. First, SMCs were already widely established. Second, SMCs were merely a circulation device—they could not directly intervene in agricultural production and could not give farmers direct guidance. Thinking the question through with his superior Lai Ruoyu, Wang Qian envisioned a formula that would organize peasant farmers into economic units and keep them in step with the party. The Soviet collective farm was an obvious model. Most likely aware of the chaos that had accompanied collectivization in the USSR, Wang Qian feared that peasant farmers might resist attempts to organize them in this way and thus impair agricultural production. Unwilling to take these risks, Wang switched his attention to an arrangement that focused on communal property as the first step to collective farms. His choice fell on mutual aid teams.[44]

It is likely that Wang and Lai were inspired by Gao Gang, who was experiencing a rapid rise within the CCP's core leadership. Between 1950 and 1952, newspapers like the *Shanxi Daily* reprinted many of Gao Gang's speeches and followed his agenda closely. On January 4, 1950, the *Northeast Daily* published Gao Gang's speech urging that the mutual aid organizations be improved. In March 1950, the *Shanxi Daily* echoed Gao's sentiments in an article of its own.[45] This pattern was repeated in the media until 1952.

43. Moshe Lewin, *Russian Peasants and Soviet Power*.
44. Zhang Guoxiang, "Xin Zhongguo nongye shengchan hezuoshe de youlai," 31.
45. *Shanxi Daily*, March 5, 1950.

On May 30, 1950, Wang Qian submitted a report entitled "Focusing on mutual aid teams in Changzhi" to the party's Shanxi provincial branch. The report began by outlining the history of mutual aid teams in Changzhi, dating back to 1943. It claimed that between 1943 and spring 1947, peasant farmers had embraced mutual aid teams, established intimate working relationships, and become accustomed to helping each other in the fields. After years of working in these organizations, they had acquired the habit of working collectively. Indeed, individuals were unwilling to work the land on their own. However, the mutual aid movement had lost traction when it was undermined by "leftist" errors during the land reforms of 1947. In 1948, these aberrations were corrected and the peasants had again shifted their attention to farming. Slowly, mutual aid teams had re-formed. By spring 1950, 70 percent of households in the older liberated regions had joined the teams. The truth was, Wang Qian asserted in the report, that while peasant farmers aspired to raise production and become wealthy, they did not know how to go about it. The answer lay in improving the quality of agricultural equipment, introducing new technology, and getting better organized. Cleverly combining ideas drawn from Mao Zedong, Gao Gang, and Liu Shaoqi, Wang Qian came up with a new slogan for the mutual aid teams: "Get organized, improve the technology, increase production and make money."[46]

Reading the report today, there can be no doubt that Wang Qian rewrote the history of the mutual aid movement in Changzhi. The formation of mutual aid teams in 1943 occurred in response to Mao's call to "get organized" at a time when there was an extreme labor shortage due to war service. Between 1945 and 1946, most mutual aid teams were not formed voluntarily, but were imposed on the peasants by the local CCP authorities, who assigned them a variety of political, military, and economic tasks. Not surprisingly, enrollment rates in the teams were high, at least on paper. When radical land reform was criticized in 1948 and local government was warned not to adopt methods involving coercion and "commandism," mutual aid teams fell apart.[47] Whether or not aware of Wang Qian's distortions in the report, the Shanxi provincial branch approved Wang's report and autho-

---

46. Wang Qian, "Changzhi zhuanqu nongye huzhu zuzhi de qingkuang he jinhou de fangxiang he zuofa" (The situation of the agricultural mutual aid organizations in Changzhi district and future development and methods) (May 30, 1950), SPA, 21.7.34.

47. "Shanxi sheng zuzhi qilai de lishi qingkuang," 593–595.

rized "Get organized, improve the technology" as the new slogan for peasant farmers.[48] However, surviving records of internal discussions within the Shanxi branch reveal different reasons for the adoption of the slogan. What concerned Shanxi officials was not that peasants did not know *how* to increase production, but that many lacked incentives to do so. While poor peasants usually worked hard in order to reach the living standards enjoyed by middle-ranking peasants, they tended to lose their impetus once they had achieved this goal. The old slogan "Work harder, accumulate wealth" had little appeal for them. However, the government needed them to increase agricultural outputs. If they could not do it themselves, the party would intervene to help—for example, by organizing peasants into mutual aid teams. Despite the fact that there was a labor surplus in Shanxi, rather than a shortage, the official rhetoric put the situation rather differently: "On the basis of voluntarism and the enjoyment of equal benefits, [the party must] organize the peasants into mutual aid teams, overcome the labor shortage and animal power shortage, restore rural production levels, and encourage the habit of working collectively."[49]

In the months to come, party branches from village to prefecture level in Shanxi held meetings at which the message of organizing peasant farmers into mutual aid teams was hammered home. Officials from Tunliu County in Changzhi prefecture reported that 2,000 to 3,000 people attended local meetings in 1950. The head of the county regarded the message as a call to political mobilization and diligently disseminated it. However, at the village level, even after rounds of meetings, the policy was still a mystery to most party members and village heads, and the vast majority of farmers wanted to carry on working as they always had done.[50] Reports from Wuxiang County also revealed a negative response from peasants, even though Wu-xiang would play a key role in the coming years in promoting the movement. With few exceptions, peasants in Wuxiang regarded mutual aid teams as an emergency measure, to be implemented only during a labor shortage. As laborers returned home from military service and

---

48. "Zhonggong Shanxi Shengwei di 19 ci Changwei Huiyi," 258.

49. "Shengwei kuoda huiyi," 63.

50. "Nongcun fangxian guanche zhuanti baogao" (A special report on implementing rural development policy) (October 30, 1950), JMA, 24.1.1.

rural production improved, the need for mutual aid teams diminished. After 1948, as rural production climbed, the movement declined further. Most peasants were inclined to work on their own account. Some mutual aid teams remained, but they comprised peasants with similar economic conditions; few peasants were willing to work with the poor, the disabled, the elderly, and women.[51] The Wuxiang report completely failed to mention the latter alleged peasant "mentality," which inclined them toward collective labor.

The lack of support from farmers in the region did not prevent the Shanxi government from proceeding with its plans in the name of the peasants. On June 7, 1950, the *Shanxi Daily* published Gao Gang's speech emphasizing the need for mutual aid teams. In the same month, the newspaper published multiple stories about successful mutual aid teams. One article, "A Couple of Problems Affecting the Mutual Aid Movement in the Older Liberated Areas," is of particular interest. The writer questioned the conventional wisdom that farmers joined mutual aid teams to overcome difficulties in production, and that they tended to withdraw when these problems no longer existed. Quite the opposite was true, the article argued—members withdrew because, in their current form, mutual aid teams could not meet the farmers' need to increase production. The writer called on the party to expand the functions carried out by mutual aid teams—for example, organizing members to collectively reclaim wasteland.[52] The article implied that villagers would embrace the movement and work together effectively if mutual aid teams included more activities within their remit.

This article constituted a crucial statement in the theory of the mutual aid movement and precisely echoed the views of Shanxi officials on the question. It immediately triggered vigorous debates, although it is not clear whether specific political forces lay behind these discussions. In hindsight, however, it is clear that the article set out a new explanation, formulated by provincial party leaders, for the peasants' failure to support mutual aid teams and their guidelines for the future development of the movement.

The *Shanxi Daily* piece indicated that Lai Ruoyu and his confidants were gathering their resources for a major breakthrough on the agricultural pro-

---

51. "Wuxiang xianwei dangqian nongye huzhu qingkuang yu xu zhongshi jiejue de wenti" (The current situation of agricultural mutual aids in Wuxiang county branch and problems that need to be fixed), JMA, 1.1.24.

52. *Shanxi Daily*, June 11, 1950.

duction front. As a precautionary measure, or simply an attempt to gather more statistics to back the plans, in the summer of 1950, the Shanxi Agricultural Bureau in Wuxiang County of Changzhi prefecture conducted an investigation that produced a wealth of data. Drawing on these statistics, officials at the county, prefecture, and provincial level each produced a series of reports. Many reached Beijing and some were published in the *People's Daily*, thrusting Shanxi Province onto the national stage. What follows is an investigation of a selection of these reports and an examination of how the information they contained was channeled (or mischanneled) through progressively higher levels.

Losing Touch with Reality: Local Reports Moving up the Chain

Before discussing these reports, the first question to ask is why the investigation was conducted in Wuxiang County. The selection of Wuxiang as the study site was probably not a casual decision. During the revolutionary years, Wuxiang County had built up a strong record as a site for Communist social experiments and was recognized as a radical center in terms of social reform. Some background information on Wuxiang's history sheds lights on why Shanxi party leaders made it the site of an important case study.

Wuxiang was the center of the Taihang base area, both geographically and organizationally.[53] Its socioeconomic makeup differed from many of its neighbors in Shanxi. By the 1920s Wuxiang had established a rural-based, small-scale industrial sector that reflected the emergence of a substantial rural working class. The economic crisis of the early 1930s, coupled with a run of poor harvests, compelled many farmers, including wealthy peasants and landlords, to hand over a large proportion of their land to creditors. By the end of the 1930s, although there were fewer landlords in Wuxiang than in other counties in the Taihang region, they were wealthier than elsewhere in the region.[54] Some villages were owned by a single landowner, who was often an absentee landlord, while the villagers themselves were poor tenant

---

53. David Goodman, *Social and Political Change in Revolutionary China*, 16–17.
54. According to Goodman, in the Taihang region landlord households made up to 2.8 percent of total households and owned 26.3 percent of the land; in Wu-

farmers. Assessed by average incomes, Wuxiang was one of the poorest counties in Taihang. The high degree of land concentration and intense poverty paralleled the situation in Yan'an.[55]

As happened in Yan'an, the CCP penetrated Wuxiang with unusual success. In the 1930s, the CCP recruited large numbers of workers (including farmhands, tenant farmers, artisans, and industrial workers) there, which accounted for 20 percent of the party membership, while in the Taihang base areas the average figure was less than 10 percent. In Wuxiang, the proportion of middle-ranking peasants among party members was less than 10 percent, while the figure in Taihang was about 40 percent. In May 1939, Wuxiang County held direct elections in the villages, and CCP candidates ended up with 85 percent of the seats. These new village leaders were predominantly factory workers, shepherds, and farm laborers.[56] As a result of its success there, Wuxiang was frequently selected by the CCP as an experimental site for various programs the party wished to try out.

In 1939, Li Xuefeng, party secretary of the Taihang base area, designated Wuxiang as the trial site for the CCP's rent and interest reduction program. While, in theory, this program was not designed to eliminate private ownership or to displace landowners, party members and peasants in Wuxiang understood it differently. They believed that the proletarian revolution stage of the Communist movement had arrived and that economic growth was no longer a top priority. It was time to exterminate the landlord and rich peasant class and to abolish private property. They attacked landlords and wealthy peasants throughout the county and confiscated and redistributed their land. Arbitrary arrests and executions of the "class enemy" were carried out.[57] Economic production plunged, and local officials admitted that

---

xiang, forty-four landlords owned half of the land. David Goodman, *Social and Political Change in Revolutionary China*.

55. For the peculiar land conditions in Yan'an, see Pauline B. Keating, *Two Revolutions*.

56. David Goodman, *Social and Political Change in Revolutionary China*, 110.

57. Peng Tao, director of the Propaganda Department in the Taihang base area, estimated that in the over seven hundred "struggle meetings" organized in Wuxiang, more than eighty landlords and rich peasants were physically attacked, most of whom died. David Goodman, *Social and Political Change in Revolutionary China*, 211–212.

"there was an urgent need to implement a new policy toward landlords, rich peasants and even intellectuals."[58]

In April 1940, senior CCP officials from the Taihang base area censured the party branch in Wuxiang, replacing its native leader, Li Youjiu, with an outsider, Wen Jianping. Wen was a displaced student from Northeast China and a protégé of Liu Shaoqi. Arriving in Wuxiang, he was determined to reform the branch and expelled over five hundred local members from the party. He also refocused the county's agenda on agricultural production and away from class conflict. However, rank-and-file party members resisted his attempts at reorganization. Although the details are unclear, Wen Jianping left his new post in 1941 and Li Youjiu was reinstated along with all the other local members who had been dismissed. There was no further attempt from above to restrict the activities of the Wuxiang party branch, which in 1942 resumed its role as a laboratory for social experimentation.[59]

Following the rent and interest reduction program, the numbers of middle-ranking peasants increased to the point that they became the majority of the rural population in the district. As a result, during 1941–1942, the CCP in the Taihang base area decided to focus on this group rather than poor peasants as the core of its future social reforms. However, officials' efforts to elevate the political status of middle-ranking peasants met with strong resistance from below, especially in Wuxiang, where party members were the most vocal critics of this change in strategy. According to Ma Guishu, party secretary in Wuxiang between 1942 and 1944, "It was the middle-ranking peasants who were responsible for making troubles."[60] He insisted that this group could—and should—be part of the new political entity in the region, but only if they were led by poor peasants and workers.[61] Wuxiang was unwilling to promote middle-ranking peasants to serve as village heads; during the rectification campaign of 1947–1948 the dominance of poor peasants in local leadership roles was further consolidated in the county.

In sum, Wuxiang had a long history of radicalism and had gained a reputation for supporting the party's social programs, factors that help explain

---

58. Ibid., 216.
59. Ibid., 205–223.
60. Ibid., 219.
61. Ibid., 220.

why Lai Ruoyu and Wang Qian chose the county as their study site. Three of the many reports produced during the party's investigations in Wuxiang bear examining.

THE WUXIANG COUNTY'S REPORT

The first of these reports, "An Investigation of the Organization of Mutual Aid Teams and Agricultural Production in Six Villages in Wuxiang County," was produced by Wuxiang County officials and submitted to the Agricultural Bureau of Shanxi Province on August 7, 1950. Basing its analysis on this report, the province submitted a report of its own, "An Investigation of Villages in the Older Liberated Areas of Wuxiang County," to the North China Bureau on August 25, 1950. This second report was later published in the *Shanxi Daily* on October 12, 1950. On November 14, a report issued by the Changzhi prefecture, "On the Current Situation and Problems Associated with Getting Organized," was published in the *People's Daily*.

The original county-level report summarized developments in the villages, along with fresh problems that had arisen. According to the report, following land reform middle-ranking peasants comprised 86 percent of the rural population. Agricultural production had recovered and farmers had improved their livelihoods: 3.14 percent of households contained stocks of 10 dan of surplus grain, 6.7 percent had more than 5 dan, and 33.5 percent had access to over 1 dan of surplus grain. At the same time, 47.2 percent of households could barely feed themselves, and 6.5 percent had fallen below the subsistence line. According to the report, the main problem in the villages was the increase in surplus labor, the result of large numbers of demobilized soldiers returning to their home villages. The report suggested expanding investment in agriculture—devising careful planting regimes in order to absorb the surplus labor force. The report noted that class polarization was becoming apparent and that land sales were taking place: 4.33 percent of households were involved in trading land and a few had even sold off their entire holdings.

The report concluded that in areas where peasants had been organized into mutual aid teams, the pace of class differentiation was slower and the scale smaller. However, it also acknowledged that these social changes were closely related to peasant farmers' access to loans and credit and suggested that credits and loans be made more readily available. As for the issue of mutual aid teams, the report acknowledged that fewer households were participating in them. Peasants of similar economic status were more likely to form a mutual aid team. Most had failed to make long-term production plans. The report explained the decline of mutual aid teams under three main heads:

1 First, peasants feared that their property would be "socialized" in the near future, and thus lacked a motive to invest in farming.
2. Second, with the increase in surplus labor, peasants did not feel the need to "get organized."
3. Third, for rural cadres, organizing the peasants was a low priority.[62]

In sum, though emphasizing the prosperity apparent in the countryside, the county report acknowledged the existence of a number of problems, especially the upsurge in surplus labor and the lack of available credit to boost agricultural production. It admitted that peasants had neither wanted mutual aid teams nor called on the party for guidance in relation to them. On the contrary, the report implied that many peasants did not withdraw from mutual aid teams only out of fear of being labeled "laggards," choosing to support them in name only. While the report underlined the importance of organizing peasants into mutual aid teams, it said little about a future socialist state or the long-term goal of collectivization. Rather, it suggested that the party provide additional economic incentives to attract peasants to join mutual aid teams. While supporting the party's program and endorsing the mutual aid movement as a viable way of increasing agricultural productivity, this original report offered no evidence that the peasant farmers of Wuxiang were in favor of mutual aid teams, let alone mutual aid teams that had been developed as an initiative by the peasants themselves.

THE SHANXI PROVINCE'S REPORT

In Shanxi Province's report to the North China Bureau, although the statistics presented were in accordance with the Wuxiang county report, the characterization of the issues at stake was very different. The focus shifted to the alleged problem of class polarization and the phenomenon of land concentration. This second report emphasized that a small number of families

---

62. "Wuxiang liuge cun nongye shengchan zhong zuzhi huzhu de kaocha baogao" (An investigation into the movement to organize mutual aid in agricultural production in six villages of Wuxiang) (August 7, 1950), SPA, C77.04.0002.

had doubled their landholdings in two years, and it alerted the party to this negative trend. After discussing several cases, the report claimed that villages that had embraced the "Get organized" campaign had undergone fewer land transactions or none at all. As for the county's mutual aid teams, results were mixed: some were developing well while others were declining. The Shanxi report argued that these results did not show that peasants were unwilling to join mutual aid teams—on the contrary, they were reluctant to abandon them. It asserted that after the party had enabled the peasants to acquire land, their political consciousness had risen and they had gradually formed the habit of working collectively. Hence, the report concluded that although peasant farmers as small producers were inclined to work as private individuals, they had the potential, and even the desire, to be organized along more socialist lines. Accordingly, the party should follow the advice of Chairman Mao, who had stated that the critical issue was the education of the peasantry. The report concluded on a confident note: "When we did things right, there was no problem getting the peasants organized."[63]

Unlike the original Wuxiang county report that was circulated only internally, this provincial-level report was published in the *Shanxi Daily* and widely publicized. It told a story of peasant aspirations to work in mutual aid teams and proposed steering peasant culture toward increasingly collective work habits. It also signaled the reemergence of class polarization as a pressing issue in the countryside and called on the party to identify and eradicate the problem. Because of the slant given to the provincial report, many other problems afflicting the countryside were downplayed in the article, if not totally ignored.

THE CHANGZHI PREFECTURE'S REPORT IN THE *PEOPLE'S DAILY*

The Changzhi prefectural report, which was published in the *People's Daily*, painted an even more simplistic picture. First, it presented rural life as swimming in abundance and wealth. Without providing supporting statistics, it stated that in the Changzhi region, some exceptional villages had produced 50 percent more than their prewar output, or even doubled it. The peasants were growing wealthier and had more surplus grain than before.

---

63. "Laoqu Wuxiang nongcun kaocha baogao" (August 25, 1950) (An investigation of villages in the older liberated region of Wuxiang County), in *Shanxi sheng nongye hezuo shi wenjian huibian juan*, 258–265.

For example, in Wulihou village, the majority of households had accumulated stocks of surplus grain in excess of 5 dan. In addition, the *People's Daily* article asserted, there was abundant "idle money" or capital available in the countryside that needed to be properly channeled by the party. The situation had reached a crisis point: while peasant farmers were demanding further progress, the party was unable to supply them with the guidance they needed. As a result, farmers had embraced the notion of "working individually" (*dangan*), and the mutual aid teams were falling apart. Such developments were dangerous. If things were allowed to continue, a few peasants would become rich while the majority would go bankrupt. Rural cadres, the report warned, must not ignore the situation.

The Changzhi report frequently quoted Mao's writings from the mid-1940s and stressed that the party must resist the idea of "leaving the peasants to their own devices" and must strive to put them on the road to collectivization. In Changzhi, the authorities had married mutual aid teams with new technology by encouraging team members to purchase farm tools collectively. According to the *People's Daily*, this approach had been shown to work well and a revolution in agricultural production was already underway.

The *People's Daily* article took a very different approach from those of the other published versions of the Wuxiang study. First, the statistics used were inconsistent with those cited in the first two reports. They were simply too good to be true. Even if the figures were valid in specific instances, they did not represent the overall situation. Even official records showed a slower pace of recovery in Shanxi Province, taken as a whole, than the report claimed. Shanxi's grain output in 1936 was 6.7 billion catties, 5.2 billion in 1949, 6 billion in 1950, and 6.4 billion in 1951. Not until 1952 did grain production reach 1936 levels again, and this was after the CCP had conducted a massive campaign to find "hidden" land and reassess agricultural output, measures to be discussed in more detail in Chapter 6.[64] Second, the article did not rely on data to back up its claims, but simply quoted Mao Zedong's words to prove its points. Being ideologically driven, it was permeated with references to the long-term goal of collectivization. From this point of view, peasant farmers' tendency to work individually and the presence of rich peasants in the community were considered undesirable. The report emphasized that farmers who preferred to work as individuals stood

---

64. Liang Quanzhi, *Shanxi nongzheng yaolan 1949–1989*, 4–42.

in opposition to the goal of collectivization, and it expressed a clear resolve to curb this trend.

Of the three reports, the prefectural document probably reflected the least about rural realities. Unfortunately, this was the most influential report of the three, and by being published in the *People's Daily*, its message reached the whole nation.[65] Subsequent reports from Shanxi followed its tone and drifted further from reality.

By comparing the three reports, we see that during the process of transmission from the local to the central level and from internal circulation to public dissemination, reality was sacrificed, and the central message was increasingly distorted at each successive level. The development of agricultural production in the countryside was exaggerated, especially in the *People's Daily* article, to emphasize that the time had arrived to prioritize the party's ideological agendas because the economy had already been boosted. It is likely that Changzhi prefectural leaders were aware of the inflation their report had undergone. In an internally circulated summary of agricultural production in the prefecture, a marginal note pointed out that data purporting to show an increase of over 40 percent in output were totally unreliable; agricultural production in 1949 was only slightly above prewar levels, and a third of the villages in the prefecture were yet to reach their prewar production levels.[66]

At the same time, developments such as alleged class polarization and land sales were increasingly emphasized from one report to the next, while their complex causes, including natural disasters, personal difficulties, and the lack of agricultural credit, were entirely overlooked. While the contributing factors were not analyzed, the solution offered was crystal clear: form mutual aid teams and get the peasants organized. The diversity of views among peasant farmers was not explored. Instead, peasants were categorized into two groups: those who wanted to work individually to accumulate family wealth and those who were keen to form mutual aid teams, but had thus far not received meaningful assistance from the party. Although no evidence was provided to support it, the *People's Daily* article asserted that, deep in their hearts, most peasants nurtured a desire to work in mutual aid

---

65. *People's Daily*, November 14, 1950.

66. "Changzhi diwei 1949 nian yilai nongye shengchan zongjie" (Summary of agricultural production in Changzhi prefecture for 1949), JMA, 004.2.

teams and move toward collectivization. Given this situation, it was naturally the party's responsibility to make every effort to educate and to guide them. The fact that many farmers were in desperate need of credit and loans was not highlighted. On the contrary, the newspaper was happy to promulgate the myth that the countryside was awash with abundant idle money available for investment.

In sum, Shanxi leaders, through the *People's Daily*, sent out a clear message as analyzed below. The peasants had reached a bottleneck in rural production and were in need of guidance before further development goals could be achieved. Only mutual aid teams could help farmers improve their lives, while putting them on the road to collectivization. Mao's writings on mutual aid and China's socialist future were reiterated and held up as embodying self-evident truths. Once the task of guiding the peasants toward collectivization became a central issue, mutual aid teams were no longer viewed as merely economic organizations, but had political implications. The need to move toward collectivization in the future pointed to the necessity of developing mutual aid teams in the present. Blinkered by this narrow focus, many other pressing issues in the countryside were neglected. The disbanding of mutual aid teams was thus increasingly regarded as a serious concern that needed to be addressed immediately.

Even the original Wuxiang county report was produced for the specific purpose of promoting mutual aid teams, and probably did not fully reflect what the peasants were thinking or what they needed. But with a dearth of statistical information at the village level, it is prudent not to question the Wuxiang report. However, given its reputation as a radical heartland and the rapid agricultural recovery it had experienced, Wuxiang was hardly representative of rural reality in China.

The higher up the administrative level a report was sent, the simpler its message became. During the process of communication and channeling, a succession of politically motivated interpretations was interpolated into the document, each having a specific purpose. Although their real concerns and circumstances were misrepresented, most of the reports gave the impression that they represented the views of rural people and often utilized peasant voices and language. Plans, suggestions, and innovations were commonly represented as coming directly from the peasants or as the party's earnest responses to their requests.

Lai Ruoyu saw no problem in distorting and suppressing the peasants' voices in this way. He even published an article in the *Shanxi Daily* discussing how the opinions of the masses should be correctly gauged and acted on. Lai asserted that it was counterproductive to begin investigations such as those undertaken in Wuxiang with the raw reality. Research without a theory would result in vital intrinsic relationships being overlooked. The slogan "Everything comes from the masses" did not mean a slavish adherence to the people's views—rather, it meant that one should first collect their opinions and then synthesize them into a collective viewpoint. It was then up to the party to advocate and to explain this collective perspective to the masses, and indeed to make it their own opinion. Lai reiterated that theory and practice must be unified. Practice without guidance from theory was nothing more than a hollow empiricism.[67] Lai's article contained unambiguous echoes of Mao's talks at the Yan'an forum on literature and art, especially his assertion that "[the revolutionary statesman's] task is to collect the opinions of these mass statesmen, sift and refine them, and return them to the masses, who then take them and put them into practice."[68] Lai went a step further by arguing that when the result of an investigation failed to fit the theory behind it (advanced by Mao Zedong, for example), or the opinion of the masses was out of step with the theory, then one should amend the investigation results—or the people's opinions—in order to fit the theory. The reports produced by Shanxi Province perfectly reflected Lai's approach to the issue.

High-ranking leaders like Mao Zedong were presented on a daily basis with numerous official reports that had been subjected to round after round of censorship, editing, and interpretation. Little wonder that the complexities of the rural situation were lost in the process of communication. What the peasants were thinking was not as important as what they *should* be thinking. In the end, these deeply flawed reports, where error was compounded by error, proved sufficiently plausible to convince Mao that the peasants had genuinely embraced the notion of farming collectively.

Despite the flawed nature of the Wuxiang reports, it is still worth asking whether peasant farmers were interested in forming mutual aid teams. There had been cases of successful teams, such as Geng Changsuo and his

---

67. *Shanxi Daily*, July 1, 1951.

68. Mao Zedong, "Talks at the Yenan Forum on Literature and Art," in *Selected Works of Mao Tse-tung*, vol. 3, 69–98.

followers in Wugong village in neighboring Hebei Province.[69] But such successes were rare. In 1950, in places where there was no special guidance from the party, farmers were overwhelmingly reluctant, if not resistant, to joining mutual aid teams. A case in point is Li Shunda, head of Xigou village of Changzhi prefecture. In the 1940s, Li had been a model laborer in the mutual aid movement. He would emerge as the symbol of the cooperativization movement and become the most celebrated model laborer in the nation—his story would become the subject of a series of books, comic books, and even operas widely distributed across the nation.[70] But in 1949, even his team was falling apart and Li himself was thinking of relocating to a neighboring town, upsetting Changzhi prefecture leaders. In response, Changzhi officials decided to reinforce the "special guidance" offered to Li Shunda and his village. In late 1949, a work team consisting of cadres from different levels was stationed in Xigou village. They provided Li with advice, helped him with research, made work plans for his team and, most importantly, manufactured reports for him. The prefecture even assigned Li a secretary to host receptions. In addition to these personnel, Li received a great deal of material support.[71] It was on the back of this extensive support that Li Shunda rose to become a national figure in the early 1950s.

Many decades later, Tao Lujia, then head of the Propaganda Department in Shanxi Province, shed light on instances like these. When asked in an interview, "Did the peasants practice cooperative farming or have aspirations to do so?" Tao replied candidly, "The peasants themselves had no such aspirations. The key was the guidance we offered."[72]

---

69. Edward Friedman, Paul G. Pickowicz, and Mark Selden, *Chinese Village, Socialist State*.

70. For example, books include Kang Tianxiang, *Li Shunda* (Beijing: Qingnian chubanshe, 1952); (comic book) Zhao Fengchuan, *Li Shunda* (Beijing, Huabei renmin chubanshe, 1953). The opera "Li Shunda" was widely performed in China in the 1950s.

71. "Youguan Li Shunda he Xigoucun xiang shengwei he Huabeiju de baogao" (A report to the provincial government and the North China Bureau on Li Shunda and Xigou village) (June 10, 1951), JMA, 44.1.1.

72. Gao Jie's interview of Tao Lujia, April 19, 2007, unpublished. Gao Jie had been a graduate student in history at Renmin University at the time.

Shanxi's Invention of the Agricultural Producers' Cooperative

As discussed, in the summer of 1950 Shanxi leaders decided that endowing mutual aid teams with additional functions would make them more appealing to farmers. What would these new functions involve? It was becoming clear to party bosses that if they were to demonstrate a higher commitment to socialism, the teams must have the capability to shape their members' production plans and be provided with more collectively owned property. Most importantly for Shanxi officials, a new name was needed for the expanded teams, and the task fell to Wang Qian. Unsurprisingly, Wang referred to Soviet sources for inspiration. Having read Lenin's "On Cooperation," he concluded that Lenin was proposing SMCs rather than collective farms. He then switched his attention to Stalin and found an article entitled "The Agricultural Producers' Cooperative." Although this work too dealt with SMCs, Wang Qian was taken by the title and suggested the term "Agricultural Producers' Cooperative" to Lai Ruoyu. Lai immediately approved and the concept of the agricultural producers' cooperative was born.[73] In July 1950, the *Shanxi Daily* began referring to a new form of "agricultural producers' cooperative." According to the newspaper, in these organizations, while peasants pooled their privately owned land as shareholders and farmed the aggregated land collectively, the land and output remained in the owners' hands.[74] Getting the peasants to work collectively certainly entailed an element of socialism. Changzhi prefecture regarded it as an appealing idea, yet was cautious about implementing it too soon, no doubt because this new idea threatened the preservation of private ownership that was an essential component of New Democracy.

In numerous reports published in the *Shanxi Daily*, mutual aid teams were consistently described in glowing terms. The reality was not so reassuring and Shanxi leaders knew this all too well. The idea of combining mutual aid teams with new technology was impractical and had few positive results. It did not reverse the trend of the teams breaking up into individual household units—a point that even Lai Ruoyu had to concede: "Experience had proven that, without proper guidance, the peasants cannot get orga-

---

73. Zhang Guoxiang, "Xin Zhongguo nongye shengchan hezuoshe de youlai," 31.
74. *Shanxi Daily*, July 22, 1950.

nized."[75] But guiding the peasants was no easy task. Village heads kept asking awkward questions such as, How should we guide the peasants while respecting the principle of voluntarism? and If this principle (voluntarism) is to be honored, then should mutual aid teams be allowed to disband?[76] Some heads merely convened a meeting to announce the policy of "getting organized" and made no further efforts to enforce it.[77] Changzhi prefectural cadres repeatedly instructed their counterparts at village level to publicize good examples of collective work practices so that other peasants would emulate them. More often than not, these good examples were hard to find. Village heads cried out for detailed guidance.

In addition to instructions, it was clear that something more substantial had to be offered. In the winter of 1950, Changzhi prefectural cadres issued a new call asking peasant farmers to purchase new farming tools and to overcome these unexpected difficulties. To reinforce this request, mutual aid teams were asked to collect community funds (*gongjijin*) from members. A further reason for this new approach was the party's concern over the manipulation of mutual aid teams. Because hiring laborers was considered politically risky, wealthy peasants would set up mutual aid teams as a screen in order to recruit poor peasants to work for them. Changzhi prefectural cadres were determined to clamp down on such activities. To discourage these abuses, Wang Qian announced three rules:

1. The community funds were to be collected according to the amount of private land held by individual farmers, but were to be shared equally among all members.
2. If a member exited a team, his share of the funds must remain with the team.
3. The funds were to be used to cover the costs involved in reinvestment and community welfare.

---

75. Lai Ruoyu, "Guanyu changzhiqu shiban nongyeshe de yijian" (Opinions on the trial establishment of agricultural cooperatives in the Changzhi area) (March 1951), in *Shanxi sheng nongye hezuo shi wenjian huibian juan*, 273; "Shengchan huzhu yundong zongjie baogao" (Summary of the production and mutual aid movement) (January 17, 1951), SPA, C77.04.0001.

76. "Shengchan huzhu yundong zongjie baogao."

77. Ibid.

Beginning in December 1950, the practice of collecting community funds was enforced in Changzhi prefecture.[78]

Taking money out of the peasants' pockets was not a popular policy. Those with more land were especially resentful. They disputed the stated use of the community funds and rejected the idea that they could not take their share with them if they left the team. Despite this opposition, Wang Qian believed that "community funds might be a way of introducing the peasants to agricultural collectivization while at the same time keeping wealthy peasants out of the mutual aid teams."[79] Grassroots opposition failed to overturn the policy, and it certainly did not prevent Shanxi leaders from issuing numerous reports praising its suitability for the region.

In February 1951, Wang Qian took a step further. The fact that some mutual aid teams now had increased public assets, partly due to the forced accumulation of community funds and partly due to the rewards in kind that high-performing teams received from the government, confirmed Wang's belief that "as mutual aid teams operate well, the accumulation of public assets is inevitable."[80] Aware of the problems involved in collecting community funds from peasant farmers, Wang Qian predicted that the task would be made much easier in agricultural producers' cooperatives in which funds would be deducted from farmers' incomes before being distributed to individual peasants.[81]

Disheartened by the numbers of mutual aid teams that had broken up, but encouraged by new developments such as community funds and the accumulation of public assets, Lai Ruoyu recognized that the mutual aid movement had reached a turning point. He reasoned that the only way to save the teams from collapse was to actively encourage them to reinvent themselves as higher-level socialist organizations. Following Wang Qian's suggestions, Lai proposed setting up experimental agricultural producers' cooperatives in Changzhi prefecture in March 1951.[82] While Wang Qian stipulated the basic structure of the new organization, operational details

---

78. "Changzhi zhuanqu huzhuzu zhong de gonggong caichan yu gongjijin wenti," 271–273.

79. Ibid.

80. Ibid.

81. Ibid.

82. "Zhonggong Shanxi shengwei shuji Lai Ruoyu guanyu sheng di'erci dang daibiao huiyi zhuyao neirong xiang Huabei jubing Mao zhuxi de baogao," 63–64.

would be worked out between local CCP agents and the farmers themselves, rather than exactly as Wang Qian had prescribed (see Chapter 4).

A closer examination of how Shanxi leaders came up with the idea of agricultural producers' cooperatives suggests that it was not the success of mutual aid teams, but rather their failures that prompted Lai Ruoyu and Wang Qian to adopt a more "progressive" formula and thus move one step closer to their ultimate goal of collectivization. However, this decision was to trigger a bitter personal struggle between Lai Ruoyu and Liu Shaoqi.

Lai Ruoyu and Liu Shaoqi at Odds

In pushing for the new structure, Shanxi leaders had echoed the frequently expressed views of Gao Gang, a fact to which Liu Shaoqi was not blind. When Lai Ruoyu and Wang Qian moved to collect community funds from peasant farmers and restrict their freedom of exit, Liu Shaoqi saw this as a violation of the New Democracy principles. Unfortunately for them, the Shanxi party bosses were directly answerable in the CCP hierarchy to the North China Bureau, which was under Liu Shaoqi's influence. Exacerbating the situation was the bitter personal rivalry between Lai Ruoyu and the third secretary of the North China Bureau, Liu Lantao. When Lai Ruoyu died in 1958, Liu Lantao launched a purge and slapped Lai with the damning posthumous label of "extreme rightist opportunist."[83] With personal grudges and policy disagreements muddying the waters, the Shanxi leaders took their tentative steps toward collectivization. The North China Bureau put obstacles in their path and did not hesitate to chastise them. Liu Shaoqi and his North China Bureau went as far as to use the term "agrarian utopian socialism," an expression that had been publicly denounced in 1948, to refer to the Shanxi proposal. Although previous research on the Liu–Lai disagreement has been mainly based on Bo Yibo's memoir and has focused on the heated disputes between Shanxi provincial leaders and Liu Shaoqi in mid-1951,[84] the battle had in fact begun a year earlier.

On April 28, 1950, when Wang Qian was occupied with investigating mutual aid teams in Changzhi, the North China Bureau sent a directive de-

---

83. Ren Fuxing's interviews with Han Chunde, March 9 and March 12, 2003, Beijing.

84. Bo Yibo, *Ruogan zhongda juece yu shijian de huigu*, vol. 1.

manding "the rectification of simplistic notions of agrarian utopian social-ism." The order made it clear that the right direction for rural development was contained in the New Democracy policy, which was based on the private economy.[85] This directive had little impact on Wang Qian, who immediately submitted his doctored report praising mutual aid teams and called for them to be upgraded. Over the next few months, the *Shanxi Daily* published multiple reports in favor of mutual aid teams. The North China Bureau was not ignorant of these reports. On July 10, 1950, the bureau published an editorial entitled "Striving to Increase the Wealth of Peasants in North China" in the *People's Daily*. It stated that the most urgent problem affecting peasant farmers was their reluctance to work harder out of fear of the future redistribution of private property. The solution was to reassert New Democracy policies and to reassure rural people that a "rich peasant" economy was legitimate, and that prosperous peasants were protected by law. The article sought to reassure readers that full-fledged socialism was still in the very distant future and that the mutual aid movement would never be forced on peasant farmers.[86]

In August, the North China Bureau issued a further internal directive, harsher in tone, demanding that cadres repress "agrarian utopian socialism" and reject the move to force peasant farmers to "get organized." Without naming its specific target, the directive asserted that "some branches have still not seriously implemented the North China Bureau's directive to rectify the simplistic notion of agrarian utopian socialism. They are expected to carry out an in-depth investigation into the matter and thoroughly expunge their errors."[87] The main branch in question was undoubtedly the Shanxi branch.

In response, Shanxi leaders chose to let the facts speak for them. They submitted their report titled "An Investigation of Villages in the Older Liberated Areas of Wuxiang County" to the North China Bureau. As we saw, this report claimed that since many peasants were unwilling to withdraw from mutual aid teams, far from suppressing them the party should provide guidance to such teams and expand their functions to meet their members'

---

85. *Zhonggong zhongyang Huabeiju zhongyao wenjian huibian,* vol. 1 (hereafter as *Huibian*), 638–639.

86. *People's Daily,* July 10, 1950.

87. *Shanxi sheng nongye hezuo shi wenjian huibian juan,* 638–639.

needs.[88] In November, Changzhi prefecture managed to get its report on mutual aid teams published in the *People's Daily*, in which the collective purchase of farming implements was recommended.[89] Following Changzhi prefecture's published article titled, "On the Current Situation and Problems Associated with Getting Organized,"[90] on December 30, 1950, the Shanxi party branch submitted a report on mutual aid teams to the North China Bureau that claimed that the movement was flourishing. A survey of fifty-seven villages claimed to show that total output now surpassed prewar levels by 80 percent. As the teams were using new equipment and making efficient use of available labor, unit yields had improved significantly. Moreover, many teams had collectively purchased large-scale farm equipment, and some groups had taken the initiative to collect community funds for further investment and members' welfare.[91]

When in March 1951 Lai Ruoyu proposed setting up experimental agricultural producers' cooperatives in Changzhi and Wang Qian convened a meeting to mobilize peasant farmers, the North China Bureau reacted with irritation. The bureau sent a work team to the meeting as its representative and later recommended that Lai's experiment not be conducted in haste (see Chapter 4). Wang Qian refused to budge. When the bureau's work team confronted Lai Ruoyu, Lai took Wang Qian's side and reasserted his support for Wang.[92] No compromise was reached. Wang Qian went on to establish ten experimental agricultural producers' cooperatives, and Lai Ruoyu wrote to the North China Bureau formally proposing the establishment of further experimental cooperatives in Changzhi. For its part, the bureau sided with its work team, declaring agricultural producers' cooperatives as inappropriate and in conflict with New Democracy. The episode presented a rare scenario showing how the CCP resolved policy differences and adopted measures within its own rules and beyond.

As the conflict unfolded, the North China Bureau decided to confront the Shanxi leaders directly and apply greater pressure on them—and not just in words. It decided to convene a conference, "The Developments in

---

88. "Laoqu Wuxiang nongcun kaocha baogao," 258–265.

89. *People's Daily*, November 14, 1950.

90. Ibid.

91. "Zhonggong Shanxi shengwei xiang Huabeiju zhuanbao nongyeting guanyu 1950 nian shengchan huzhu yundong de zongjie baogao," 49–57.

92. Tao Lujia, "Mao zhuxi zhichi Shanxi sheng shiban hezuoshe," 635–654.

Mutual Aid and Cooperatives in Five Provinces and Cities in North China," to discuss the issue of agricultural producers' cooperatives.[93] Learning of the upcoming conference, Shanxi provincial leaders met, approved a draft by Lai Ruoyu titled "Upgrading Mutual Aid and Cooperative Organization," and submitted it to the North China Bureau for consideration at the conference. In this report, Lai argued that mutual aid teams had reached a crucial point—they would either decline and become organizations dominated by wealthy peasant farmers or they would successfully advance a socialist agenda. Lai proposed reforming the mutual aid movement and setting up agricultural producers' cooperatives as a way of checking the "spontaneous tendencies" of individual farmers. He insisted that accumulating community funds and distributing profits according to labor were two key principles that could not be sacrificed.[94]

Running contrary to the principles of New Democracy, such claims no doubt angered Liu Shaoqi. A short time later, Liu and the North China Bureau dealt a counterpunch at "The Developments in Mutual Aid and Cooperatives in Five Provinces and Cities in North China" conference held on April 22, 1951. Wang Qian and Wu Guangtang, who had overseen the investigations in Wuxiang County during the summer of 1950, represented Shanxi Province at the conference. Even half a century later, Wang Qian retained bitter memories of this event. As he recalled, the first day was quiet, but, on day two, the conference host, a high-ranking cadre from the North China Bureau, opened proceedings with a provocative statement: "Shanxi Province has built ten agricultural productive cooperatives, as they mentioned yesterday. I don't agree with this, and the North China Bureau doesn't agree with it either." He then encouraged attendees to discuss the issue and not to worry about "seeing blood on the floor." Prompted by this invitation, a flood of criticism overwhelmed the Shanxi delegates. The majority argued that under the New Democracy policy, it was wrong to eliminate private ownership and that there could be no true collectivization without mechanization. Some participants attacked Wang Qian personally, condemning him for "seeking the limelight" (*chu fengtou*).

On the defensive, Wang Qian justified Shanxi's position by citing the

---

93. Zhang Guoxiang, "Xin Zhongguo nongye shengchan hezuoshe de youlai," 33.

94. "Ba laoqu huzhu zuzhi tigao yibu" (Taking the reform of the mutual aid movement one step further in the older liberated areas) (April 17, 1951), *Huibian*, 35–36.

example of the Soviet Union and rural reforms in Eastern Europe, reminding delegates that when the USSR began its successful collectivization program, there were few machines available. And when Bulgaria launched its collectivization effort, the land had not yet been nationalized. Therefore, Wang argued, mechanization and nationalization of land were not absolute preconditions for collectivization. "Could we not at least try?"[95] he asked.

The debate soured. On day four of the conference, the North China Bureau advised that it "had reported to the Central Committee, and the Central Committee did not approve Shanxi's plan to build agricultural producers' cooperatives."[96] Following the conference, Liu Lantao told Wang Qian, "Comrade Liu Shaoqi does not agree with the Shanxi report. When you return, tell the provincial branch not to endorse the errors in the report. You should read some books on the subject and report back to the North China Bureau."[97] For its part, the bureau was awaiting Shanxi's self-criticism.

The bureau's rejection of the plans generated disputes among Shanxi provincial leaders. First party secretary Cheng Zihua came out in support of the North China Bureau and asserted that Shanxi should follow its instructions. Lai Ruoyu disagreed. Wang Qian sided with Lai and delivered a speech drawing on Mao's writings of the 1940s, which advocated mutual aid teams and collectivization in order to underscore the necessity of getting peasant farmers organized. Although Wang Qian acknowledged that farmers were enthusiastic about the private economy, he insisted that they also wanted to "get organized." Wang Qian concluded that to put rural development on the right path, agricultural producers' cooperatives should be formed.[98]

In the end, Lai Ruoyu's views prevailed over Cheng Zihua's. Lai drafted a formal reply to the North China Bureau, which denied the bulk of the charges leveled against the prefecture.[99] In response to Liu Lantao's advice to "read more books," the Shanxi leaders turned to the Marxist classics to find theoretical support for their own position. On the question of mechaniza-

---

95. Zhang Guoxiang, "Xin Zhongguo nongye shengchan hezuoshe de youlai," 34.
96. Ibid.
97. Tao Lujia. "Mao zhuxi zhichi shanxi sheng shiban hezuoshe."
98. *Shanxi sheng nongye hezuo shi wenjian huibian juan*, 282–292.
99. Details of this report and the North China Bureau's response are found in Bo Yibo, *Ruogan zhongda juece yu shijian de huigu*, 193–194.

tion as a precondition for collectivization, they discovered that, in *Capital*, Karl Marx had stated: "All fully developed machinery consists of three essentially different parts, the motor mechanism, the transmitting mechanism, and finally the tool or working machine," and "The tool or working-machine is that part of the machinery with which the industrial revolution of the 18th century started."[100] Lai Ruoyu concluded that new "tools," such as large-scale farm equipment made of iron and pulled by horses, were the "working-machines" Marx had referred to. Compared to China's traditional wooden farming tools, these new tools represented a significant technological advance. Organizing cooperatives and encouraging the use of such new tools was an important component of mechanization. Tractors, he quipped, should not be regarded as the only modern machine of relevance to rural people.

As for the question of when collective farms should be initiated, the Shanxi leaders found another apposite text, this time from Engels: "It will serve us naught to wait with this transformation until capitalist production has developed everywhere to its utmost consequences, until the last small handicraftsman and the last small peasant have fallen victim to capitalist large-scale production."[101] This provided useful ammunition with which to rebut Liu Shaoqi's support for the development of New Democracy–style capitalism. Shanxi leaders were eager to promote Engels' ideas on the transformation of small-peasant private enterprises and private property into cooperative enterprises and collectively owned property as the best method of liberating the peasants.[102] Taking Marx and Engels as their theoretical guides, Lai Ruoyu and his associates asserted that their plans had nothing to do with utopian socialism. They refused to yield.

Accordingly, no word of self-criticism reached the North China Bureau from Shanxi. Infuriated, on May 4, 1951, the bureau issued a formal criticism of the Shanxi leaders for their proposal to establish experimental cooperatives, declaring that "collecting community funds and making distribution according to labor input" was erroneous. Liu Shaoqi joined the crusade against Shanxi in person. On May 7, at the National Propaganda

---

100. Cited in Tao Lujia, *Mao zhuxi jiao women dang shengwei shuji*.

101. Frederick Engels, "The Peasant Question in France and Germany," cited in Tao Lujia, *Mao Zhuxi jiao women dang shengwei shuji*.

102. Tao Lujia, *Mao zhuxi jiao women dang shengwei shuji*, 205–206.

Conference, he stated that it was almost impossible to guide China's agricultural sector toward socialism by organizing mutual aid teams or agricultural producers' cooperatives. Rather unusually, Liu publicly named Shanxi provincial leaders as the targets of his criticism, and labeled their policies "utopian agricultural socialism."[103] On several occasions between May and July 25 Liu Shaoqi criticized Lai Ruoyu in front of a variety of audiences.[104] In this barrage of criticism, Liu Shaoqi made his objections crystal clear: he did not regard mutual aid teams as appropriate precursors to socialism, and agricultural producers' cooperatives had no future. Rich peasants, Liu argued, would flourish and even control their villages if the party could not constrain them. For the following decade at least, the party should give no thought to building socialism in the rural sector. Liu introduced two major principles to be followed. First, no attempt should be made to undermine private ownership in the countryside. Second, mechanization was to be accepted as a precondition for collectivization. Liu Shaoqi again accused those who wanted to undertake collectivization in the countryside of pursuing "utopian socialism."[105] Bo Yibo commented in his memoir that it was unusual for a figure like Liu Shaoqi to level his serious accusations against another provincial leader in a semipublic setting without first consulting Mao.[106]

On June 29, Bo Yibo published an article in the *People's Daily* that had been revised and approved by Liu Shaoqi. Bo asserted that it was sheer fantasy to believe that the gradual development of mutual aid teams and cooperative organizations could "weaken and negate private ownership" and thus pave the way for the collectivization of agriculture. Such an idea was a manifestation of "utopian socialist" thinking. Bo Yibo insisted that mutual aid teams were intended to protect, not undermine, private property. Any further development of these teams should build on the foundation of the individual economy and private property. Bo cautioned rural officials not to criticize individual farmers and wealthy peasants. Collectiv-

103. Bo Yibo, *Ruogan zhongda juece yu shijian de huigu*, 194.
104. Zhang Guoxiang, "Xin Zhongguo nongye shengchan hezuoshe de youlai," 35.
105. Bo Yibo, *Ruogan zhongda juece yu shijian de huigu*, 195.
106. Ibid., 212.

ization would eventually become a reality in the countryside, but it would have to be based on mechanization, Bo reiterated.[107]

Shanxi leaders were now coming under enormous pressure. Lai Ruoyu claimed sick leave and went to Beijing for medical treatment. In his absence, Xie Xuegong, an official from the Jinsui base area and not a member of the Taihang clique, took charge of provincial affairs in Shanxi. Meanwhile, representatives from Shanxi were on their way to Beijing, ready to make acts of self-criticism. However, Wang Qian had no intention of giving up. He wrote to Mao Zedong, attaching a copy of the Changzhi report that had been published in the People's Daily along with his own piece on the party's leadership of agricultural production that was filled with excerpts from Mao's own writings. It was a gamble. Despite failing to consult with the Shanxi party branch, or send his message through official channels, Wang Qian's material succeeded in reaching Mao.[108]

Apparently, Wang Qian's material appealed to Mao. As we saw in Chapter 1, Mao strongly believed that mutual aid teams should form the first stage toward collectivization. More precisely, while he was clear about the starting point (mutual aid teams) and the end point (collectivization) of the process of transforming the countryside along socialist lines, Mao had failed to formulate the intermediate stages. Mao now saw that Shanxi's proposal for agricultural producers' cooperatives had made his vision viable. Mao was possibly also offended by Liu Shaoqi's contempt for the mutual aid movement and the fact that Liu had acted behind his back.

Mao decided to intervene and did so in two stages. First, he sent his secretary Chen Boda, an acquaintance of Lai Ruoyu, to visit Lai in the hospital. Chen told Lai that the case against him had been overturned and that Mao was supporting him. Lai left the hospital the next day and returned to Shanxi. Second, in August 1951, Mao Zedong summoned Liu Shaoqi, Bo Yibo, and Liu Lantao and made clear to them his personal endorsement of the Shanxi proposal. Mao rejected the notions that mutual aid teams could not develop into collective farms and that it would be a mistake to weaken the private economy at the current stage, as both Liu Shaoqi and Bo Yibo had insisted.[109] Mao referred to statements by Stalin in the *Foundations of*

---

107. *People's Daily*, June 29, 1951.
108. Ma Shexiang, "Interview with Tao Lujia," 72–74.
109. Ibid.

Leninism, asserting that just as the British "putting-out system" had provided the foundations for a new set of production relations associated with industrialization, so Chinese mutual aid teams could perform a similar function in the development of new production relations associated with socialism.[110]

Chinese scholar Xin Ziling argues that this analogy provided the cornerstone for Mao's final endorsement of Shanxi's plan. Although Mao himself did not elaborate on the analogy, his secretary Chen Boda argued that since the major difference between the British putting-out system and agricultural producers' cooperatives was that British workers were proletarians who had nothing whereas Chinese peasants were small producers who owned something, the shortest way to erase the difference was to deprive Chinese peasants of their private property and turn them into agricultural laborers. The irony here was that Mao, whose own grasp of Marx's *Capital* was less than expert, had once asserted that Chen Boda's main weakness, as his secretary, was his poor understanding of Marx's *Capital*.[111] Such niceties aside, Chen Boda's theoretical breakthrough added weight to the Shanxi leaders' manufactured "evidence." Convinced or not, Liu Shaoqi, Bo Yibo, and Liu Lantao appeared to have been "persuaded by Mao's arguments" and immediately abandoned their previous position.[112]

Mao's intervention ended the dispute and overturned several of the leading principles that Liu Shaoqi had previously insisted on. First of all, there was nothing to stop the state from intervening to weaken the private economy. Second, mutual aid teams would be allowed to develop into agricultural producers' cooperatives, which could develop further into collective farms. Third, mechanization was not to be regarded as a prerequisite for collectivization. Mao instructed Chen Boda to organize a national conference—"with a limited audience"—focusing on mutual aid and cooperatives.[113]

---

110. Bo Yibo, *Ruogan zhongda juece yu shijian de huigu*, 191.
111. Xin Ziling, "Nongye jitihua lilun shi zenyang shizu de."
112. Ma Shexiang, "Interview with Tao Lujia."
113. Zhang Guoxiang, "Xin Zhongguo nongye shengchan hezuoshe de youlai."

The Mutual Aid and Cooperation Movements Taking Off

Chen Boda, formerly a professional writer with little knowledge of agriculture, moved swiftly to convene the conference. Following Mao's instructions, he invited representatives from only a few areas, including Northeast China and Shanxi Province. In September 1951, the First National Mutual Aid and Cooperative Conference was convened in Beijing. Although Liu Shaoqi had written a keynote speech, it was shelved and not included in the conference agenda. Instead, Chen Boda presented a draft of his paper, "A Resolution on Mutual Aid and Cooperation in Agriculture." During the conference, representatives from Northeast China proudly shared stories of their success in upgrading mutual aid teams, while the Shanxi representatives eulogized the province's ten experimental agricultural producers' cooperatives. In the end, Chen Boda's draft document was adopted as the conference resolution. It emphasized the aspirations of peasant farmers to work collectively and to join mutual aid teams.

After the conference, Mao consulted Zhao Shuli, a highly respected novelist who wrote about peasants and rural life, about Chen's resolution. Zhao replied candidly that peasants had no desire to join mutual aid teams and only wanted to work for themselves. Following the interview with Zhao, Mao instructed Chen to revise the conference document, which was thereafter known as the "Resolution on Mutual Aid and Cooperation in Agriculture (Draft)" (the Draft). The first paragraph of this revised version stated that Chinese peasant farmers were attracted to both working for themselves and working collectively.[114] After acknowledging their dual character, the Draft urged that their collective inclinations be encouraged and their individual proclivities checked.

The Draft clarified the point that *now* was the time—not ten years hence—to make the transition to socialism. Most importantly, it offered a clear blueprint of the path to collectivization: first the mutual aid teams, followed by lower-stage agricultural producers' cooperatives, progressing finally to a more advanced form of producers' cooperative that would take the form of a collective farm in a fully socialist mold. The structure of the agricultural producers' cooperative emphasized in the Draft was clearly modeled on the Shanxi prototype: peasant farmers were to invest in their land by

---

114. Du Runsheng, *Dangdai Zhongguo de nongye hezuo zhi*, vol. 1, 143.

holding shares and farming the land collectively. The Draft called on local cadres to organize farmers into mutual aid teams throughout the country. In selected areas, local cadres should encourage and help peasants form agricultural producers' cooperatives.[115]

The contents of the Draft were arbitrary—there was no hard evidence to support the notion that the peasants had a dual character. The Draft was heavily influenced by a series of reports submitted by the Shanxi leaders and was based more on what the party wanted the peasants to be rather than the reality on the ground. It was approved by a narrow range of delegates, likely drawn from areas that already favored agricultural producers' cooperatives, just as Mao and Chen Boda intended. Nevertheless, this document served as the foundation for a series of future rural initiatives, and its assertion of the dual character of the Chinese peasantry was never challenged during the Mao era. The notion that peasants were willing to work collectively answered the question of whether or not it was time to start the collectivization process, while the idea that they were also inclined to work individually naturally invited guidance from the party.

On October 14, 1951, Gao Gang presented Mao with a report he had written on mutual aid and cooperation in Northeast China. He claimed that peasant farmers in the northeast were not reluctant to increase production—in fact, they were demanding a rapid boost in outputs. Hence the party needed to step in and actively develop mutual aid teams based on the principle of volunteerism, upon which it could then organize more advanced forms of collective farming. Gao Gang seconded Shanxi's proposal. Mao Zedong approved Gao's report and ordered that it be circulated to party branches across the nation. Mao added the following rider: "This report is accurate, and all party branches throughout China that have completed the land reform process should seriously get to work on this issue, organizing peasants into various kinds of mutual aid teams based on private ownership, while not penalizing those who refuse to participate." This was Mao's first official directive on mutual aid and cooperative questions following the founding of the PRC.[116] The North China Bureau backed away from its earlier criticism of Shanxi by affirming that agricultural producers' cooperatives were the only means of making the transition to socialism.[117]

115. Ye Yangbing, *Zhongguo nongye hezuohua yundong yanjiu*, 198–199.
116. Du Runsheng, *Dangdai Zhongguo de nongye hezuo zhi*, 138.
117. Ibid., 139.

Why did Mao Zedong, in 1951, choose to step into the debate and proclaim a vision for the future of China's agricultural sector that was in conflict with the official New Democracy ideology? The reasons were many. In addition to Mao's longtime personal predilection for the mutual aid movement, the many problems land reform had produced, and the powerful case presented by Shanxi Province, the outbreak of the Korean War in 1950 also played a crucial role in his thinking. New Democracy was grounded on the premise of continuing peace. China's prolonged engagement in the Korean War led Mao to reassess the relevance of New Democracy, regarding which he already entertained some doubts. The involvement of the United States in the Korean War revealed its willingness and capacity to intervene in East Asia affairs. The threat from the United States was not only immediate, but it showed every sign of persisting. Even after the Korean War was over, the U.S. threat would remain through its alliances with Taiwan, South Korea, and Japan. The Korean War convinced CCP leaders, especially Mao, that China was surrounded by hostile neighbors, just as the Soviet Union had been in the 1930s. The Soviet Union seemed to be an exception and it was also the most likely model for pursuing socialism.

The party modified its domestic agenda to meet these perceived threats. In November 1950, the Financial and Economic Committee gave national defense top priority in the state budget. In spring 1951, the CCP established a six-member committee, three of whom were from the army, to prepare a draft of China's first five year plan.[118] In the fall of 1951, heavy industry and defense together replaced agriculture as the core of China's new economic strategy, and this situation would remain in place for several decades.[119] The simple fact that the Chinese army was fighting in Korea paved the way for reapplying the economic methods that the CCP had adopted during the revolutionary wars, which heavily focused on state intervention and state oversight. The year 1951 proved to be the right time for Lai Ruoyu to put forward his proposal.

---

118. Shinji Yamaguchi, "Lun Mao Zedong fangqi xin minzhu zhuyi de zhanlue yanbian," 194.

119. Ibid.

Conclusion

By the end of 1951, the debate over the agricultural producers' cooperatives was officially over. Lai Ruoyu had won. The internal voice of dissent in Shanxi, Cheng Zihua, was transferred to a post in another province, clearing the way for the launch of the agricultural cooperativization in Shanxi.[120] In the years to come, Liu Shaoqi repeatedly criticized his own "mistakes" over the question.

Looking back on the unfolding of the debate, the Shanxi leaders, especially Lai Ruoyu, had stood unusually firm in confronting their superiors in the party, both in words and action. Lai Ruoyu had instructed Wang Qian to set up experimental APCs despite the North China Bureau's explicit opposition. And when the bureau was expecting Lai's self-criticism, he issued a rebuttal instead. For two months he had simply refused to bend to Liu Shaoqi, the second-most powerful figure in the CCP. What had caused Lai to act so confidently, even recklessly? He was likely sincere in his faith in collectivization, but faith alone was not sufficient to defy Liu Shaoqi. Speculation that Lai had an axe to grind with the North China Bureau and was frustrated by Beijing's appointments to the Shanxi leadership post-1949 might help explain his motivations, but hardly accounts for his courage. One possible factor is that Lai Ruoyu was aware of Mao Zedong's disapproval of Liu Shaoqi's approach to peasant issues and chose to exploit it to his advantage. Whatever the precise details, in retrospect Lai Ruoyu seemed to have taken a calculated risk. He and Wang Qian regarded Mao's views as self-evident and were constantly quoting his sayings. At the same time, it was clear that Gao Gang was the rising star in the party and Mao's favorite at the time, and it was only sensible to follow in Gao's footsteps.

Whatever motivated Lai Ruoyu and his clique to challenge Liu Shaoqi, they eventually succeeded and were well rewarded for their persistence. The Taihang clique consolidated its rule of Shanxi and dominated the province for the next two decades. It was not long before Lai Ruoyu was promoted to first secretary of the Shanxi branch of the CCP, the position to which he had long aspired. A year later he was appointed secretary of the National Labor Union and left Shanxi for Beijing.[121] Xie Xuegong, who hailed from the Jinsui

---

120. Gao Jie's interview with Tao Lujia at Beijing, April 19, 2007.

121. Lai Ruoyu's political career in the 1950s followed an unusual path. His development of agricultural producers' cooperatives certainly impressed Mao Zedong.

base area and who had served as interim secretary of Shanxi when Lai Ruoyu went on sick leave, was pushed out of Shanxi. In his place, Tao Lujia, head of the Propaganda Department under Lai Ruoyu, served as first secretary of Shanxi between 1953 and 1960, and was then appointed director of the North China Bureau. He had certainly learned his lessons well. In the 1960s, Tao was the first to draw Mao Zedong's attention to the experience of Dazhai village, where the village heads had mobilized the peasants to carry out massive public projects to restore damage to the environment and to raise agricultural productivity. As a result, Mao launched a nationwide campaign, Learning from Dazhai in Agriculture, which carried on until his death in 1976.

Wang Qian, head of Changzhi prefecture in Shanxi, became a well-known figure and continued to build his reputation as a specialist on the peasant economy. He was rapidly appointed head of the Policy Research Center of the North China Bureau and subsequently vice-minister of the bureau's Rural Work Department. Between 1954 and 1956 Wang worked as vice-secretary of the Central Rural Work Department, a crucial post in terms of formulating the CCP's rural policies. In 1956 he became vice-secretary of the Shanxi provincial branch of the CCP, and in the 1970s he was the party's first secretary in Shanxi.

The success in 1951 was only the beginning of Shanxi's long journey for rural socialist transformation. Wang Qian and his colleagues found they still had to defend their zone of influence, and further battles between Shanxi and the North China Bureau would follow.

In 1952 Mao handpicked Lai Ruoyu to lead the National Labor Union, an institution that had hitherto been controlled by Liu Shaoqi. At the time, Lai Ruoyu had just finished consolidating his governance of Shanxi and knew little about labor unions. After seeking advice from his former superior Bo Yibo—whom he had no doubt alienated during Lai's conflict with Liu Shaoqi—Bo told him coldly that as Mao had chosen him, Lai would have to leave; if he knew nothing about labor unions, then he should learn. In his new—and probably lesser—position as secretary of the National Labor Union in Beijing, Lai Ruoyu became embroiled in a controversy over the principles underlying the Labor Union, a debate that once again involved Liu Shaoqi. Lai Ruoyu was purged in 1958 and died of cancer the same year. Li Guiren, *Lai Ruoyu Zhuan*.

4

Peasants Outmaneuvering the Party

The masses are like pecan nuts—you have to smash them so you can eat them.

—motto for some CCP cadres in Changzhi[1]

Get organized to accumulate the family fortune.

—peasant saying, April 1952[2]

(Mutual aid teams were) formed in the spring, came undone in the summer, collapsed in the fall. [This pattern] will repeat itself next year.

—peasant saying, Changzhi, June 1952[3]

In March 1951, Lai Ruoyu set out a proposal for establishing experimental agricultural producers' cooperatives in Shanxi. In these organizations, members would pool their land as shares and farm collectively, and distribute the net profits according to both labor input and land shares. In addition, the

---

1. *Neibu cankao*, February 28, 1951.
2. *Neibu cankao*, April 29, 1952.
3. "Changzhi diwei guanyu bannian lai nongcun shengchan huzhu hezuo yundong zonghe baogao" (Changzhi prefecture's report on the Mutual Aid and Cooperation movement during the last six months) (June 30, 1952), JMA, 92.1.1.

cooperatives would collect community funds and accumulate public assets.[4] Lai Ruoyu was confident about his plan, arguing that it was grounded in the fact that peasant farmers already had experience of accumulating such assets in mutual aid teams. But, as we saw in Chapter 3, this "fact" had substance only because it had been imposed by the party.

Once experimental agricultural producers' cooperatives were initiated and established in Shanxi, the decision to approve them and make them universal was evidently made from the top down. Lai Ruoyu and Wang Qian made no attempt to disguise their direct involvement in the initiation of the policy. Following Lai Ruoyu's proposal, on March 27, Wang Qian convened a mobilization meeting in Changzhi prefecture with the heads of mutual aid teams and "discussed" the details involved in creating and operating the new organizations. Wang made a passionate appeal to his audience by outlining the ultimate goals of collectivization and modernization. The joint purchase of farm implements would advance collectivization and the acquisition of community funds would accumulate assets. In order to facilitate the transition to collectivization, he not only drew up the blueprint for the new cooperatives, but he also spelled out some specific rules. He recommended that peasants pool at least two-thirds of their land to form the cooperatives and farm collectively. In Wang Qian's estimation, each experimental cooperative should consist of approximately twenty households. The distribution of profits according to land input should be lower than land rents, which were about 30 percent of land output. Landowners would be responsible for the cost of supplying seed and fertilizers and would cover agricultural taxes. At least half the profits would be distributed according to labor input, and 20 percent would go into community funds. If members withdraw from the cooperative, they would not be entitled to a share of the community funds. To improve the chances of success, Wang Qian set some ground rules: the experimental cooperatives should be led by experienced party cadres and model laborers; they must be located in areas with good soils and convenient access to resources, and close to party headquarters.[5] Wang Qian promised state loans and reduced agricultural taxes as financial

---

4. "Zhonggong shanxi shengwei shuji Lai Ruoyu guanyu sheng di'erci dang daibiao huiyi zhuyao neirong xiang Huabei jubing Mao zhuxi de baogao," 63–64.

5. Wang Qian, "Zai changzhi qu huzhu daibiaohui shang guanyu shiban nongye shengchan hezuoshe de baogao," 274–276.

incentives. In his closing remarks, he nonetheless warned attendees not to spread news of new ventures in order to avoid unnecessary disruption.[6]

As mentioned in Chapter 3, the North China Bureau sent a work team as its representative at the meeting and to check any hasty decisions. The work team immediately raised concerns and disagreements with Wang Qian's plans. First, it pointed out that the timing was bad. The farmers had had no advance warning, and local mutual aid teams had made no material preparations. The spring sowing season had already begun. Thus it was both premature and imprudent to begin the trial immediately.

The work team certainly had a point. There was a Catch-22 element in the CCP's principles to mobilize the peasants. While the party could launch political and agricultural campaigns during the off-season (usually the winter, when work on the land was suspended), it needed to withdraw with the start of the spring sowing season and to let the peasants farm their land undisturbed. Failure of the spring sowing would condemn that year's crop and damage the following year's as well. However, Lai Ruoyu and Wang Qian were so zealous in pressing their case that they completely disregarded these considerations. In their estimation, the political stakes were too high to let such things stand in their way. Another contentious issue concerned the proposed community fund. The work team thought it would unfairly impact the well-off peasants and it strongly opposed Wang Qian's proposal for retaining monies paid into the fund when members left. The work team believed that this proposal violated the principle of protecting private ownership. In addition, deciding how the funds were to be used was likely to generate conflict among members.[7]

In face of these criticisms, Lai Ruoyu and Wang Qian refused to back down.[8] They filed a report with the North China Bureau defending their proposals, which eventually triggered the conference held in April, "On Mutual Aid and Cooperatives in Five Provinces and Cities in North China," as

---

6. "Wang Qian tongzhi sanyue 29 ri zai huzhu daibiaohui shang de zongjie baogao" (Wang Qian's report on a Mutual Aid and Cooperation conference of heads of mutual aid teams) (March 29, 1951), SPA, C77.4.5.

7. "Chungeng gongzuodui Shanxi xiaozu guanyu Changzhi zhuanqu huzhu daibiao huiyi qingkuang de baogao" (The Shanxi branch of the spring planting work team on the Mutual Aid and Cooperation conference of heads of mutual aid teams in Changzhi prefecture) (March 30, 1951), SPA, C54.2003.47.

8. Ibid.

discussed in Chapter 3. At the same time, Wang Qian continued to work on the scheme.

According to the official records, following the March mobilization meeting the attendees unanimously agreed that agricultural producers' co-operatives would increase rural productivity and many signed up for the venture. Opting for quality over quantity, Wang Qian decided to limit the scope of the trial to ten cooperatives, ensuring that Changzhi prefecture could allocate adequate resources to the experiment and so make it a dazzling success.[9] It was interesting that Changzhi officials declined a request from the region's most celebrated model laborer, Li Shunda, for fear that any failure on Li's part would draw unwelcome attention to the scheme and put a damper on the whole experiment.[10]

Changzhi's Experimental Cooperatives: The Success Stories

In April 1951, China's first experimental agricultural producers' coopera-tives were established in Changzhi prefecture. Wuxiang County, not sur-prisingly, was chosen as a major site for the trial. Five days after the mobili-zation meeting, Wuxiang County officials put out a call for volunteers. Two weeks later, four experimental cooperatives had been established in three villages, each based on a former mutual aid team. It was an enormous task. In the words of one cadre, "We put in a massive effort consolidating the cooperatives."[11] Within this brief time span, eighty-seven households—all middle-ranking peasants—had joined the four cooperatives in Wuxiang, pooling 77.9 percent of their land into the venture. Of the eighty-seven households involved, thirty-five included party members and twelve had communist youth league members. With respect to potential income distri-bution, 50 percent of total farming production would be credited according

9. "Guanyu nongye shengchan hezuoshe chunji shenchan diwei xiang shengwei baogao" (October 4, 1951) (The prefect's report to the province on the spring pro-duction figures from agricultural producers' cooperatives), SPA, C77.4.5.

10. Tao Lujia, "Mao Zhuxi zhichi shanxi sheng shiban hezuoshe."

11. "Guanyu shijian nongye shengchan hezuoshe gongzuo de zongjie baogao" (A review of the establishment of experimental agricultural producers' cooperatives) (April 30, 1951), SPA, C77.4.5.

to labor input, 30 percent to land shares, and 20 percent would go into community funds. As for the income gained through sidelines, 20 percent would be collected as community funds, and the remainder distributed solely according to labor input. Meanwhile, landowners were to take responsibility for taxes, seeds, and fertilizers. In each cooperative, one head and one deputy head (or sometimes two) were selected, plus an accountant. (This distribution complied precisely with Wang Qian's suggestions.)

According to the above formula, the share of land contributed by farmers bore little relationship to the profits they accrued. A rough calculation tells us that the common land share would receive only 30 percent of total agricultural output. Taxes—a combination of state agricultural tax and local surcharges—would account for between 15 and 25 percent of land output. The cost of seed, animal fodder, and fertilizers would easily account for 20 percent of total profits. Local farmers were suspicious that the costs incurred by landowners would exceed returns.[12] The great majority of older peasants in Wuxiang harbored grave doubts that these experimental cooperatives would succeed. The father of a deputy head in Jianzhang village openly questioned the formula. He calculated that land inputs would be such that they would deliver no net income, sidelines would require large financial input, and loans would need to be repaid. He saw no benefits for peasants to participate in the experiment. In addition, a cooperative would need to support three or four "leaders" who did not farm full time. How could it possibly be done? Not to mention the common sense reasoning that even if family members were to be divided up (fenjia), how could twenty or thirty households work together? Trouble was on the way, this critic predicted.[13] Nevertheless, dozens of peasants signed themselves up for the scheme. Did they not know how to add?

While farmers certainly knew how to do their sums, each made a different set of calculations. A series of surveys taken in Wuxiang found that peasants joined these experimental cooperatives for a variety of reasons.

---

12. In the case of Yaoshanggou cooperative, expenditure on seed, fodder, and fertilizer amounted to 106 dan out of a total land output of 501 dan. "Wuxiang Yaoshanggou 1951 nian shi ban nongye shengchan hezuoshe de zuihou baogao" (The final report from Yaoshanggou village of Wuxiang County on the establishment of experimental agricultural producers' cooperatives in 1951) (October 23, 1951), JMA, 50.1.1.

13. "Guanyu shijian nongye shengchan hezuoshe gongzuo de zongjie baogao."

Political ambition was the spur for forty-five households, mainly party members and activists, to join the cooperatives. Their political aspirations and ambitions for the future convinced them to follow the party's call. For this group, financial returns were not the whole story. Another group of fifteen households was less progressive politically but did not want to be left behind. Seven households vacillated: while they expected to suffer some economic loss, they were afraid of being considered politically backward, which may have proved even more damaging. In the end, after "being inspired and educated" by party members, they decided to participate, even though it was a painful decision.[14]

A third group consisted of villagers who were either relatives or close friends of the cooperative heads and were easily "persuaded" to join the scheme. Thirteen households fell into this category. The fourth group adopted a different approach. These households were well known by locals for their shrewdness—after carefully accounting for every detail, they calculated that they would benefit economically by joining the trial. Households with extra laborers but little land counted on benefiting from the cooperatives' distribution formula. Others were pure opportunists. Their past experience had convinced them that when the CCP called for volunteers, joining at the first call would doubtless result in handsome profits as the party could be counted on to ensure that any experimental schemes it initiated were successes.[15] Thus, based on a variety of motives, eighty-seven households in Wuxiang County formed four cooperatives, all expecting solid rewards one way or another and of one kind or another.

However, the majority of peasants in Changzhi were not optimistic about the trials; indeed, they were dismayed by the prospect. Most village activists were faced with a dilemma—while their superiors urged them to join the scheme, they knew they would suffer economic loss if they did. They feared that they would be forced to join in any case. Those with extensive landholdings or land of good quality did not want to be part of any cooperative venture. Peasant farmers had long feared the advent of communism, and now it seemed that their fears were coming true: private property was to be collectivized. In response, some peasants immediately stopped

14. Ibid.
15. Ibid.

investing in their land. Villages earmarked for trial cooperatives, as well as neighboring villages, followed developments with trepidation.[16]

Confronted with sharp critiques from the North China Bureau and serious doubts from below, those advocating Wuxiang's ten experimental cooperatives were playing for high stakes. Wuxiang county officials did all they could to aid the four experimental cooperatives under their jurisdiction. They helped draw up production plans designed to double outputs. They placed strict constraints on the members' ability to withdraw from the scheme: while the principle of volunteerism was honored and members were allowed to withdraw, if someone left the cooperative, he could not take out his land for the current year. Wuxiang officials also published regulations designed to monitor farmers' work habits.[17]

In May 1951, Wuxiang County submitted a follow-up report to Changzhi prefecture emphasizing the success of its four cooperatives. In just one month, the four schemes had successfully devised methods allowing them to substantially increase their output. The most efficient of these was planting additional cash crops. Another technique was to increase investment in sideline work. All four cooperatives had doubled or tripled the area of land sown in cash crops, primarily cotton and tobacco.

However, there were some clouds on the horizon. Surplus labor had become the most pressing issue for the peasants themselves, if not yet for the party. Yaoshanggou village cooperative, led by Wang Jinyun, offered a good illustration of the problem. The cooperative consisted of twenty-eight full-time laborers and 367 mu of sown land. As only ten laborers were needed to work the land, the cooperative assigned the remaining eighteen to raise pigs, make terrines, produce vinegar, sell eggs, and even planned to send some to work in nearby cities.[18] Aid from the state was crucial to underpin these ambitious plans. In April, Wuxiang officials promised strong support for the cooperative. Within a month, two loans totaling 12,000,000 RMB (old currency) were granted to Yaoshanggou.[19]

---

16. Ibid.

17. Ibid.

18. "Guanyu nongye shengchan hezuoshe gonggu gongzuo de zongjie baogao" (Consolidating agricultural producers' cooperatives—a review) (June 1, 1951), SPA, C77.4.5.

19. Ibid.

By October 1951, the party's efforts had paid off, at least on paper. Local reports showed that the Yaoshanggou cooperative's average unit yield was 1.8 dan per mu—25.5 percent higher than the figure for 1950 and 12 percent more than the highest unit yield achieved by mutual aid teams in the same village. Profit from sideline ventures was even higher. Overall, yield per capita was 1485 catties (sideline products were converted into grain), 73.4 percent higher than that in 1950, and 33 percent more than the results achieved by mutual aid teams in 1951. However, while these results appeared impressive, they failed to meet the original production targets set by Wuxiang County.[20]

Perhaps surprisingly, on the question of net income distribution, the formula developed by Wang Qian was amended by the peasants themselves. After many rounds of discussion among cooperative members, a more flexible solution was adopted. The new formula substantially reduced the share allocated to community funds, which were now to be levied progressively, starting at 2 and rising to 15 percent.[21] Members were to be allowed to take most of their community fund contribution with them if they withdrew from the cooperative. Income distribution based on land input was to vary from 37 to 42 percent of land output, while remuneration based on labor accounted for no more than 56 but not less than 48 percent. Landowners were to be compensated by the cooperative for what they spent on seeds, fodder, and fertilizers.

In Yaoshanggou cooperative, the final distribution was worked out as follows: total income (from agricultural and sideline sources) for 1951 was 693 dan of grain. Of this, 328 dan was apportioned to labor input, 136 dan to land input, 106 dan was allocated to the cost of cattle, fodder, seeds, and fertilizers, 51 dan was collected for the community funds, and 70 dan was used to repay state loans.[22] Although all households in the cooperative

---

20. "Wuxiang Yaoshanggou 1951 nian shi ban nongye shengchan hezuoshe de zuihou baogao."

21. The formula was calculated as follows: where the unit yield was approximately equal to the village's average yield, 2 percent of output was collected as community funds; where the unit yield was 25 percent higher than the village average, 5 percent of output was collected; where the unit yield was 50 percent higher, a rate ranging between 10 and 15 percent was set. "Wuxiang Yaoshanggou 1951 nian shi ban nongye shengchan hezuoshe de zuihou baogao."

22. The figures add up to 691, not 693, but these are the numbers the report

earned more than they had in 1950, the extent of the increase varied. Those with less land but more laborers doubled their incomes, while those with more land received only slightly more remuneration.[23]

This outcome was promising. The Yaoshanggou report listed ten reasons why cooperatives could do better than mutual aid teams or individual farmers, mostly because of the advantages of large-scale cultivation and additional opportunities for sideline work. At the theoretical level, there was an impressive case to be made. By pooling land, uneconomic strips were abolished, scattered land was consolidated, and additional acreage was obtained. At the same time, more rational cropping patterns could be introduced and surplus laborers could work on sideline projects. (In the future, such theoretical advantages would be repeatedly presented as accomplished facts.) The report also attributed the trials' success to the assistance from local party leaders—which indeed was indispensable, as discussed below.

In addition, the report outlined suggestions for further developing the cooperatives. It alleged that the unit yield from land that members kept as their private portion (*ziliudi*) was lower than that from collectively held land and that conflicts between members over the time and energy to be expended on each type of tillage were frequent. Following a democratic decision, it was agreed that the private portion should henceforth be reduced to 5 percent per household and limited to the least fertile land.[24] The report also conceded that approximately half the cooperative's surplus laborers had not been used, and a more scientific way of allocating surplus labor needed to be found. Finally, the report urged that given the immense contribution made by the cooperative's heads, their workload should be assessed on a separate scale and they should be better compensated.[25]

According to official accounts, most of the other nine experimental producers' cooperatives in Changzhi prefecture were just as successful as

provides.

23. "Wuxiang Yaoshanggou 1951 nian shi ban nongye shengchan hezuoshe de zuihou baogao."

24. This finding contradicted common sense. As data from the late 1950s and 1960s shows, unit yields from farmers' "private portion" were consistently much higher than yields from the pooled area. See Gao Wangling, *Renmin gongshe shiqi Zhongguo nongmin fanxingwei tiaocha*.

25. "Wuxiang Yaoshanggou 1951 nian shi ban nongye shengchan hezuoshe de zuihou baogao."

the Yaoshanggou venture. Almost all the surviving documentation found in local archives indicates that they were regarded as an unqualified triumph. Each county where cooperatives were located submitted a report to Changzhi prefecture, which in turn produced a summary of each cooperative's results and passed them higher up the chain together with an overall account. Not surprisingly, during this process, figures were inflated. For example, where Wuxiang County had reported that the unit yield of the Yaoshanggou cooperative was 1.8 dan, the prefecture raised this figure to 2.6 dan when reporting to Shanxi Province. In addition, Changzhi's report emphasized that the Yaoshanggou cooperative had channeled resources into arranging for local farmers to study politics, disciplining wayward members, organizing criticism and self-criticism sessions, and educating the peasants to subordinate their personal interests to the interests of the state.[26] None of this was mentioned in the Wuxiang County–level report.

Again, the reports drafted by higher authorities had an influence on issues at higher levels. Based on the versions produced by Changzhi prefecture, a special dossier was compiled at the national level for this set of documents, and was frequently referred to in the mid-1950s. In the 1970s, a collection was published under the title "Several historical documents regarding the establishment of experimental agricultural producers' cooperatives in the Changzhi area."[27]

At the experimental stage, Shanxi's ten cooperatives were established in response to orders from above and were closely monitored by cadres at county and prefecture level. Nevertheless, the peasants were not merely passive recipients—as we have seen, they made their own calculations and made their own decisions about whether to join. Political ambition, respect, fear of the CCP, personal ties, economic considerations, and opportunism all played a role. To a certain extent, farmers managed to modify the rules to their own advantage.

The clearest example relates to community funds. Few peasants liked the idea of 20 percent of their total output being taken away from them for this purpose—it was almost as steep as the tax rate. Although the negotiations between villagers and local party cadres were never documented, the

---

26. "Guanyu 10 ge nongye shengchan hezuoshe de zongjie" (A review of the ten agricultural producers' cooperatives) (November 1951), SPA, 53.1.1

27. Shanxi nongcun zhengzhi gongzuo bu, *Changzhi diqu shiban he fazhan nongye shengchan hezuoshe de ruogan lishi ziliao.*

farmers did end up paying a much lower rate. This change was later acknowledged by the party. In early 1952, the North China Bureau ruled that the rate for community funds should be set between 1 and 5 percent of total income and should not significantly affect members' annual earnings. Farmers also succeeded in increasing their return on land input. They succeeded in getting the cooperative to bear the cost of seeds, fodder, and fertilizers, which in the original scheme was to be shouldered by the landowners. These changes reflected the bargaining that went on between peasants concerned with the needs of the individual household and CCP cadres who wanted to inject more socialist elements into the cooperatives. In the end, the cadres made concessions as they came to see the need for material incentives. These changes were ultimately acknowledged at the local government level and later became a common standard that many agricultural producers' cooperatives, both inside Shanxi Province and elsewhere, took as a model. Thus, to a certain degree, the earliest agricultural cooperatives were what peasant farmers and local officials made of them.

Underside of Success Stories

The success of Shanxi's ten experimental agricultural producers' cooperatives sounded almost too good to be true, although no evidence has yet been uncovered that would prove otherwise. A consideration of some of the circumstances surrounding those cooperatives might help us in arriving at a balanced assessment.

One significant factor was the collection of agricultural tax. In the early 1950s, taxation was a complex issue. Tax rates varied dramatically from year to year and across different regions, as discussed in Chapter 6. In Shanxi Province, before 1952, agricultural tax was theoretically collected as a proportional of the "normative yield." Taking into account factors such as the amount of sown land, soil fertility, planting customs, and harvests in normal years, a perennial land yield (*changnian yingchanliang*) for each household was struck through democratic discussions among the farmers, and this figure was then ratified by local government. But the rate differed each year, being adjusted to the needs of the party, generally ranging between 15 and 25 percent.[28] Actual land yields played a relatively minor role in the way

---

28. Zhongguo nongmin fudanshi bianji weiyuan hui, *Zhongguo nongmin*

land tax was calculated. In practice, however, tax matters were often simplified. In 1949 and 1950, in Shanxi, each mu attracted a levy of 22 catties of millet for the state agricultural tax and 5 catties for local surcharges. In 1951 and 1952, the state agricultural tax was 21 catties per mu, with surcharges on top of that.[29] Thus, the tax farmers paid had little to do with their actual production. In other words, no matter how high the land yield claimed may have been, peasants were not required to pay more tax immediately.

In the short term, fabricating a high yield would not cost peasants a penny. On the contrary, if the unit yield was high enough to impress local cadres, the latter were likely to reward farmers with substantial bonuses—perhaps a draught animal, or an expensive farm implement. Furthermore, farmers who rose to official notice in this way might receive benefits such as priority in obtaining government loans or being nominated as model laborers. Those chosen for the latter role would have the chance to travel to the provincial capital, to Beijing, or even to the Soviet Union. Such prestige could bring peasants and their families even more benefits. For example, through the networks he had formed with party cadres, Geng Changsuo, a national figure well known for his work in forming mutual aid teams in Hebei, managed to secure his sons comfortable jobs in major cities.[30] In addition, promoting the activists who made a name for themselves during a particular campaign had become common practice within the party. As a result, local activists tended to overfulfill their established goals in return for promotions and rewards.[31]

For peasant farmers in Changzhi prefecture, achieving "enhanced" results was a tempting option. As one of the established liberated regions, Changzhi had produced a large number of native cadres who were sent by the party out of Shanxi Province to the south to help in administering the newly liberated areas. At the same time, the province's bureaucratic infrastructure was expanding, leading to a shortage of administrative personnel. In August 1951, the Shanxi party branch decided to promote ten thousand

---

fudanshi, 47.

29. Ibid., vol. 4, 76–77. This tax system started to change in 1952 and the amount of tax was increasingly linked to the land's actual output.

30. Edward Friedman, Paul Pickowicz, and Mark Selden, *Chinese Village, Socialist State.*

31. Yu Liu, "Why did it go so high?" 740.

new cadres, who would work either for the party or for the government.[32] In Changzhi prefecture, the plan was to recruit one thousand new cadres of peasant origin, who would be relieved of agricultural duties and put on the state payroll; two hundred would be selected from rural model laborers.[33]

It was hardly surprising that many villagers aspired to become state employees, as a peasant's life was full of hardships. Totally depending on a natural environment that was hard and unpredictable, engaging in backbreaking labor in the fields marked by periods of intense hard work, living in small rural communities—the average peasant knew little of the amenities offered by urban civilization.[34] Getting onto the state payroll meant a farewell to this harsh lifestyle. Furthermore, one cadre's salary was sufficient to feed an entire family. When such rare opportunities presented themselves, rural party members, village model laborers, and activists were only too eager to take advantage of them. As mere peasants, villagers enjoyed limited means of gaining their superiors' attention. The experimental cooperatives that party bosses were promoting so vigorously provided a channel through which villagers could interact with county heads and cadres of even higher rank.

Considering the low tax costs and the potentially high returns in these other areas, farmers commonly inflated data. Although evidence is lacking to suggest that such practices were followed in the ten Shanxi cooperatives in the trial stage (1951), later, in 1952 and 1953, the heads of these same cooperative were exposed for falsifying their accounts (see Chapter 5). Yaoshanggou cooperative, for example, had a reputation for overreporting its harvests.

The absence of any mention of problems in Changzhi's reports on its experimental cooperatives invites suspicion in itself. Even assuming that the data provided by the prefecture were reliable, and those farmers did in fact produce more in cooperatives, could they have sustained their initial success? The answers suggested by the surviving evidence are hardly positive.

First of all, it should be noted that agricultural taxes were not included in cooperatives' accounts. If taxes had been included, households owning

---

32. "Wei yingjie xin de jianshe gaochao daliang peiyang tiba ganbu de tishi" (A notice regarding the promotion of a large number of cadres to meet the needs created by the new surge in development) (August 18, 1951), JMA, 39.1.1.

33. "1950 nian changzhi diwei youguan ganbu xun lian jihua" (Changzhi prefecture's plan for training cadres in 1950), JMA, 43.5.1.

34. Moshe Lewin, *Russian Peasants and Soviet Power,* 22–30.

more land would have barely increased their incomes. At the same time, few reports acknowledged the significance of government loans in contributing to the success of the trial farms. In the case of Yaoshanggou, the cooperative obtained at least 12 million yuan worth of loans, sufficient to purchase 670 dan of grain at the local market. This figure almost equaled the cooperative's total income in 1951, combining agricultural income and returns from sideline work. This high level of government investment was a common policy in the province's ten experimental cooperatives. To cite another example, Guo Yu'en's cooperative in Pingshun County received a loan of 6.8 million yuan, the equivalent of 51 percent of its total income. The interest on the loan accounted for 59 percent of its increased agricultural production. In both these cases, the cooperatives involved were unable to repay their state loans within the year—they could barely afford the interest. Repaying state loans rapidly became a heavy burden for cooperatives. For its part, the state could not sustain this excessive level of investment, let alone extend it further. Troubled by this situation, the North China Bureau implored local governments to cap their investment in agricultural producers' cooperatives.[35]

The most potentially lucrative part of the cooperative economy was its ability to organize surplus laborers into sideline work. However, in many cases, the cooperatives acknowledged that the supply of labor was outstripping demand. The success of sideline work depended largely on the strength of demand from urban markets. However, following the founding of the PRC, urban markets were shrinking at a rapid pace. For rural traders, finding short-term jobs in the cities would become more and more difficult and later became illegal after the household registration system was introduced.

There was another way for the cooperatives to raise their income levels. If the high production rates reported by the experimental cooperatives were accurate, planting cash crops was a surefire way of increasing profits. Until 1952, farmers paid the same agricultural tax on cash crops as they did on grain, and profits from sideline ventures involved no tax at all.[36] Such a plan was possible in 1951 when the central government was in need of industrial materials, such as cotton, and encouraged peasants to plant them. But in

---

35. "Huabeiju nongye shengchan hezuoshe de qingkuang yu jingyan" (The situation of agricultural producers' cooperatives in the North China Bureau's jurisdiction and lessons to be learned), *Huibian*, vol. 2, 586–589.

36. Zhongguo nongmin fudanshi bianji weiyuan hui, *Zhongguo nongmin fudanshi*, 44–80.

1952, this trend was reversed. In its annual plan the central government made it clear, "Grain output must be substantially increased—the acreage dedicated to growing it can in no way be reduced." Accordingly, cash crops were not to exceed 1951 levels, at least as far as acreage was concerned.[37] In 1952, a higher tax was also levied on cash crops. Thus cooperatives hoping to profit from cash crops ran up against government policy. In formulating its five year plan—involving increasing the area dedicated to cash crops from 590,000 to 2,230,000 mu, while reducing grain crops from 8,490,000 to 6,910,000 mu—Changzhi prefecture attracted criticism for its emphasis on cash crops, which threatened the state's grain supply plan.[38] Shanxi leaders were furious when they discovered that the province had to supply more grain to the villages than to the cities.[39]

From the moment the experimental agricultural producers' cooperatives were launched, administrative problems became evident. How were labor inputs to be calculated? Who should work on a specific piece of land? How could all members be encouraged to maintain the same work rates? As cooperative heads did not usually engage in farming per se, how could their labor inputs be calculated? Because draught animals were borrowed from individual members, how should they be compensated and on what basis? How much land should each family retain as their private portion? These were certainly thorny questions, and farmers spent days and nights contesting every detail with cooperative heads. If the latter were overwhelmed, so were the local party cadres. No doubt for their own convenience, some cadres suggested a number of shortcuts—pooling all peasant-owned land into cooperatives, purchasing all livestock and farming implements from members and putting them at the permanent disposal of the cooperative, and severing the link between leaders' income and their labor input as farmers. One after another, these suggestions would be put into practice in the mid-1950s. Although Chinese historians have tended to explain these innovations as "leftist" errors, documents from the early stages of the movement show that they were not purely ideological in intent. Rather, they were derived from the everyday practices involved in operating a cooperative. In

37. "Zhongyang renmin zhengwuyuan guanyu 1952 nian nongye shengchan de jueding," 43.
38. "Bixu kefu zai lingdao nongye shengchan zhong de yanzhong mangmu xing."
39. Ibid.

other words, they were part of the mechanism of agricultural producers' cooperatives.

Shanxi's ten experimental cooperatives were composed of middle-ranking peasants. Given the distribution formula that favored labor input, poor peasants who tended to have less land should have been the most enthusiastic about joining cooperatives. In reality, however, this was not the case. Although the reasons for this situation have not been documented, it seems likely that either poor peasants refused to join, or that cooperative heads declined to admit them. The party was not yet ready for this development.

Indeed, in their hearts, the Shanxi leaders knew that they had effectively dismissed any opposition to their plans, thus leaving it up to them to succeed or fail on their own terms. They were aware that they had paid insufficient attention to local conditions and regional diversity, and that they had overestimated the popularity of both mutual aid teams and agricultural producers' cooperatives. On central issues, such as compensation for land inputs, community funds, and public assets, they had pursued their own ideological agenda. Yet over the next two years, they did their best to conceal these problems and offered only positive views of the ten experimental cooperatives.[40]

What if agricultural producers' cooperatives had been left to the peasant farmers themselves? While it is difficult to address this question directly, the experience of Sichuan Province might begin to provide some answers. Sichuan is located in southwest China and was liberated in 1950. It was considered a "backward" region in terms of where the CCP's strength lay. In the spring of 1952 and in response to the party's call for establishing experimental cooperatives, twenty-five cooperatives were established in Zizhong County in Sichuan. Most were organized by village heads who had attended only a single party meeting. Zizhong County failed to provide much guidance; the peasants formulated a number of rules themselves. Of the twenty-five initial cooperatives, only two were still operating after the fall harvest of that year.[41]

Of the two survivors, Sun Xianhe cooperative was the better docu-

---

40. Tao Lujia, "Zai di 190 ci shengwei changweihui shang de fayan," 333–334.
41. "Cong Zizhong xian qige nongye shengchan hezuoshe tiaocha zhong suo kandao de jige wenti" (Several problems discovered in Zizhong County's report on seven agricultural producers' cooperatives) (October 24, 1952), Sichuan Provincial Archive, Agricultural Committee, vol. 362.

mented. In the spring of 1952, a cooperative was formed there, and members were required to pool all their land. All the property that peasants had registered during land reform was counted as shares, regardless of the actual amount of land they owned or its suitability for farming. Although this arrangement worked to the disadvantage of farmers who owned land of better quality and who had "hidden" land, it was a convenient way of avoiding disputes as each household had a certificate identifying the land it held. Cooperative members later complained about this arbitrary policy and requested some private land to plant vegetables, with the result that each household was able to reclaim a small share (about 2 percent) of their land.

The cooperative purchased members' draught animals using credits and put the animals to collective use. Following the harvest, the cooperative was unable to honor these credits and went into heavy debt, which was then transferred to poor members who originally did not own livestock. The cooperative set a fixed wage for laborers of only half a catty of rice per work point, with a maximum of five points per day. As sideline income was listed under land output, landowners could take a share of sideline income too. As a result, in the Sun Xianhe cooperative, labor input accounted for only 20 percent of total income, whereas land input formed a much larger proportion. In essence, the cooperative was in the business of hiring laborers, only wages were lower than the market rate. Different from Wang Qian's original vision, Sun Xianhe cooperative provides a unique perspective on running a successful cooperative from the peasants' point of view.[42]

In Zizhong County, as in Shanxi, the overwhelming majority of agricultural producers' cooperatives were controlled by middle-ranking peasants, although it was not uncommon for poor peasants to serve as their nominal heads for the purpose of acquiring state loans. As one cooperative head, a party member and also a middle-ranking peasant, remarked: "We, the middle-ranking peasants, are able to coordinate them, the poor peasants, because only we have the necessary resources."[43] The key distinction here was between "we" and "they." All the cooperatives in Zizhong County, with the exception of Sun Xianhe, were divided into an "upper courtyard" and a "lower courtyard." The former accommodated middle-ranking peasants and their property, while the latter was reserved for poor peasants and their belongings. The former accused the latter of being lazy, while the latter were

---

42. Ibid.
43. Ibid.

jealous of their better-off counterparts. The two groups did not trust each other and frequently spied on each other. Conflict between the two "courtyards" often led to the collapse of cooperatives.

Poor peasants were wary about becoming involved in cooperatives. At the first sign of trouble, they were usually the first to jump ship, and this group pressed most firmly for the right to withdraw. While middle-ranking peasants sometimes formed cooperatives with the express purpose of exploiting poor peasants, the latter were not always passive. In some cases, poor peasants were active in forming cooperatives, inviting farmers with more resources but suspect class backgrounds to join them. Sadly, such cooperatives tended to collapse even sooner than most.[44]

In Changzhi, cases of failures were well-kept secrets and rarely came to light. The stark contrast between the experience of Changzhi and that of Sichuan shows the difference that effective party leadership could possibly make.

In addition to their efficiency, cadres from Changzhi were well known for their commandist approach to leadership. An internal investigation revealed that cadres in the prefecture had low levels of literacy and knew little about New Democracy. They believed that as the advent of socialism was only two or three years away, there was no need to protect private ownership. Thus, they were lukewarm at best when it came to issuing land certificates to peasants. When exhorted to "guide" the peasants, they simply resorted to command and coercion. They were known for such sayings as, "The masses are like pecan nuts—you have to smash them so you can eat them," and "One horsewhip works better than thousands of fine words." Some cadres went about equipped with handcuffs and there were even cases reported of peasants being tortured to death. These cadres had developed a variety of methods to persuade villagers to accept their suggestions. Holding meetings day after day until the peasants agreed to adopt whatever the cadres asked was a common practice. They would also question peasants one on one. A typical conversation might have run as follows. Cadre: "Who encouraged you to become a master?" Peasant: "Chairman Mao." The next question followed: "Do you support Chairman Mao?" and the answer was, of course, "Yes." Then came the clincher: "Chairman Mao has issued a call to get organized—so why don't you support it?" Another trick question was, "Who doesn't support Chairman Mao?" The answer was counterrevolutionaries—but who would dare to align himself with them? By practicing such

---

44. Ibid.

tough methods, cadres in Changzhi enjoyed considerable success in having their orders carried out.[45] Establishing successful producers' cooperatives in 1951 was at the top of their agenda.

Stage One (1951–1952): Peasants Adapting Party Policies

As Changzhi prefecture was setting up its pioneering agricultural producers' cooperatives, organizing peasants into mutual aid teams was put on the national agenda. In September 1951, the Draft was passed, projecting a three-stage plan to advance peasant farmers from mutual aid teams to agricultural producers' cooperatives and finally to advanced agricultural producers' cooperatives (in nature, collective farms). The Draft set a short-term target of 40 percent of the rural population organized into mutual aid teams by the end of 1952.[46] In October 1951, Mao circulated the report issued by the Northeast China Bureau calling on party members to discourage peasant farmers from working on their own account.[47] In December 1951, Mao ordered that the provisions of the Draft be carried out. Between the winter of 1951 and the spring of 1952, a campaign was conducted with the aim of educating farmers to "get organized." In February 1952, the State Council released the "Decisions on Agricultural Production for 1952," urging that "in the older liberated regions, 80–90 percent of the rural population should get organized within two years; in the newly liberated regions this task should be completed within three years."[48] It also encouraged the upgrading of a select number of mutual aid teams to agricultural producers' cooperatives, albeit with caution.

Following the directive from the State Council, each province set its own timetable. The Agriculture Ministry and the People's Bank issued decrees promising state loans at low interest rates to peasants' organizations such as mutual aid teams and agricultural producers' cooperatives.[49] Thus the Mu-

45. *Neibu cankao*, February 28, 1951.

46. Zhu Yonghong, "Reflections on the Party's Policy," 29.

47. Ye Yangbing, *Zhongguo nongye hezuohua yundong yanjiu*, 201–202.

48. "Nongyebu, Zhongguo renmin yinhang guanyu 1952 nian nongdai gongzuo de zhishi" (Directives from the Agricultural Ministry and the People's Bank regarding agricultural loans, 1952) (January 25, 1952), *Nongye juan*, 154–155.

49. Ibid.

tual Aid and Cooperation movement officially unfolded across China. In what follows, we move beyond the borders of Changzhi prefecture and observe how peasants across the nation responded to the call to "get organized."

Although Mao Zedong had specifically instructed CCP cadres to "regard mutual aid teams and agricultural producers' cooperatives as important issues,"[50] cadres at the county level and higher did not regard this as their most urgent task. Their attention was fully occupied by the Three-Anti movement, which was initiated in late 1951. The Three-Anti movement was the most prominent political movement in China in 1951–1952. It aimed to eliminate three organizational vices: corruption, waste, and obstructionist bureaucracy. Primary targets were party members, bureaucratic officials, and the managers of factories and other businesses.[51] As targets themselves, party members were understandably preoccupied with this campaign.

However, as it was launched the party declared that the Three-Anti movement would not be extended to the countryside, at least for the time being. For example, the North China Bureau stated that although corruption at district and village levels was serious, the movement would not be extended to district or below. At the county level and above, tensions were heating up. Fearing that once the movement took off in the countryside, it would be difficult to contain, the North China Bureau ordered that if any village started the Three-Anti movement on its own initiative, the county should immediately send a work team to suppress it. Village cadres were not encouraged to confess to their failings and ordinary peasants were forbidden to bring accusations of corruption against rural cadres.[52]

As a result of these measures, the Three-Anti movement did not directly affect party members in the rural areas. Nevertheless, by paralyzing the machinery of government, the movement caused serious setbacks to the rural economy. In the case of Shanxi Province, its departments dealing with trading, finance, and taxation were in a state of chaos and daily business operations were frequently suspended. The circulation of commodities was reduced by half, and market-based trading fell by a third. The previously

---

50. *Shanxi sheng nongye hezuo shi wenjian huibian juan*, 37.

51. Jonathan D. Spence, *Search For Modern China*, 509.

52. "Huabeiju guanyu qu, cun liangji muqian jianjue bu jinxing sanfan gei Caha'er shengwei de zhishi" (The North China Bureau's directive to Caha'er Province on terminating the Three-Anti movement at district and village levels), *Huibian*, vol. 2, 434.

congested rail network now had almost nothing to carry and two-thirds of cargo trains were empty. The state ceased purchasing cash crops in the villages and state-owned grain stores often refused to sell grain to the peasants.[53] It was an especially difficult time for farmers who had planted cash crops. But all these changes did not happen overnight. It took months for the Three-Anti movement to substantially affect peasant farmers, as discussed in Chapter 5.

Preoccupied with the Three-Anti movement, cadres at county level and above gave little thought to other issues. In Changzhi prefecture, following the launch of the movement, county-level cadres stopped visiting the villages for two months.[54] Lacking consistent direction from above, village cadres took control of the Mutual Aid and Cooperation movement. In North China, for example, during the spring of 1952 more than three thousand agricultural producers' cooperatives were organized, mostly by village heads, rural activists, and peasants, and with very little guidance from above.[55]

Left to their own devices, rural cadres responded to the call to "get organized" in their own ways. Many simply had no interest in "getting organized." For example, in Sichuan Province, after land reform had been completed rural cadres turned their attention to increasing agricultural productivity. Their catchcry was: "To carry out land reform we must rely on the poor peasants; to increase rural productivity we need to rely on the middle-ranking peasants." In selecting model laborers, they took agricultural productivity as the sole criterion, regardless of a farmer's class background. As a result, 90 percent of the model laborers in Sichuan were middle-ranking and wealthy peasants. Local cadres simply disregarded their responsibility to organize peasants into mutual aid teams.[56] Some doubted that mutual aid teams had a positive future and treated the task casually.[57]

On the other hand, cadres in other regions interpreted the call to "get organized" as yet another political campaign and faithfully passed the message down the line. In Guizhou Province in southwest China, villagers were informed, "Building mutual aid teams is an order from above. Everyone must join them. Those who refuse to do so are only making trouble for us."

---

53. *Neibu cankao*, March 12, 1952.
54. Ibid., March 20, 1952.
55. Ibid., June 18, 1952.
56. Ibid., July 5, 1952.
57. Ibid., July 5, 1952.

The party secretary in one village told peasants, "If you don't join the mutual aid teams, you should not consider yourselves under the direction of the CCP. Unless you want to go and live in Taiwan, this is an order from the state [that you are bound to obey]."[58] In Jiangxi Province in central-south China, many peasants were told that joining mutual aid teams was an obligation.[59] In the northeast, village cadres coined the slogan, "Joining agricultural producers' cooperatives is following Mao Zedong's road—not joining them is following [U.S. President] Truman's road." In 1951, Chinese troops were fighting American forces in Korea, and President Truman and the Guomindang leader, Chiang Kai-shek, exiled in Taiwan, were potent symbols of evil. Taking their side was doubtless a counterrevolutionary crime of the highest order. Some village cadres told villagers: "If you don't join the mutual aid teams now, when socialism arrives you will be forced to write confessions."[60]

Given these pressures, the decision was not hard to make for most rural people. Mutual aid teams and agricultural producers' cooperatives sprang up throughout the nation. Not surprisingly, a large number were extremely short-lived and many only existed on paper in official reports. For example, in Ba County in Sichuan Province, while the county head claimed that 13,000 mutual aid teams had been established, it turned out that 85 percent were complete fakes. It was not uncommon for teams to be formed at a meeting convened by rural cadres and then disbanded immediately after the meeting.[61] In the "number one" village of Taihe County in Jiangxi Province, of eighteen mutual aid teams established in a single morning, ten were dissolved in the afternoon of the same day. In the remaining eight teams, members did not even know who their head was.[62] To fulfill their quota, in some counties of Southwest China rural cadres formed mutual aid teams according to administrative convenience, totally regardless of the peasants' own wishes, and reported their "achievement" to their superiors. Teams formed under such circumstances simply never got off the ground.

In stark contrast to these attempts at deception, a few rural cadres were willing to go further than the Draft had indicated as a way of getting their names known in official circles. Sporadic cases of "rash tendencies" were

---

58. Ibid., September 21, 1952.
59. Ibid., April 22, 1952.
60. Ibid., June 18, 1952.
61. Ibid., August 25, 1952.
62. Ibid., July 5, 1952.

reported.[63] In Muliu village of Shanxi Province, in an effort to have their village reported in the newspaper, a demobilized soldier, a village head, and a party member resolved to establish a collective farm instead of a mutual aid team. The scheme was nothing if not ambitious. Their plan was to pool all available land and have the peasants work and eat together. The harvest would be stored in two warehouses and members would be provided with whatever they needed. Each day members would follow a fixed schedule: work for eight hours, study for six hours, and rest for eight hours. The three organizers held a village meeting to discuss "organizing a collective farm and practicing socialism," although most villagers remained silent when asked their opinions. When the organizers then accused those who had refused to join of being unpatriotic, some relented while others remained skeptical. Eventually, the three organizers were criticized from above.[64]

At the same time, many rural cadres saw the movement as an economic opportunity, partly because the Draft had emphasized increasing production. They used economic incentives to attract peasant farmers to join up. Offering agricultural loans to mutual aid teams and agricultural producers' cooperatives was quite common. "The government will lend peasants whatever a mutual aid team needs," rural cadres promised villagers. In this way, Junchu County organized eighteen teams, sixteen of which immediately disbanded after receiving agricultural loans.[65] Because they had not been given specific instructions on how to manage mutual aid teams, many rural cadres were inclined to give farmers more "freedom." The peasants were thus able to make their own rules.

If local cadres varied in their responses, so did the peasants. Village heads, activists, model laborers, and (some) CCP members were usually the first to answer the party's call. Like the villagers of Changzhi prefecture, their motivations were multiple: genuine faith in the CCP, the habit of sticking closely to CCP directives, which so far had been well rewarded, a desire for respect and even fame, ambition to succeed in local politics, and the lure of material incentives were all part of the mix. The rewards were potentially significant. Performing well as part of a mutual aid team or cooperative would substantially increase an individual's chances of being selected as a model laborer and raise their social status, thus enhancing their influence in

---

63. Ibid., April 14, 1952.
64. Ibid., July 8, 1952.
65. Ibid., August 25, 1952.

village affairs. Model laborers with good reputations and effective networks were capable of challenging local cadres, and even resisting their orders.

For ordinary villagers, economic incentives were important. Agricultural loans offered by the state were especially tempting. In the older liberated areas, these loans were almost exclusively limited to mutual aid teams and agricultural producers' cooperatives. Rewards and honors were regularly bestowed on those who had proved themselves in the fields. From the end of 1951, the title of model laborer was highly recommended, if not reserved, for heads of mutual aid teams and agricultural producers' cooperatives, as were the rewards that went with it. While the organizations concerned might be nominal, the prizes were substantial. In 1952, the first mutual aid team established in Jieyang County of Guangdong Province in South China was rewarded with a buffalo, an invaluable asset for peasant farmers.

In the countryside, those with undesirable class backgrounds sought alliances with people of better standing in the eyes of the Communist regime. It was reported that rich peasants, and sometimes former landlords, volunteered to join mutual aid teams and offered to lend, even transfer, their draught animals and tools to their peers. They hoped that such economic sacrifices would enable them to befriend and seek protection from the rural majority. In most cases, these better-off villagers were welcomed by both mutual aid teams and agricultural producers' cooperatives.

If managed well, farmers indeed profited from their membership of mutual aid teams. By making their own distribution rules, middle-ranking peasants, sometimes allied with their wealthy counterparts, were able to reduce the cost of labor and make more money than they could by working on their own account. In cases when economic gain was the main motivation, middle-ranking peasants usually dominated. For example, Tong'an village was a relatively wealthy village situated in Keshan County in Northeast China. In 1952, seventy-three middle-ranking peasants, twenty-one peasants from upper-middle backgrounds, six rich peasants, and forty-nine poor villagers and hired laborers were living in Tong'an. Four of the six wealthy peasants were party members—one was secretary of the village party branch, one was a former deputy village head, and a third was a model laborer well-known at provincial level. All were engaged in "capitalist" business enterprises in 1951. When the Mutual Aid and Cooperation movement was launched, many mutual aid teams and agricultural producers' cooperatives were formed in which wealthy peasants played leading roles. Economic imperatives were the driving force behind them. An investigation into eight agricultural producers' cooperatives in Keshan County revealed that most were controlled by rich peasants. Income distribution favored land input and the input of production materials; seven had actually hired their own farm laborers.[66]

Wealthy peasants frequently used collective organizations as a screen to "exploit" the poor. For example, one rich peasant, Wang Fa, together with three other wealthy families, established a mutual aid team. The team also included five poor peasants who were living at Wang's home, following his orders and working for him. Although these five villagers were essentially hired laborers, they were reported as team members and one was actually the nominal team head. Using a similar system, another rich peasant, Chen Qingshan, boosted his personal income by 20 percent in 1952 in his agricultural producers' cooperative, which included two hired laborers. Chen himself did not farm any land at all. It was not uncommon for rich peasants to hire laborers and pay them wages at a lower rate than the market price, all in the name of cooperative labor. Moreover, mutual aid teams and agricultural producers' cooperatives tended to scorn poor peasants and to discriminate against them: land belonging to poor farmers was usually the last to be cultivated.[67]

The rules set down for mutual aid teams and agricultural producers' cooperatives varied from place to place. Some favored land input, others labor input. Some mandated the collection of community funds regardless of members' opposition, while others did not. Despite different rules, the organizations had problems in common. Members fought each other over the distribution of resources. Nearly all these cooperative bodies lacked democracy and were effectively controlled by one person. Financial accounting was patchy at best. Few members wanted to work hard and fewer still were keen to assist other members.

One outcome that particularly disappointed the party was the lack of improvement in villagers' cultural life. A report from the North China News Agency highlighted the absence of political education in mutual aid teams. After interviewing a large number of mutual aid teams in Shanxi, the agency concluded that most members saw them as an economic organization and had only vague opinions as to their future. In spring 1952, the mutual aid

---

66. Ibid., September 17 and September 29, 1952.
67. Ibid.

movement mushroomed in Shanxi, but few peasants joined it as a way of ushering in a socialist future. As we have seen, some used the teams as a cover for hiring their own laborers and others were attracted by economic incentives. It was rare that peasants joined because of their political consciousness. Even in those organizations that claimed success, the established mentality remained intact. Peasants continued to care little about socialism—they preferred to seek individual profits and short-term gains. The heads of mutual aid teams and producers' cooperatives paid little attention to training peasants in the principles of socialism. In some cases, they feared to do so. One village head in Shanxi Province said candidly, "I got the peasants organized, but I dared not say anything more about the future of socialism. Had I done so, the peasants would not have joined up." Even cadres at the county level did not attempt to introduce courses in socialist education for peasant farmers.[68]

In August 1952 an investigation into agricultural production in Shanxi revealed widespread cases of false reporting. Village reports inflated production and exaggerated peasants' participation in political education and levels of political consciousness. For example, an exemplary village, Dongtai in Luchen County, reported that "following education in patriotism, the masses were confident about increasing agricultural production." However, when the investigation team interviewed eight villagers, five knew nothing about these educational sessions. The same report claimed that all villagers were involved in making production plans and competed among themselves. The follow-up interview revealed that only a single mutual aid team had formulated a production plan and that it was unrealistic at best. And whereas the same report stated that 90 percent of laborers of both sexes had joined mutual aid teams, the investigation revealed that 191 female laborers in the village were not involved in farming at all. Likewise, model laborer Dong Zhongzheng, from Xinzhuang village in Wanquan, reported that his mutual aid team had established a work points system, subscribed to the *Shanxi Daily* and the *Shanxi Peasant Daily*, and had organized members into study groups that met three times every ten days. He even attached work point tickets and accounts to his report. The unglamorous reality was that Dong's team only worked together during the busy season, had never subscribed to newspapers, and had never even sat down to read together. Production records are often unreliable. Inflating agricultural output was

---

68. Ibid., April 29, 1952.

common. For example, while it was reported that grain production by mutual aid teams in Jiluo village of Zhao County had increased by 50 catties per mu, in reality production had *dropped* by 50 catties per mu.[69]

If the official records were to be believed, Shanxi's mutual aid teams and agricultural producers' cooperatives both appeared to have multiplied. By spring 1952, 278 producers' cooperatives had been established in Changzhi prefecture alone, and the number of peasants who had "gotten organized" rose from 52 percent in 1951 to 80 percent in 1952. Nevertheless, even Shanxi provincial leaders admitted things were not perfect. Progress was uneven. In some counties, 95 percent of peasants were organized, yet in others where rural cadres had failed to support the Mutual Aid and Cooperation movement, the rate was as low as 10 percent. As for producers' cooperatives, a third of them were distributing their resources more according to land input than labor input, reversing Wang Qian's priorities.[70] Many peasants had formed sham mutual aid teams to cover their private farming activities, while others sought to acquire material incentives. Political education was scant, and Shanxi peasant farmers remained unchanged in their basic outlook, continuing to put their own interests first. For example, they frequently took advantage of the illness of other members, did not hesitate to work their colleagues' cattle to death, and were single-minded in the pursuit of personal profit. The peasants' cynical take on the party slogan was, "Get organized to accumulate the family fortune."[71]

In Changzhi, local investigations showed that a quarter of the villages in the prefecture had failed to develop successful mutual aid teams. More than five thousand of these teams were purely nominal, and either lacked a leader or a viable plan. Many "mutual aid teams for private farming" were created. As the peasants themselves put it, "[mutual aid teams were] formed in the spring, came undone in the summer, collapsed in the fall. [This pattern] will repeat itself next year." Even the teams that survived did not always please the party. As we have seen elsewhere, members used mutual aid teams to take advantage of their fellow villagers. For example, in Luchengxi village,

---

69. Ibid., August 22, 1952.

70. "Bo Yibo, Liu Lantao tongzhi guanyu Huabei nongye huzhu yundong de fangzhen he renwu xiang Mao zhuxi de zonghe baogao" (The reports by Bo Yibo and Liu Lantao to Chairman Mao on the development of the Mutual Aid and Cooperation movement in north China), *Huibian*, vol. 2, 598.

71. *Neibu cankao*, April 29, 1952.

one herd of cattle was the equivalent of eleven human laborers. In the party's eyes, better-off peasants who could afford to keep draught animals were exploiting the poor. Gender discrimination was rife, too. Female laborers received less than half of what male laborers earned.[72]

Conclusion

Many of the features that characterized the early Mutual Aid and Cooperation movement—coercing peasant farmers to join mutual aid teams and agricultural producers' cooperatives, commandism, false registrations, the use of economic incentives, sporadic outbreaks of "rash tendencies"—would all be repeated by the future agricultural cooperativization movement. Still, compared with what the future had in store, the early stages had some unique features.

First, there was absence of significant intervention or "guidance" from above. Rural cadres at village level played the leading role in the early movement; they took more account of their personal stake in village life and local specifics than the higher-ranking cadres who came after them. At the same time, because the party emphasized the dual goals of increasing production and moving toward socialism, local cadres enjoyed considerable leeway in interpreting official policy. Ideology was not yet a dominant factor. Many cadres chose to interpret the movement as an economic campaign and gave priority to rural production. To a large degree, the peasants were left to make their own choices. Except in areas where local party cadres enjoyed exceptional influence, farmers could choose whether to join a cooperative organization or not. At the very least, they could choose to be part of a nominal mutual aid team that did not interfere with their lives. Those who chose to keep farming on their own account did not commonly suffer discrimination. Because the party failed to provide detailed instructions on running mutual aid teams, farmers were given plenty of leeway to work things out for themselves. At the village level, rural cadres and peasants together shaped the system and often managed to profit from it. They could adjust party policy to suit local conditions and protect themselves from ad-

---

72. "Changzhi diwei guanyu bannian lai nongcun shengchan huzhu hezuo yundong zonghe baogao" (Changzhi prefecture's report on the Mutual Aid and Cooperation movement during the last six months) (June 30, 1952), JMA, 92.1.1.

verse consequences. Peasants were rational people—they made their choices after careful consideration of all relevant factors. Some peasants chose to form their own organizations to avoid being organized by outsiders.[73]

Despite the central government's stress on the socialist character of mutual aid teams, few peasants were aware of it; fewer still cared.[74] By spring 1952, agricultural producers' cooperatives were still at the experimental stage. Except in Shanxi Province and in Northeast China, permission was required from the provincial authorities to set up a cooperative and the numbers remained low. In Shanxi and Northeast China, the regulations were more flexible. For example, in Shanxi, permission from the district authorities was sufficient to start a cooperative. In Northeast China, the counties could issue the necessary permission. Nevertheless, in all regions, prudence was emphasized, at least on paper. Certain conditions were required to be met before an experimental cooperative could be set up. Although they varied from region to region, these conditions largely reflected the criteria that Wang Qian had established.

In sum, in the first half of 1952, agricultural producers' cooperatives were little more than a showcase—the mutual aid teams still dominated the scene.[75] During this early stage, while commandism was evident, the degree of coercion used to enforce decisions was mild. With minimal intervention from above, the leading roles fell to village cadres. Peasant farmers themselves dealt with the practicalities of running a mutual aid team or cooperative and retained the capacity to steer the movement to their advantage. They could protect their own interests, for a short time at least. However, as the political atmosphere intensified, the party revised the ground rules for the Mutual Aid and Cooperation movement and set rigorous standards for new cooperatives to meet, as discussed in the following chapter.

---

73. *Neibu cankao,* May 15, 1952.

74. Ibid., April 29, 1952.

75. Ye Yangbing, *Zhongguo nongye hezuohua yundong yanjiu,* 230.

5

The Party's Revenge

Agricultural producers' cooperatives are like a train, and the party is like the engine; they lead us as we walk toward a society full of happiness.
> —peasants' statement as quoted in the *People's Daily*[1]

Encircle [the enemy] on all levels, attack from both within and without, prepare task forces, succeed in a single night.
> —village slogan in Shanxi to describe how to carry out the Mutual Aid and Cooperation movement[2]

Let it be. We have nothing to eat—but neither does the state. My flesh is the only thing I have left. You [cadres] can do whatever you want to me.
> —comments by Shanxi peasants who were forced to join agricultural producers' cooperative and thus refused to work hard[3]

The people's government is a government that is killing people.
> —peasant from Subei on the spring famine of 1953[4]

1. *People's Daily,* October 20, 1952.
2. Ibid., March 30, 1953.
3. "Guanxin nongmin shenghuo, gaishan nongcun gongzuo, an'ding nongcun shengchan" [Upgrade the peasants' living standards; improve (the Party's) work with the peasants and stabilize rural production](April 23, 1953), *Jianshe,* no. 215.
4. *Neibu cankao,* January 22, 1953.

The Three-Anti Movement Merging with the Mutual Aid and Cooperation

In the first half of 1952, the party attempted to protect the countryside from the turmoil of the Three-Anti movement. Since corruption was rife in the countryside, rural cadres were deeply concerned about the movement, and set about their work with unusual caution to avoid upsetting the peasants. (The new, "relaxed" attitude adopted by party functionaries at this period is analyzed in Chapter 4.) The cadres of Shanxi were no exception. For example, in the spring of 1952 rural cadres in the province were reluctant to intervene in farmers' production plans for fear of generating unnecessary friction.[5] However, this did not last long. The Three-Anti movement created an atmosphere that supported a sustained attack against the forces of capitalism. Although, at first, the central government targeted corrupt officials and corrupt capitalists, the campaign was soon extended to capitalists and capitalist activities in general.

In January 1952, at an internal meeting of the Northeast China Bureau, Gao Gang initiated the crusade against capitalism. He asserted that corruption, waste, and bureaucracy were fundamentally derived from capitalism. He characterized the attitude that tolerated capitalism as "rightist" and claimed that it was undermining the party. Gao Gang was particularly concerned with its influence on the direction of agricultural production. To him, rightist tendencies manifested themselves in two main attitudes among party members: the failure to curb the peasants' aspirations to acquire wealth, and the failure to advocate their immediate progression to collectivization. If such attitudes were allowed to persist, Gao Gang warned, the countryside would ultimately go down the path of capitalism. He labeled a number of activities commonly practiced by peasant farmers as capitalist in nature, including borrowing and lending money, hiring laborers, engaging in trade in the pursuit of individual profit, private farming, and the use of material incentives. Quoting passages from the writings of Lenin, Stalin, and Mao Zedong, Gao Gang demonstrated that apathy toward the Mutual Aid and Cooperation movement was a "rightist" error. He announced that "the primary task is to convert the current small-scale producers' economy step by step into an agricultural cooperative economy." To attain this goal,

---

5. Ibid., March 20, 1952.

Gao Gang argued that party members should be prohibited from engaging in capitalist activities of any kind, and he urged them to actively participate in the Mutual Aid and Cooperation movement. He demanded that any elementsof capitalism and leniency toward rich peasants be eliminated from the party.[6]

Gao Gang's talk was published in the *People's Daily* on January 24, 1952, under the headline, "Overcoming the Encroachment of Capitalism in the Party, Combating Rightist Ideas in the Party." Regarded as an indicator of which way the political wind was blowing, Gao Gang's article created a major stir both inside and outside party circles. In 1952, the influential party magazine *Study* (*Xuexi*) published a series of articles that thoroughly refuted those who claimed the necessity of preserving capitalism in New Democracy. These articles focused on the "counterrevolutionary" nature of capitalism and implied that capitalists should be eliminated as a class. Although *Study* magazine later received an internal rebuke from the Propaganda Ministry for its "leftist" errors, the articles published in its first three issues of the year reflected the widespread and growing disapproval in China for capitalism in all its guises.[7] Wealthy peasants were commonly characterized as rural capitalists by the media, which called for their activities to be aggressively curtailed.

In May 1952, the Northeast China Bureau presented a proposal to develop agricultural producers' cooperatives on a large scale, moving beyond the experimental stage. It issued a draft document entitled "Launching the Agricultural Cooperativization Movement," which claimed that agricultural development in Northeast China could take one of two paths. One path led in the direction of capitalism and would become a reality if the peasants continued to operate as individual farmers. The other option was to move further along the road of "getting organized," a path that would lead rural society from mutual aid teams to agricultural producers' cooperatives, and ultimately to collectivization. The proposal asserted that any notion of allowing the rich-peasant economy to prosper was a serious error; on the contrary, it must be restrained. The fact that this proposal omitted spelling out the reasons why capitalism had to be curbed reflected the contemporary

---

6. Gao Gang, "Kefu Zichan Jieji xixiang dui dang de qinshi, fandui dangnei de youqing sixiang" (Overcoming the encroachment of capitalism in the Party, combating rightist ideas in the Party), *People's Daily*, January 24, 1952.

7. *Jianshe*, no. 154, April 9, 1952.

view that regarded any level of capitalism as undesirable. It announced that agricultural producers' cooperatives, replacing mutual aid teams, would become the mainstay of the Mutual Aid and Cooperation movement.[8]

This proposal was markedly at odds with earlier documents. The annual agricultural production plan for 1951, issued by the State Council in February 1952, explicitly supported the growth of the wealthy-peasant economy and permitted the hiring of labor.[9] The Draft that followed the first national conference on the Mutual Aid and Cooperation movement, issued at the end of 1951, also acknowledged the farmers' right to work as individuals. But this new proposal condemned private farming as a capitalist activity and urged rural cadres and party members to prevent wealthy peasants from joining the Mutual Aid and Cooperation movement. Most importantly, it designated agricultural producers' cooperatives, rather than mutual aid teams, as the way forward for the movement. Despite incorporating these radical new elements, the proposal was endorsed by the Central Committee in Beijing and was dispatched to regional, provincial, and prefectural party bureaus throughout the country.

In effect, the party decided to aggressively restrain the private economy in the countryside, working under the assumption that prosperity achieved under such conditions would pose a threat to the development of the Mutual Aid and Cooperation movement.[10] To shore up its position, the party carried out a number of investigations aimed at assessing the state of capitalism in the countryside. For example, in Shanxi Province during the summer of 1952, the party launched at least three inquiries: one into the development of capitalism in the countryside, another into rural class relationships, and a third into the potential of agricultural production in the province. The first two inquiries were aimed at unearthing the extent of capitalism's penetration in the countryside. The third inquiry, considered as supplementary to the first two, resulted in excessively optimistic estimations

---

8. "Zhongyang pizhuan dongbeiju guanyu tuixing nongye hezuohua de jueyi" (The Central Committee's endorsement of the Northeast China Bureau's decision on promoting agricultural cooperativization) (April 1952), *Jianshe,* no. 161, May 30, 1952.

9. "Zhongyang renmin zhengwuyuan guanyu 1951 nian nonglin shengchan de jueding" (The State Council's decision on agricultural and forest production in 1951) (February 15, 1952), *Nongye juan,* 39.

10. Zhu Yonghong, "Reflections on the Party's Policy," 55.

of the possibilities of rural development under socialism. In the years to follow, these investigations would serve as the statistical basis for socialist transformation movements. In the politically charged environment of the day, even the North China Bureau, which in 1951 had boldly asserted it would protect the "rights" of capitalist farmers and wealthy peasants, was forced to change course and agree to curb the excesses of capitalism.[11]

The changes that followed went far beyond mere bureaucratic assertions. By May 1952, the Three-Anti movement had already done enormous damage to the urban economy. Many capitalists had abandoned their enterprises and fled the country; the national economy had ground to a standstill, and urban unemployment had risen dramatically. Regardless, the central party decided to extend it to the countryside.

The North China Bureau reluctantly agreed with the decision, but it proceeded with caution. It suggested restricting the movement to the county level until the fall harvest. On the question of the methods to be adopted, the bureau steered away from the measures employed in the cities and suggested that the right approach was through internal reform of the party. Well aware that the abuses described by the Three-Anti movement (corruption, waste, and bureaucracy) were widespread in the countryside, the bureau sought not to penalize cadres who had committed offences in the past, but to prevent them from repeating their errors in the future. The bureau assured most cadres that they could survive the purge by engaging in acts of self-criticism. To discourage peasants from taking the initiative and attacking offending cadres, the bureau decided that cadres should not return seized land and property to their former owners or redistribute them as the "fruits of victory," which had been standard practice during the land reform era. It seems that the bureau intended to discipline local cadres, but not to purge them, and it did not link it with the Mutual Aid and Cooperation movement.

However, the local cadres had different ideas. For example, cadres in Changzhi prefecture immediately seized on anticapitalism as the central pil-

---

11. "Bo Yibo tongzhi xiang Mao zhuxi, zhongyang zhuan bao Huabeiju zhengce yanjiushi guanyu nongcun ziben zhuyi fazhan qingkuang he duice de baogao" (Comrade Bo Yibo's report to Chairman Mao and the Central Committee on the findings of the Policy Research Office of the North China Bureau on problems and solutions relating to the development of capitalism in the countryside) (September 6, 1952), *Huibian*, 611.

lar of the Three-Anti movement and adopted Gao Gang's proposals as their guidelines. Changzhi prefecture reported that "under the influence of the Three-Anti movement, more than 80 percent of party branches have studied comrade Gao Gang's article 'Overcoming the Encroachment of Capitalism in the Party, Combating Rightist Ideas in the Party'"; they had "rigidly criticized these rightist errors and challenged the beliefs of the wealthy peasants." Party members thus flocked to enroll themselves in mutual aid teams and agricultural producers' cooperatives.[12]

This was likely to have been a strategic move: local cadres would understandably be keen to switch the focus of the Three-Anti movement so as to protect themselves. By focusing on anticapitalism, local functionaries could distract attention away from their own failings and redirect the blame onto wealthy peasants, or they could make up for their own shortcomings by taking a firm stand against capitalism. In the countryside, the major target of the Three-Anti movement thus became capitalist thinking and capitalist practice. At the county level, expunging all traces of capitalist thinking became an essential goal of the movement. At the district level and lower, the main task was to constrain and limit exploitative capitalist practices. By comparison, curbing corruption was seen as a minor issue.[13] By this point and given the political orientation of the Three-Anti movement, the Mutual Aid and Cooperation movement had largely lost its identity as an economic program. Together, both movements would be deployed with the full range of the party's resources and administrative support. At this stage, local party members who had survived the initial turmoil of the Three-Anti movement began scrutinizing peasants' attitudes to the Mutual Aid and Cooperation movement, with the aim of weeding out any remaining capitalist elements.

The North China Bureau sought a compromise between its approach to the Three-Anti movement and the Northeast China Bureau's proposals by

---

12. "Changzhi diwei guanyu bannian lai nongcun shengchan huzhu hezuo yundong zonghe baogao" (June 30, 1952) (Changzhi prefecture's report on the Mutual Aid and Cooperation movement during the last six months), JMA, 92.1.1.

13. "Zhonggong zhongyang dongbei ju guanyu xianqu cun ji zhengdang yu dui dang yuan gugong fangzai deng wenti de zhishi (draft)" (The Northeast China Bureau's directive on the Party's rectification campaign at county, district and village levels, and on the issue of Party members hiring laborers) (August 12, 1952), JMA, 84.1.1.

opposing corruption, waste, and bureaucracy as its primary task, while designating anticapitalism as a secondary objective.[14] This dual approach left plenty of room for subjective interpretation in implementation. For example, Shanxi Province defined the Party Rectification movement as a combination of education in the tenets of communism and a campaign against rightist trends within the party. Changzhi prefecture went further by setting the elimination of "all exploitative thoughts and deeds" as its goal.[15] Consciously or not, the Mutual Aid and Cooperation movement thus became heavily interlinked with the Party Rectification and Three-Anti movements.

Combating rightists and working for a socialist future became urgent tasks. For example, before this point cadres from Chengjiashan village in Shanxi had shown no interest in the Mutual Aid and Cooperation movement. However, in order to meet the requirements of the Party Rectification movement, they instructed that all party members were to join agricultural producers' cooperatives. When some members showed reluctance, the village cadres told them: "After receiving three lashes an old donkey will climb a mountain; would you prefer five lashes?"[16]

The combined weight of the Three-Anti and Party Rectification movements imposed direct political pressure on local cadres to push for the implementation of the Mutual Aid and Cooperation movement. In October 1952 the second National Agricultural Work Conference was convened, and set the goal of organizing 60 percent of China's rural population into some form of cooperative farming by the end of 1953. In November the Central Committee of the CCP decided to establish a Rural Work Department in Beijing to monitor the nationwide rollout of the Mutual Aid and Cooperation movement.

A new stage in the Mutual Aid and Cooperation movement had thus begun. This time, however, village cadres were no longer the leaders; rather, they themselves became the targets of the movement. Officials at district

---

14. "Guanyu ganbu gongzuo he zhengdang jiandang gongzuo zhong de jige wenti" (Several problems relating to cadres and Party rectification and reconstruction) (September 1952). *Jianshe*, no. 179, October 10, 1952.

15. "Changzhi diwei guanyu nongcun zhengdang gongzuo jihua" (Changzhi prefecture's plan for a rural Party rectification campaign) (October 25, 1952), JMA, 92.1.1.

16. "Xiang Liu Lantao tongzhi de baogao" (Report to Comrade Liu Lantao) (April 21, 1953), JMA, 146.1.1.

level and higher threatened village cadres with force, beat them up, and on occasion even disbanded entire village party branches in attempts to pressure rural cadres into implementing the party's wishes. Coming under enormous pressure, village heads found themselves having to press the peasants even harder.

One phenomenon that particularly disappointed the party was the lack of improvement in the peasants' "mentality," a problem that it attributed to a lack of guidance from the party and a lack of socialist education. However, most party members had only a vague understanding of socialism themselves and knew little about collectivization. Faced with the challenge of correcting the masses' understanding of socialism, and connecting mutual aid teams and agricultural producers' cooperatives with China's socialist future in the popular mind, the CCP again turned to Soviet models.

In April 1952, the Agricultural Ministry in Beijing and the North China Bureau jointly dispatched China's first agricultural delegation, consisting of officials, peasant farmers, and agriculturists, to the Soviet Union. They returned to China in September 1952, just in time to help the CCP fine-tune the Mutual Aid and Cooperation movement with the information they had acquired there. Drawing on their experiences in the Soviet Union, delegates were expected to show Chinese citizens what a socialist country should look like, convince peasants of the bright future collectivization had to offer, and offer guidance to cadres on operating collective farms. Thus on their return, the delegates became zealous advocates for collectivization and the advancement of socialism. They toured the country giving lectures to describe the idyllic lifestyle enjoyed by Soviet farmers and aimed at inspiring local cadres and whipping up peasant enthusiasm for agricultural producers' cooperatives. The Chinese media, from the *People's Daily* to local newspapers, dutifully reported their speeches, thus advancing the party's mandate of carrying out socialist education.[17]

The four-week period between October 17 and November 17 in 1952 was declared "Sino-Soviet Friendship Month." Newspapers published a series of articles to celebrate it. A new theme emerged emphasizing that Soviet farmers contributed to making their country rich while at the same creating happy lives for themselves. Soviet peasants were only too willing to hand

---

17. For analysis on news reports on the delegation, refer to Xiaojia Hou, "Get Organized," 167–196.

their property over to the collective farms—something that, according to a report in the *Hebei Daily*, Chinese peasants had consistently refused to do.[18] In the following months, slogans such as the "Soviet road to collectivization is our peasants' bright future" were widely disseminated. At the same time, the party held up Stalin's final work, *Economic Problems of Socialism in the USSR*, as outlining how the transition from socialism to communism would be achieved and encouraged party members to become familiar with Stalin's ideas.[19] Learning from the Soviet experience was put on an increasingly formal footing. For example, on November 10, the Agriculture Ministry, the Ministry of Water Resources, and other central institutions invited Soviet officials and specialists to Beijing to address the history of Soviet collectivization and answer questions on the operation of collective farms.[20]

Taking Soviet collective farms as the new model, "getting organized" became more political. First, it was formally announced that transitioning from mutual aid teams to agricultural producers' cooperatives and then to collective farms was the only path to socialism. With the Soviet people serving as a model, the Chinese masses were instructed to work harder if they wanted a better life. "Getting organized" became the litmus test of obedience to the party line: those who refused to take the Soviet path to socialism would end up on the road to capitalism. Compared with the movement's early stage in spring 1952, economic factors were no longer a significant consideration. Concerns for political correctness dominated. Village cadres were no longer the leading figures; rather, they became the subjects of socialist education and came under increasing pressure to serve the party rather than protecting the interests of local people.

With Soviet collective farms as the model, China's Mutual Aid and Cooperation movement now became associated with large quantities of public assets, with large-scale production, and with the myth of socialism. The media, cautiously yet firmly, articulated the message that in order to serve the interests of the state, sometimes individuals would have to suffer personal losses. Soviet peasants had been through this process; it was now the turn of their Chinese counterparts. As a report in the *Hebei Daily* con-

18. *Hebei Daily,* October 30, 1952.
19. Ibid., October 29, 1952.
20. Ibid., November 13, 1952.

cluded, "All political activities should focus on mutual aid teams and agricultural producers' cooperatives."[21] By this time, the mainstream structure had become the agricultural producers' cooperatives.

Shanxi's Rapid Building of Agricultural Producers' Cooperatives

In Shanxi, the Three-Anti movement and the Party Rectification campaign were beginning to move in step with the Mutual Aid and Cooperation movement. As in 1951, provincial leaders in Shanxi continued to follow closely in Gao Gang's footsteps. In March 1952, the *Shanxi Daily* published a short piece under the headline "Everyone Should Digest Comrade Gao Gang's Article and Defeat the Capitalists' Attack on the Countryside."[22] The editorial emphasized that Gao Gang's article (discussed earlier in this chapter) contained extremely important guidelines for the development of the Mutual Aid and Cooperation movement in Shanxi.[23] Cadres at district and county levels reported their progress in studying Gao Gang's speeches on the subject. For example, Pingshun County in Changzhi prefecture planned to organize cadres of all levels, party members, and members of mutual aid teams to study comrade Gao Gang's articles so as to aid in challenging capitalism and correcting the "rightist" errors in the Mutual Aid and Cooperation movement.[24] Pingshun County even managed to have its plans published in the *People's Daily*.[25]

The following month, "after studying comrade Gao Gang's article," more than five hundred mutual aid teams in the province asked for permission to form agricultural producers' cooperatives.[26] In May, the *People's Daily* published another report on the development of the Mutual Aid and Cooperation movement in Shanxi, highlighting Gao Gang's speech as inspiring peasant farmers to join mutual aid teams.[27]

---

21. *Hebei Daily,* October 17, 1952.
22. Ibid., March 17, 1952.
23. Ibid.
24. *Shanxi Daily,* March 17, 1952.
25. *People's Daily,* April 13, 1952.
26. *Neibu cankao,* April 25, 1952.
27. *People's Daily,* May 8, 1952.

As Gao Gang's speech continued to be widely studied, ordinary party members and peasants asked how they could implement his proposed agenda. The *Shanxi Daily* published a series of columns seeking to address this issue, using a question-and-answer format. For example, one female party member reported that as her husband was sick and unable to farm their land and there were no laborers in her family, she had hired a laborer despite Gao Gang's condemnation of this practice. What should she do to survive? The newspaper replied that she should fire the laborer and join a mutual aid team. Another peasant asked, "Comrade Gao Gang has said that in mutual aid teams party members should look after other peasants in trouble. How should this ruling be implemented?" The *Shanxi Daily* answered that mutual aid teams were prohibited from excluding families with difficulties; rather, they should give them special care if needed.[28] As we have seen, when enrolling on a voluntary basis, peasants tended to form teams with partners of similar economic status and were unwilling to admit poorer members. However, the new guidelines sought to curb such tendencies. Volunteerism as the guiding principle and economic gain as the primary goal gave way to political concerns.

Officials at county, district, and village levels began monitoring "capitalist activities" in their territories.[29] "Deviations" of various kinds that had been tolerated in 1951 were no longer acceptable in the summer of 1952.[30] In Changzhi prefecture, inspections were conducted in the established agricultural producers' cooperatives. Two major findings emerged. It was discovered that the cooperatives had placed excessive emphasis on sideline work and ignored land cultivation. Cooperative members had preferred trading rather than breaking in waste ground. The report also found that as land and laborers were collectivized, the peasants also sought to pool their livestock and farm implements. However, cooperative heads were unwilling to meet these requests. The report applauded the peasants' attitude and concluded that cooperative bosses should accede to their wishes.[31]

In the summer of 1952, the Mutual Aid and Cooperation movement was revitalized and finally threw caution to the winds. On July 26, 1952, the Shanxi party branch established the Mutual Aid and Cooperation Direction

---

28. *Shanxi Daily,* June 20, 1952.
29. Ibid., March 17, 1952.
30. *Neibu cankao,* April 29, 1952.
31. Ibid., June 26, 1952.

Committee, headed by Tao Lujia. The committee's first task was a report comparing agricultural producers' cooperatives with mutual aid teams. The report affirmed remarkable advantages of the former: with more land and a larger labor force, and equipped with modern agricultural technology such as tractors, it was possible to build large-scale irrigation projects. The report suggested that the full potential of both land and laborers would be realized and that farmers' income might well double in agricultural producers' cooperatives. In addition, agricultural producers' cooperatives could also form an ideal environment to educate the peasants about collectivism and political matters. The report claimed that the average cooperative subscribed to seven or eight newspapers and that the members increasingly identified their own interests with the cooperative's interests, even to the extent of treating their fellow members as relatives. The report confidently predicted that agricultural producers' cooperatives would not only lead the rural economy toward collectivization and modernization, but also serve as excellent schools of political and cultural education. Therefore, the Shanxi committee concluded, it was time to promote agricultural producers' cooperatives with the full energy and resources of the party.[32]

On August 20, the *Shanxi Daily* published an editorial entitled "The Chinese Communist Party Is Providing the Impetus to Lead the Peasants toward Cooperativization."[33] It explicitly stated that the party's central task in the countryside was not increasing rural production, but to lead the Mutual Aid and Cooperation movement. Previously, as we have seen, the party saw its key task in the countryside as increasing productivity, with mutual aid teams as the means; now the means itself became the end, with significant political implications.

From July onward, the *Shanxi Daily* devoted numerous columns to publishing guidelines for operating agricultural producers' cooperatives, ranging from the use of community funds to the enforcement of the distribution rules. However, the rules promulgated in these newspaper articles were often too complex and even-handed to be applied in practice. For example, they asserted that the principle of voluntarism was to be upheld, as was the bias toward labor input and providing aid to the poor. As we saw in Chapter 4, these two principles were rarely compatible in practice. Now the cadres

---

32. "Shanxi sheng 1952 nian shang bannian jianli yu," 315–320.

33. *Shanxi Daily*, August 20, 1952.

encountered the dilemma between the task and the policy, as the epilogue will discuss further.

On October 10, 1952, the newly appointed first party secretary in Shanxi, Gao Kelin, identified an imbalance in the Mutual Aid and Cooperation movement and launched an enquiry. He pointed out that county cadres were unfamiliar with conditions in the countryside and were frequently deceived by false reports. They never ventured into the villages themselves and knew nothing about leadership by personal example. Gao Kelin demanded that county officials undertake in-depth inspections of rural conditions and suggested that whereas caution had been important in the past, now it needed to be cast aside.[34] In December, he asserted that peasants who had not yet "gotten organized" were still dreaming of capitalism, and he called on everyone to combat "rightist" errors such as failing to organize the peasants.[35]

With caution now a thoroughly discredited virtue, stepping up the pace and thinking in terms of larger size and greater use of public assets took priority. Military language was swiftly adopted. For example, a village in Changzhe District in Shanxi promoted the martial slogan: "Encircle [the enemy] on all levels, attack from both within and without, prepare task forces, succeed in a single night."[36] Cadres from county down to village level all subscribed to the same notion: the bigger, the better. At the same time, the ongoing education campaign to promote socialism was often simply reduced to polemical attacks on the individual-peasant economy. The need to replace private ownership with vaguely expressed "socialist elements" was stressed. Increasingly, cadres overlooked the fact that following land reform, private farming still dominated the rural scene.

Without bothering to examine real conditions in the countryside, the head of Licheng County in Changzhi prefecture promoted the slogan, "To achieve complete cooperativization in three years." When lower-ranking cadres informed him that the peasants were unwilling to form cooperatives, he criticized them for their "rightist" errors. In reality, it was the county boss who had his head in the sand. Unwilling to spend time discussing the details

<hr>

34. "Zai zhonggong Shanxi shengwei kuoda huiyi shang de zongjie baogao," 321.

35. "Zai quansheng nongye fengchan laodong mofan daibiao dahui shang de baogao" (Report on the provincial conference of model laborers' representatives) (December 19, 1952), in *Shanxi sheng nongye hezuo shi wenjian huibian juan*, 323–324.

36. *People's Daily*, March 30, 1953.

of running cooperatives, he simply demanded that more cooperatives be built. To inject more "socialist elements," Licheng County cadres ordered every established mutual aid team in the county to plant eight mu of collectively farmed high-yielding land, forcing farmers to pool much of their best land. To meet this requirement, some teams had to lease fertile land from elsewhere. The commitment to "eliminate the small private economy" stifled enthusiasm for public assets, and the obsession with collectivism trampled the voluntary principle underfoot. As part of Changzhi prefecture, cadres from Licheng County aspired to compete with Wuxiang County, whose name was regularly mentioned in the newspapers. Licheng officials asked, "If they can do it, why can't we?"[37]

Cadres at the county level rarely concerned themselves with the day-to-day operations of cooperatives as long as their quotas were fulfilled. Under pressure from their county-level supervisors, district and village cadres, who usually possessed a low level of literacy and poor understanding of socialism, interpreted the policy in very basic terms: get agricultural producers' cooperatives established. They forced peasant farmers, and themselves, to set up cooperatives despite significant resistance. These cadres seemed to have held the belief that once a cooperative was established, they had done what the party required of them. Villagers were told, "In three years, private ownership will be eliminated, all production equipment will be collectivized" and "Everyone should get organized."[38]

In theory, agricultural producers' cooperatives were to be built on successful mutual aid teams, but this rule was ignored in practice. For example, in Licheng County, fifty-eight out of ninety-eight cooperatives set up in late 1952 had no such history; officials established them arbitrarily to fulfill their quotas.[39] As the peasants complained, "Cadres at the county level don't come near the district; cadres at the district level don't come near the villages; village heads don't farm land, and ordinary peasants don't get a wink of sleep because of constant meetings."[40]

At the same time, Shanxi Province and Changzhi prefecture in particular continued to build up their national reputation as pioneers in the Mu-

---

37. "Xiang Liu Lantao tongzhi de baogao."
38. Ibid.
39. Ibid.
40. Ibid.

tual Aid and Cooperation movement. In June 1952, *People's Daily* published the success of the first ten experimental agricultural producers' cooperatives in Changzhi prefecture. The report noted two new developments in particular: increased efforts at political education and increased use of public assets. According to the article, as farmers pooled their land and labor force, they were demanding that their tools and implements be pooled as well. The report concluded that it was time to "step by step resolve the contradiction between the collective management of production and the private ownership of production equipment, which is the key to advancing the cooperatives."[41] In the same month, the success of Guo Yu'en cooperative in Changzhi prefecture was trumpeted in the *People's Daily*; it was later to be held up as a national model for agricultural producers' cooperatives. The "advanced" features of this cooperative were a larger pool of collectively farmed land, more peasants enrolled (membership had jumped from eighteen to forty-six households), a greater utilization of public assets, and improved collective working habits.[42] Later in the year, the editor-in-chief of the *People's Daily*, Fan Changjiang, produced a pamphlet on the Guo Yu'en cooperative that was published by the prestigious People's Press and widely circulated.[43]

Thanks to Gao Gang, party members were no longer permitted to work as individual farmers, meaning that once enrolled, they could not withdraw from a mutual aid team or cooperative. For example, in December 1951 the Li Shunda mutual aid team, one of the best known in the nation, was converted to an agricultural producers' cooperative. Some older members, including Lu Quanwen, wanted to leave when the changeover occurred. Born into a poor family, Lu had achieved the status of a middle-ranking peasant through sheer hard work and joined the CCP. Judging that "based on the soil conditions in our village, there is no scope for a higher yield, no matter how well we organize ourselves," he asked to leave his team and was permitted to withdraw in 1951. However, following Gao Gang's January speech, a series of investigations into rural development was conducted in summer 1952, and Lu Quanwen was publicly criticized after coming under official scrutiny. According to the reports, one after another, every party member in

41. *People's Daily*, June 5, 1952.
42. Ibid., June 3, 1952.
43. *Shanxi nongye hezuohua*, 682–683.

Li Shunda cooperative condemned Lu after studying Gao Gang's speech. In the end, Lu Quanwen was said to have burst into tears, lamenting, "I was wrong. I have betrayed the party, I have betrayed Chairman Mao, and I have betrayed my comrades' trust and the education I received." He apologized for his pursuit of personal profit and rejoined the Li Shunda cooperative.[44] Like many other similar cases from Changzhi, this episode was reported in the *People's Daily*.

In July, 1952, the *People's Daily* published another article titled "The Steady Development of Agricultural Producers' Cooperatives in North China" in praise of Shanxi. The article endorsed the five criteria that Wang Qian had set for the ten experimental cooperatives (discussed in Chapter 4), recommending that they serve as the basis for establishing additional cooperatives in North China.[45] In August, Changzhi's success in enrolling rural cadres in the Mutual Aid and Cooperation movement was again mentioned in the *People's Daily*.[46] In September, *People's Daily* reported the rapid development of mutual aid teams in Shanxi, mainly in Changzhi prefecture.[47] In October, Shanxi's experience in setting up agricultural producers' cooperatives was once again endorsed by this national party newspaper.[48]

According to these reports, by September 1952, 56.3 percent of households in Shanxi had been organized into some form of cooperative farming. The drawdown of public assets had increased substantially. Many mutual aid teams had formulated annual production plans, successfully combined sideline work with farming, adopted advanced agricultural technology, and projected a dramatic increase in their incomes.[49] At the same time, the peasants' political consciousness had been enhanced and they had gained an improved understanding of collectivism. These reports also asserted that an increasing number of peasants had voluntarily asked to be part of producers' cooperatives. The peasants were quoted as saying, "Agricultural producers' cooperatives are like a train, and the party is like the engine; they lead us as

---

44. *People's Daily*, October 24, 1952.
45. Ibid., July 18, 1952.
46. Ibid., August 7, 1952.
47. Ibid., September 3, 1952.
48. Ibid., October 20, 1952.
49. Ibid., September 3, 1952.

we walk toward a society full of happiness."[50] However, this remarkably rapid progress in reality witnessed the appearance of what were officially known as "rash tendencies," with serious consequences to follow.

Rash Tendencies

Media campaigns had denounced the hiring of laborers and money lending as forms of exploitation, which should be stamped out. Rich peasants should be beaten, a fate that had befallen landlords during land reform. Private farming was considered a form of capitalism; those farming on their own account were no longer to be tolerated, but rather to be despised. Slogans were posted up with messages, such as: "Are you still farming for yourself?" "Private farming is backward—it is a barrier to socialism," and "There is no future for private farmers—they will be isolated, flushed out and shamed."[51]

Capitalizing on this campaign, once again rural cadres displayed their ingenuity in "mobilizing" the peasants. For example, in Jincheng County of Changzhi prefecture, officials devised a wide variety of measures to discourage private farming, ranging from financial boycotts to psychological discrimination. Individual farmers were refused state loans and other financial assistance, and they were forced to shoulder a larger proportion of local levies of various kinds. For instance, whereas a mutual aid team was required to subscribe to a single copy of a party newspaper, private farmers had to take out a family subscription, regardless of whether they were literate. And even if they did not use the new farming equipment purchased by the cooperative, they still had to pay their share of the costs. In many cases, private farmers were forbidden to use village facilities such as wells or mills. Discrimination went far beyond the economic sphere. Organizationally, private farmers were placed in a separate category and were often lumped in with landlords. In some villages, they were forced to report in person twice a day to the village head. Such psychological discrimination was probably even harder to bear than the financial burdens laid on them. During village

---

50. Ibid., October 20, 1952.

51. "Zhuyi jiuzheng youguan huzhu hezuo de cuowu xuanchuan" (Strive to rectify the false propaganda surrounding the mutual aid and cooperation movement) (September 1952), *Jianshe*, no. 181.

ceremonies, especially marriages and funerals, private farmers were forced to carry a large drum on their backs, a role that according to custom was considered humiliating and performed only by slaves.[52]

Similar abuse took place in Wuxiang County as well. By December 1952, 94 percent of households were organized.[53] Party members were busy joining established cooperatives or setting up new ones.[54] Direct orders and strict enforcement seemed to work faster, if not better, than education, and they accounted for the very high compliance rate. After village heads had studied Gao Gang's January speech, they abandoned their caution and actively pushed the peasants onto the socialist path. Village cadres in Wuxiang also developed a variety of ways to discriminate against those who refused to get organized. Private farmers were seated separately at village meetings, or they were sometimes forced to stand by themselves while others sat. In Nanzhang village, village cadres forbade their peers to use their names, demanding that they be addressed as "private farmers." This form of discrimination also extended to their children, who were to be known as "sons of private farmers." Stung by such treatment, one child begged his father to join a mutual aid team; the father in his turn pleaded to join the team and offered to contribute more than the going rate for the privilege.[55]

In the face of these pressures, many private farmers gave up and joined mutual aid teams, preferably those that were nominal only. To the surprise of many, however, this option had now disappeared, partly because district and county cadres were making regular visits to the villages and partly because mutual aid teams were no longer favored by the party. Cadres were actively promoting agricultural producers' cooperatives, which were much harder to simulate. Mutual aid teams were mainly conceived as a labor-sharing mechanism and could be "created" on paper by simply drawing up a list of names. They did not necessarily require any surrender of individual property. Agricultural Producers' cooperatives differed in that they required farmers to pool their property as an initial investment. Collecting money and goods was a very different matter from listing names on a sheet of

52. "Jincheng xian huzhuzu zhong dangqian qingkuang yu cunzai de wenti" (Circumstances and problems of mutual aid teams in Jincheng County) (May 11, 1953), SPA, C29.1.17.

53. *Neibu cankao*, December 30, 1952

54. Ibid.

55. Ibid., January 22, 1953.

paper. The party was taking a much tougher attitude to enforcement, too. In addition to verbal threats, rural cadres were now also resorting to violence. The peasants had long assumed that socialism would mean the socialization of property.[56] Local cadres held tenaciously to the idea that the more public assets a cooperative had, the more successful it would be. As the agricultural producers' cooperatives were rolled out, the utilization of public assets was overwhelmingly emphasized. Regardless of the criteria set out by Wang Qian or directives from above, in the eyes of local cadres the essential difference between the two types of organization was that whereas agricultural producers' cooperatives involved the collectivization of participants' landholdings, livestock, and farm implements, mutual aid teams did not.

In nearly every county in Shanxi, it was reported that there were cooperatives that had collectivized all their members' land, livestock, and farm equipment. For example, of the one thousand newly established agricultural producers' cooperatives in Changzhi prefecture, 76 percent had collectivized all of their members' land, animals, and farm implements.[57] Even old furniture was sometimes acquired by cooperatives, regardless of whether there was any use for it. In extreme cases, some cooperatives even took away the timber people had saved for their coffins—the most valuable asset of many elderly peasants.[58] According to an incomplete statistical survey of Qinshui County in Changzhi prefecture, in forty-three cooperatives, 496 collectivized farm animals were entirely surplus to needs.

A variety of measures was introduced to "ensure" that peasants pooled their livestock. As a first step, deadlines were set, along with demands such as, "Cattle must be turned over to the cooperative within five days, horses within seven days. Following the deadline, any remaining animals will be confiscated." Second, those who failed to hand in their livestock were publicly criticized and repeatedly roll-called. Third, a quota would often be set to be filled by the villagers as a body. Fourth, all "hidden" property was

56. "Linfeng zhuanqu huzhu hezuo yundong zhuanti baogao" (Linfeng prefecture's special report on the mutual aid and cooperation movement) (May 7, 1953), SPA, C29.1.17.

57. "Jiuzheng nongye shengchan hezuoshe fazhan zhong de mangmu maojin qingxiang" (Rectify impetuous tendencies in the development of agricultural producers' cooperatives) (March 1953), *Jianshe*, no. 205.

58. Ibid.

searched and if any livestock were discovered, it was confiscated by the co-operative without compensation.[59]

After the peasants had been successfully induced to turn their property over to the cooperative, further problems surfaced. Although in theory farmers would be compensated for their collectivized property, there were no fixed compensation rates or standard procedures for assessing it. Compensation was determined on a case by case basis. In most cases, the compensation granted was significantly lower than the market value of the property requisitioned. During the campaign against capitalism, it was standard practice to privilege poor peasants at the expense of others.[60] Although there were a few cases where a cooperative gave generous compensation to attract new members, or where farmers succeeded in gaining a fairer price through bargaining, the payment process—with cash or credit—took years, if it ever materialized at all. As one woman complained, "The cooperative is getting richer, the household is getting poorer."[61]

Discriminatory practices were often endorsed by cadres at higher levels. For example, one mutual aid team asked Su San, one of its members and a middle-ranking peasant, to pay for a plough that the team wanted to buy. Su San refused and petitioned the district cadre over the matter. The cadre told him, "Your money is useless if it is kept at home. You need to donate it to realize its potential." Su San ended up having to sell his grain reserve to pay for the plough, and he determined to give up grain production altogether.[62]

Taking care of collectivized livestock was always problematic. In most cases, the burden of feeding farm animals was not fairly divided. Farmers who had recently suffered significant losses with respect to their private property rarely showed much concern for the property of "others." As a result, fat animals rapidly lost weight, and those in poor condition were unlikely to survive. In one cooperative in Huguan County in Changzhi prefecture, fourteen farm animals died. As the local wits commented, "See, this is the great advantage of agricultural producers' cooperatives—so many live-

---

59. "Guanyu huzhu hezuo mangmu maojin qingxiang diandi jiyao" (Accounts of impetuous tendencies in the mutual aid and cooperation movement) (May 12, 1953), SPA, C29.1.16.

60. Gao Huamin, "Rectifying the Problems of Impetuosity and Rash Advance," 61.

61. "Guanyu huzhu hezuo mangmu maojin qingxiang diandi jiyao."

62. "Jincheng xian huzhuzu zhong dangqian qingkuang yu cunzai de wenti."

stock could never die on family farms."[63] Similar scenes took place across the country, from northeast China to central south China.[64]

More often than not, commandeering members' property was not sufficient to establish a fully fledged agricultural producers' cooperatives. Following the example of the ten experimental cooperatives in Changzhi, newly established agricultural producers' cooperatives were not shy in demanding state loans. As befitted their "advanced" status, their requests were usually granted. Consequently, most ended up with sizeable debts. These new cooperatives were often so indebted that they could not even afford the interest payments on the loan—exactly the situation that had occurred with the initial ten experimental cooperatives.

As the allocation of public assets increased, so did the size of the cooperatives. Slogans such as, "It is better to have more than less, to have larger than smaller," and "The more the better, the bigger the better," were widely disseminated.[65] For example, in Hongjing village in Licheng County, Changzhi prefecture, one agricultural producers' cooperative consisted of twenty-seven households in the summer of 1952. In the fall, village cadres requested that its membership be increased to forty households, but this failed to satisfy the district cadre. He replied that in order to compete with the Wang Jinyun cooperative in Wuxiang County, all 101 households in Hongjing should join the cooperative. His advice was duly acted on.[66]

Drawing down public assets was only one way in which cooperatives could become more "socialist." Incorporating socialist principles into their everyday operations was important as well. Full compensation for land and cash investments was not considered ideologically correct; in most cases, compensation for land was strictly limited to 30 percent before agricultural taxes or around 10 percent after tax. Further, some cooperatives contemplated eliminating compensation for land entirely.[67]

Apart from the utilization of public assets, the best-known feature of cooperative life associated with socialism was "eating from a big pot." This

---

63. "Xiang shengwei de san yuefen zonghe baogao" (Summary report to the province for March) (March 1953), JMA, 124.1.1.

64. There were numerous reports detailing the loss of livestock in cooperatives, from each of the major regions of China. See *Neibu cankao.*

65. Gao Huamin, "Rectifying the Problems of Impetuosity and Rash Advance," 62.

66. "Xiang Liu Lantao tongzhi de baogao."

67. "Jincheng xian huzhuzu zhong dangqian qingkuang yu cunzai de wenti."

phenomenon, whereby peasants were required to eat together in a common dinner hall, was an early element in many cooperatives.[68] Other lesser known "socialist" elements defined and implemented during this period are also worthy of note. Social welfare became a promising new feature of agricultural producers' cooperatives and multiple proposals were drafted to create comprehensive welfare systems. For example, in Linfen County of Changzhi prefecture, village heads proposed measures such as these:

- "A woman with children will be paid 30 percent of her previous income even if she does not work."
- "The team will financially support women confined to the home."
- "The team will raise children under 18 years of age."
- "The team will take care of seniors aged over 50."

On the one hand, young male laborers did not want to work with women and were resentful of the rule that women were to be paid equally.[69] On the other hand, such proposals reflected ordinary peasants' aspirations for an effective social welfare system. Their demands were based on rational considerations. Because they had handed over their land and livestock to the cooperative and had also taken on large debts, they felt justified in demanding that their legitimate social needs be met. As one cooperative member said, "I did what you told me to do, and now I have nothing left; the cooperative should help me out in every way possible. After all, there is nothing more you can get out of me."[70]

Spontaneously, members turned to the cooperative for help in the face of material shortages and personal problems. In theory, one essential advantage of an agricultural producers' cooperative was to meet its members' welfare needs, yet in reality cooperatives were ill-prepared to do so. They were often forced to turn to state agencies, mostly banks and credit unions, for aid. For example, in one village in Yi County in Changzhi prefecture, after all property had been collectivized, members petitioned the cooperative head for subsidized food, medicine, and entertainment. With grain supplies

---

68. Gao Huamin, "Rectifying the Problems of Impetuosity and Rash Advance."

69. "Guanyu shencha nongye shengchan hezuoshe de jinji zhishi" (An urgent directive on inspecting agricultural producers' cooperatives) (April 3, 1953), SPA, C54.1005.34.

70. "Linfeng zhuanqu huzhu hezuo yundong zhuanti baogao."

gone, the head of the cooperative managed to get a loan of 4 million yuan from the state bank to feed his members over the winter.[71] Few cooperatives enjoyed such reliable networks. In Hongdongbei County in Changzhi prefecture, of three cooperatives incorporating a total of 122 households, 22 households were unable to make ends meet, 33 were short of seeds to plant, all the cattle were in poor condition, and the cooperative heads were at a loss as to what to do.[72] No record of their fate has survived.

As agricultural producers' cooperatives grew larger and took on additional functions, running them became increasingly difficult. A cooperative of one hundred households or more was virtually unmanageable, at least as far as the peasants themselves were concerned. While reams of regulations were published in the newspapers, literacy levels were often lower than officials assumed, and the work involved in farming was difficult to quantify. A work points system was proposed as a basic tool for quantifying labor output and assessing compensation. But in 1952, as many cases demonstrated, the cooperatives were not yet ready for this system. As most peasants tended to work as little as they could get away with, some cooperative heads ended up forcing them to work the land for long hours with intensive labor.[73] In this sense, cooperatives were certainly intruding on the peasants' everyday lives. As one investigation noted, "Some cooperatives emphasized 'united action,' which resulted in peasants having no time to take care of personal matters."[74]

At the same time, the movement vested rural cadres with wide-ranging powers—powers that were open to abuse. Rural cadres and cooperative heads were empowered to levy charges on members. For example, in Jincheng County, Changzhi prefecture, on the pretext that agricultural activity had been combined with sideline work, local cadres arbitrarily levied taxes on peasants' sideline income. In Kaiwan village, the Ji Hongfu mutual aid team issued regulations enabling it to retain 20 percent of members' income from sideline work. Even women's earnings from childcare were not exempted. Village heads even levied fees on absent workers. In Xiyao village, anyone working outside the village was required to pay 500 yuan per day to make up for their absence. In Jin village, residents' earnings, with the excep-

---

71. Ibid.

72. Ibid.

73. *Neibu cankao*, August 14, 1952.

74. "Guanyu huzhu hezuo mangmu maojin qingxiang diandi jiyao."

tion of agricultural income, were subject to a 5 percent tax for community funds.[75] With an unprecedented supply of money and credit, village cadres took the opportunity to create a local infrastructure that had previously been no more than a pipe dream: auditoriums, dining halls, libraries, and administration buildings were all established, one after another, but at the expense of a massive accumulation of debt.[76]

As a conduit between the state and peasant families, agricultural producers' cooperatives had a responsibility to pass on assistance offered by state agencies, but the peasants came to see this as more of a burden than any kind of help. For example, the state had long sought to persuade peasants to use new farm implements, such as improved models of ploughs. While the peasants themselves showed little interest in such innovative tools and simply refused to buy them, the heads of mutual aid teams and cooperatives, who were much less cautious about spending money and much more eager to please state agents, proved more willing to purchase new equipment. Whereas in 1951 in Licheng County only fifty-seven ploughs were sold, in spring 1953 sales soared to 581, mainly to mutual aid teams and cooperatives. Subscriptions to party newspapers offer another example of this dynamic. In 1952 in Licheng County, 92,117 copies of newspapers and books were sold during the entire year; whereas in the first three months of 1953, 74,996 copies were sold, again mostly to mutual aid teams and cooperatives.[77]

Last, but not least, the direction taken by the movement led to increasing levels of coercion and violence, ranging from threatening language to torture. Cases of killings and suicide were reported, and tears and grief were commonplace.

Although most commonly encountered in the cooperatives, these developments were also found in the mutual aid teams. As already mentioned, the practical difference between the two structures was the amount of property collectivized. Since agricultural producers' cooperatives were regarded as the more advanced form, rural cadres drew the conclusion that the more publicly owned assets allocated to mutual aid teams, the more the teams resembled cooperatives and the more progressive they would be. Popular slogans of the day included these:

---

75. "Jincheng xian huzhuzu zhong dangqian qingkuang yu cunzai de wenti."
76. "Guanyu shencha nongye shengchan hezuoshe de jinji zhishi."
77. "Xiang Liu Lantao tongzhi de baogao."

- "Small teams should join together to form a large one."
- "Those with less than five households are not counted as mutual aid teams."
- "It is glorious to join larger teams."[78]

In Jincheng County in Changzhi prefecture, mutual aid teams were formed on a large scale. On average, one team consisted of twenty-five households, the size of the first ten experimental producers' cooperatives. Community funds were collected, and the allocation of public assets was vastly expanded. Whereas Jincheng County's first district had specified that agricultural cooperatives needed to reserve 20 percent of their income for community funds, mutual aid teams set aside 10 to 15 percent.[79]

Another factor was responsible for the zeal shown by rural cadres in pressing for collectivization was industrialization. In 1952, the CCP announced its national industrialization plan, meaning that additional cadres were needed in industry. Plans for relocating cadres from the agricultural to the industrial sector were set in motion. Cadres who had been assigned posts in the countryside now competed to be "relocated" to urban areas.[80] This opportunity to advance their careers stimulated them to improve their performance in the field—which often meant doing more in a shorter time period.

While there were cases of peasants voluntarily joining cooperatives in this new phase of the movement, intending participants were more likely to be reacting to coercive pressures compared to those who joined the ten trial ventures in Changzhi. Many became convinced that sooner or later they were bound to follow the road. By acting earlier they would gain respect and receive more privileges from the state.[81] As the political atmosphere intensified, peasants from "undesirable" class backgrounds took fright. To demonstrate their progressive spirit and avoid being targeted by the authorities, they invited poor peasants to form cooperatives by offering them economic incentives.[82] Once the Mutual Aid and Cooperation movement was recon-

78. Gao Huamin, "Rectifying the Problems of Impetuosity and Rash Advance," 62.
79. "Jincheng xian huzhuzu zhong dangqian qingkuang yu cunzai de wenti."
80. "Zhongguo gongchandang zhongyang weiyuanhui guanyu chungeng shengchan gei geji dangwei de zhishi" (The Central Committee's directive to Party committees at all levels on the spring plowing and production) (March 16, 1953), *Nongye juan.*
81. Ye Yangbing, *Zhongguo nongye hezuohua yundong yanjiu.*
82. Ibid.

figured as a political movement, the peasants no longer had much room to maneuver. Considered from the economic perspective, most of these new cooperatives were doomed to fail.

Because the Mutual Aid and Cooperation movement was now essentially a political movement, the pursuit of profit was branded as capitalism and was to be "amended." Many of the innovations adopted by peasant farmers in 1951 were now considered unethical, if not yet illegal. Hiring laborers, encouraging sideline ventures, planting more cash crops, seeking higher levels of compensation for land and livestock, and cash investment in cooperatives were all condemned as marks of capitalism. Prudent economic considerations were thrown overboard.

The question of compensation for livestock was a case in point. Customarily, one head of cattle was calculated as the equivalent of—if not superior to—one and a half laborers. But under the new regime, this formula was condemned as exploitation, and the compensation paid for cattle was reduced to the equivalent of half a laborer, despite frequent objections that this was not sufficient to pay for fodder. The choice was a stark one: eat the animal or sell it. Under strong pressure from local cadres not to withdraw from mutual aid teams, cattle-owners increasingly saw their animals as a liability and felt that they either had to donate their cattle to the team or propose that a producers' cooperative be formed.[83] In the party's overly optimistic assessment, such actions could be wrongly interpreted as examples of the peasants' "selflessness" and their eagerness to form cooperatives. However, it is safe to assume that those involved would not be seeking to raise any more cattle.

Such trends were by no means limited to Shanxi Province. By the spring of 1953, numerous agricultural producers' cooperatives and large-scale mutual aid teams in every province (with the exception of minority administrative regions) had been established. Historian Gao Huamin has listed the features of the party's "rash advance" into collectivism at this time. According to Gao, by spring 1953 publicly owned assets were being carelessly expended as a means of developing producers' cooperatives; the party's emphasis on cooperatives had resulted in the downgrading of mutual aid teams; in some regions the use of coercion and commandism was common, undermining the earlier principle of voluntarism.[84] A party document from

---

83. *Neibu cankao*, December 4, 1952.
84. Gao Huamin, "Rectifying the Problems of Impetuosity and Rash Advance," 62.

1953 acknowledged that in the newly liberated regions, the use of "political" methods to form mutual aid teams was commonplace, which often harmed the interests of middle-ranking peasants. By contrast, in the older liberated regions, there was a tendency to place undue emphasis on agricultural producers' cooperatives, along with the heavy collectivization of farmers' assets and the introduction of a great many "new" socialist features.[85]

The Peasants' Resistance

The excesses of the Mutual Aid and Cooperation movement in late 1952 and early 1953 sapped the energy of China's peasant farmers and severely impaired agricultural production. In many counties of Shanxi Province, no one collected night soil for the entire winter, sideline work was neglected, and crops went untended. For example, in Podi (village) cooperative in Wuxiang County, members were not even interested in picking beans, which ended up as fodder for pigs. One elderly peasant worried that "the cooperative can afford to lose these beans, but I cannot afford to lose my pigs. I am afraid they will die from eating too much."[86] Although Changzhi prefectural officials showed no anxieties about the pigs, they were deeply concerned about the agricultural production plan for 1953.

Between October 1952 and April 1953, the peasants' enthusiasm for farming their land reached its lowest ebb since 1950. In two producers' cooperatives in Changzhi, 70 percent of the arable land lay unused; the farmers had refused to plant it out. Although not all peasants in Shanxi had joined cooperatives or mutual aid teams, nearly all of them had either witnessed or heard about what was occurring in cooperatives nearby. In their eyes, their neighbors had been unjustly deprived of their livestock and farm implements. Their land brought them little or no profit, and slogans like "overthrow private ownership" were in the air. Almost the entire rural population reacted with a sense of fear and foreboding: "Communism is coming!" They felt they were next in line. Many said frankly, "I am afraid of joining the cooperatives. I am afraid that I won't be given any grain after the harvest. I am afraid of starving." Pessimistic about the future, many adopted the spirit of *carpe diem*: they chopped down fruit trees, slaughtered their livestock for

85. "Zhongguo gongchandang zhongyang," *Nongye juan*, 25–26.
86. "Xiang shengwei de san yuefen zonghe baogao."

meat, and crammed their bellies full. Although Feng Zituo rarely ate meat, in the Chinese New Year of 1953 he slaughtered three pigs and claimed that he still felt unsatisfied. In Wuji village in Changzhi prefecture, eight households sold all their livestock, and some even sold additional houses that they owned. Tingcheng village in Qin County had provided enough work for at least eight blacksmiths between 1950 and 1952, and dozens of carriages had been sold each year. Yet in 1953 only one blacksmith remained in the village, and he had gone out of business, unable to sell even a single carriage. Peasants refused to spread fertilizer on their land, saying, "Why bother? After the fall of 1953 everything will belong to the cooperatives."[87] The peasants had little interest in maintaining their farming activities at the present level, let alone expanding them.

Excesses in the movement were by no means isolated to Shanxi Province. The northeast region experienced its own run of "rash tendencies." In 1952, over twelve hundred agricultural producers' cooperatives were established in Northeast China. On average, members received compensation worth less than half of their output, and some cooperatives went bankrupt.[88] In the end, both Shanxi and the northeast region suffered significant falls in grain production. In Northeast China, while projected production for the year was 44 billion catties of grain, the actual figure was 37 billion catties at best. In Shanxi, wheat production fell by 600 million catties.[89] The impact of the Mutual Aid and Cooperation movement went far beyond crushing peasants' incentives for farming the land and disrupting the state's grain projections. Signs of even more perilous consequences were beginning to appear.

Peasant farmers had lost heart for life on the land: "For the whole year we have worked as hard as we can, yet we still can't feed the state." They concluded, "There is no future in farming. We would do much better to leave the village and find a job in cities."[90] Land became a burden. Certainly no one wanted to purchase it, and the myth of "selling land for free" became a harsh reality. In Licheng County, in 1951 1 mu of arable land was worth 6–7 dan of millet. In 1953, no peasant was willing to purchase additional land, regardless of the price. In order to get rid of some of his land, peasant

---

87. "Linfeng zhuanqu huzhu hezuo yundong zhuanti baogao."
88. *Neibu cankao*, December 23, 1952.
89. *Dangdai Zhongguo liangshi gongzuo shiliao*, 150–167.
90. "Linfeng zhuanqu huzhu hezuo yundong zhuanti baogao."

Wang Changsuo not only gave away 6 mu of arable land, but also offered the buyer a cash bonus.[91] When peasants felt better off abandoning their land, the government should have been alerted to an impending crisis and reexamined its rural policies.

The abandonment of land had some predictable consequences. Cadres in Changzhi prefecture found that their job of recruiting for the army was getting much easier; peasants were joining up with enthusiasm. "In past years, it had been difficult to recruit peasants into the army; this year, it is difficult to persuade them to go back home [from the recruiting stations]."[92] This dramatic turn, probably partly also due to the winding down of the Korean War, reflected the peasants' pessimism about their future in the countryside. At the same time, large numbers of youths left their home villages for the cities, seeking new opportunities. Their primary motivation, according to an inquiry conducted by Changzhi prefecture, was that they felt that "any profession is better than tilling the land." Compared with other occupations, farming was hard work, yet the gains were now very tenuous. With additional taxes and other miscellaneous levies to pay for, many peasants saw no future in farming, and complained that they were now unable to keep half their output. They calculated that two weeks of a worker's salary was now equivalent in value to what one farmer could make from the fall harvest.[93]

The peasants' hostility toward the state increased. When freezing winter weather threatened the grain harvest, the farmers responded with resignation: "Let it be. We have nothing to eat—but neither does the state" and "My flesh is the only thing I have left. You [cadres] can do whatever you want to me." Although most peasants adopted passive methods of resistance, some chose to stand and fight. Even in Changzhi prefecture, an older liberated region where the party had deep roots, when the peasants were pressed too hard in 1953, they embraced millenarianism. The movement witnessed the revival of a sect known as the Wholehearted Worship of the "Tao" of Heaven and the Dragon China Society (*yixin tiandao longhua hui*) and thousands were recruited as part of a conspiracy to rebel. The revolt was put down even before it started, but the people's attitude appalled local party leaders. Acknowledging that unrest in the countryside had reached unprecedented lev-

---

91. Ibid.
92. "Xiang shengwei de san yuefen zonghe baogao."
93. Ibid.

els since 1949, local cadres were also well aware of its causes: the party had made some serious mistakes in implementing its rural polices, and ordinary peasants could not make ends meet. It was time to consider seriously such questions as the peasants' standard of living and to improve the party's work in the countryside.[94]

At this point, prefectural cadres in Changzhi were forced to acknowledge that the most dangerous trend of all was the continuation of "rash tendencies" in the Mutual Aid and Cooperation movement. These excesses had triggered peasants' deep distrust of cooperatives; even those who had joined up voluntarily had been alienated. Farmers had lost a significant amount of private property. In Changzhi prefecture, officials were becoming anxious about the production plan for 1953, which was clearly going to be difficult to meet; the spring sowing program was already in difficulty. Another alarming sign was the outbreak of popular religious fervor. After 1949, the old superstitions had seemingly disappeared, yet in 1953, the peasants once again began praying to emperors and gods for help. Considering all these factors, the Changzhi prefecture concluded that the undermining of the interests of the middle-ranking peasant class had shaken the foundations of the new China.[95]

Given the pioneering role of Changzhi prefecture in the Mutual Aid and Cooperation movement and the stakes that it had vested in its outcome, the prefecture's acknowledgment of conditions in the countryside indicated the severity of the situation. The spring famine that subsequently broke out in 1953 stopped the Mutual Aid and Cooperation movement in its tracks.

The "Rectification" in Spring 1953

In 1953, spring famine spread its way across China. In Shandong Province, 4 million people experienced food shortages;[96] in central–south China, in the provinces of Henan, Hubei, Guangdong, Guangxi, Hunan, and Jiangxi,

---

94. "Guanxin nongmin shenghuo, gaishan nongcun gongzuo, anding nongcun shengchan" (Take care of the peasants' living standards; improve the Party's work with the peasants and stabilize rural production) (April 23, 1953), *Jianshe*, no. 215.
95. "Xiang shengwei de san yuefen zonghe baogao."
96. *Neibu cankao*, March 25, 1953.

over 10 million people were getting by on insufficient food;[97] in east China, 16.57 million people suffered serious hunger;[98] in northwest China, 1.8 million peasants found themselves in the midst of a full-blown famine.[99] Reactions were extreme: peasants abandoned their land, fled to the cities, sold their children, starved to death, and even committed suicide. The Mutual Aid and Cooperation movement did not save Shanxi Province from the spring famine; on the contrary, the province was badly hit. In some areas of Shanxi, by April 20, 6 percent of the rural population had no food at all and an equal number had food supplies for only five more days.[100] In the seventeen villages in Tunliu County of Changzhi prefecture, 672 households could not make ends meet. In Nanxinzhuan village and three others, one child was sold, fifty-five peasants fled the district, and seventeen took to begging.[101]

Multiple factors lay behind the spring famine. Although natural disasters had affected some regions, they alone were insufficient to produce a spring famine on such a scale. Most official reports attributed the famine primarily to natural causes, yet recent research on meteorological data has shown that 1952 was a good year for Chinese agriculture, and 1953 was an average year.[102] Based on internal reports produced by the CCP, two major factors contributed to the outbreak of large-scale spring famine in 1953. The first was the Surveying Land and Fixing *Production* Quotas campaign (*chatian dingchan*), which dealt a powerful blow to peasants in the newly liberated regions (discussed in detail in Chapter 6). The other was the violence and panic generated by the Mutual Aid and Cooperation movement, especially in North China and Northeast China. Official reports could blame natural disasters for the famine, but the peasants were not fooled: it was the governments, not "heaven," that had unleashed a series of policies that had harmed them so severely. For example, peasants in Subei were furious about what was happening around them: "The people's government is a government that is killing people." Local cadres sensed that riots might break out at any time.[103]

---

97. Ibid., May 9, 1953.
98. Ibid.
99. Ibid., April 21, 1953.
100. Ibid., April 20, 1953.
101. Ibid.
102. Kenneth Walker, *Food Grain Procurement and Consumption in China*, 31.
103. *Neibu cankao*, January 22, 1953.

Even before the spring famine, the party leaders in Beijing had been fielding concerns over what was going on in the countryside. In November 1952, the Shandong provincial prosecutor filed an internal report exposing the excesses and misdeeds of local CCP cadres. He found that commandism was rampant among rural cadres and that, more often than not, it was the only method they used to implement policies. They had developed a variety of measures to impose their will on local people, like political threats, never-ending meetings with no breaks for food and rest, and the use of police and militia forces. Beatings, arrests, detention, private hearings, and forced confessions were all common. Cases were reported in which local cadres were said to have shot peasants out of line in response to a single negative comment. In addition, village cadres enforced their will by raping local women; often, a whole group of village cadres was involved—sometimes resulting in the victim's death.[104]

Appalled by the Shandong report, the Central Committee of the CCP asked other regions to conduct their own investigations. In the following months, a flow of reports reached the Central Committee, documenting a catalog of systematic abuse. In early 1953, the Agricultural Ministry in Beijing initiated a series of investigations into false production reports. On February 9, 1953, the *People's Daily* published a report exposing this kind of fraud. It became clear that inflating production figures to boost a cooperative's tally of model laborers was not a rare occurrence; it was the same story all across China, from the older liberated regions to the newer ones. It was discovered that cadres at township and county level were encouraging these activities, rather than restraining them; some even took the initiative in falsifying reports, as happened in Shanxi Province.[105]

These centralized investigations exposed a poorly disciplined rural community to the scrutiny of high-ranking CCP cadres. In response, the party launched a period of self-examination, focusing on its shortcomings in the area of rural policy. In early 1953 a new "Three-Anti" movement was launched in the countryside, this time targeting commandism, bureaucratism, and violation of the law. As this new campaign unfolded, further

---

104. "Shandong fenju jilu jiancha weiyuanhui guanyu fandui guanliao zhuyi fan-dui mingling zhuyi fandui weifa luanji de yijian de baogao" (A report and commentary by the law enforcement committee of the Shandong Party branch on anti-bureaucratism, anti-commandism and anti-lawbreaking) (November 1952), *Jianshe*, no. 197.

105. *People's Daily*, February 9, 1953.

abuses committed in the name of the Mutual Aid and Cooperation movement were uncovered and reported to Beijing. In effect, if not in design, the new Three-Anti movement acted as a brake on the anticapitalism campaign in the countryside and provided the Central Committee with the opportunity to check the "rash tendencies" they had discovered at work in the Mutual Aid and Cooperation movement.

Timing also played a role. Deeply concerned about unrest in the countryside and the peasants' resistance to party policies, the government was at pains to appease peasant farmers, especially as the spring sowing season of 1953 was about to start. The party decided to restrict the activities of the Mutual Aid and Cooperation movement so as to focus it once more on agricultural production. The North China Bureau was the first to act. On January 31, 1953, Liu Lantao, vice-secretary of the North China Bureau, issued a statement titled "A Reply to All County Committee Secretaries on the Question of [How to] Lead Agricultural Production," instructing county heads that "in terms of guiding the cooperatives, there is a tendency of rash advancement as manifested in striving for more and larger cooperatives." The tendency of "blindly going after higher forms, blindly adding elements of socialism, and expanding public assets excessively and impatiently, must be checked and rectified."[106]

In response to Liu's directive, in early February 1953 Changzhi prefecture convened a meeting to criticize these organizational abuses.[107] However, the meeting resulted in very little action. To reinforce the new policy, on March 2, 1953, the North China Bureau issued another directive titled "Rectifying the Tendency to Blind and Rash Advances in the Development of Agricultural Producers' Cooperatives." It demanded that "party committees at all levels must pay great attention to the serious consequences produced by the mistakes of leftist adventurism" and must intervene and rectify them.[108] The directive especially criticized Changzhi prefecture for its pervasive impetuousness. It demanded a halt to building new agricultural producers' cooperatives and a reassessment of all established ones.[109]

---

106. Gao Huamin, "Rectifying the Problems of Impetuosity and Rash Advance," 63.

107. "1953 nian nongye shengchan hezuoshe de jiben zongjie" (A basic summary of agricultural producers' cooperatives in Changzhi in 1953) (January 25, 1954), JMA, 124.1.1.

108. Gao Huamin, "Rectifying the Problems of Impetuosity and Rash Advance," 64.

109. "Zhengdun nongye shengchan hezuoshe zhong de mangmu maojin qiang-

It was not long before the Central Committee of the CCP took similar action. On February 15, 1953, the Central Committee issued the directive titled "A Resolution on Mutual Aid and Cooperation in Agriculture," followed soon after by the "Directive to Party Committees at all Levels on the Spring Plowing and Production." On March 26, the *People's Daily* published both documents, along with an editorial entitled "The Key to Leading Agricultural Production." These three pieces were put together as a pamphlet under the title *Guide to Current Rural Work* and published by the People's Press at the request of the Central Committee. The pamphlet was widely circulated and served as the party's official guide for those charged with leading the peasants.[110] Cadres commonly referred to the pamphlet as the "Three Documents" (*sanda wenjian*). All three pieces called for a check on the excesses of the Mutual Aid and Cooperation movement, for an end to commandism as a way of organizing the peasantry, and for encouraging farmers to produce more crops. One after another, the Three Documents raised theoretical challenges to the ideas underlying the rapid development of the Mutual Aid and Cooperation movement in 1952.

The first document in the collection, "A Resolution on Mutual Aid and Cooperation in Agriculture," acknowledged that Chinese peasants' inclination to private farming was deeply rooted and should not be ignored or simply curbed. While not denying that the party's ultimate goal was collectivization, the directive emphasized that mutual aid teams and agricultural producers' cooperatives were both still grounded in private ownership. The party must consolidate its ties with middle-ranking peasants and leave the wealthy peasants to prosper. The directive condemned both the attitude of passively "letting the peasants take their own course" and the "rash tendency" to intervene as deviations from the correct path, and it focused on attacking the latter. It emphasized the central importance of the principle of voluntarism and the principle of mutual benefit.

Coincidentally or otherwise, this document placed economic considerations at the center: the sole criterion of a successful mutual aid team or producers' cooperative should be high agricultural productivity—more than individual farmers could achieve—and increased income for its members. The directive repeated the preconditions for establishing cooperatives:

---

xiang" (Rectifying the tendency to blind and rash advances in the development of agricultural producers' cooperatives) (March 2, 1953), SPA, C54.1005.34.

110. *Nongye juan*, 24.

they should be set up at the peasants' request; have a solid basis built on mutual aid teams; and be distinguished by good leadership, peasant activism, and sufficient preparation. It further announced thirteen rules to regulate agricultural producers' cooperatives. For example, sideline work was to be encouraged and considerable autonomy was given to members, such as the right to make decisions about community funds and income distribution. It even allowed cooperatives to hire short-term laborers and technicians. In conclusion, the directive asked that private farmers be respected and treated fairly. In brief, the document vindicated the right of members to pursue their personal interest and material profits in mutual aid teams and agricultural producers' cooperatives. It was intended to depoliticize agricultural producers' cooperatives and treat them as economic entities.[111]

"A Resolution on Mutual Aid and Cooperation in Agriculture" was not well received by local cadres. One month later, the second "Directive to Party Committees at All Levels on the Spring Plowing and Production" was released. It explicitly stated, "The Central Committee requires each comrade at prefecture, county, and district level to study the Central Committee's directive on mutual aid and cooperation in agriculture." This new directive launched a blistering attack on "rash tendencies," adding a detailed list of reckless actions, most of them outlined above. It condemned the use of coercion and threats and required all party members to accept wellfounded criticism from the peasants and to rectify their leftist mistakes. It urged cadres to keep their feet on the ground when dealing with the peasants: "In forming mutual aid teams and cooperatives, don't forget to begin with the peasants' actual political consciousness and their own personal experiences, and to start from the peasants' practical needs and the existing production methods used by small producers." This directive reinstated the four freedoms (to hire laborers, to lend money, to trade, and to strengthen the peasant economy in the countryside) that had been denounced during the Three-Anti movement. In sum, this second directive made it very clear that the critical task in the countryside was the spring plowing: any action that threatened to compromise it, such as the radical activities associated

---

111. "Zhonggong zhongyang guanyu nongye shengchan huzhu hezuo de jueyi" (A resolution [by the Central Committee] on Mutual Aid and Cooperation in agriculture), *Nongye juan*, 125–135.

with the Mutual Aid and Cooperation movement, should be modified, delayed, or cancelled.[112]

The *People's Daily*'s editorial "The Key to Leading Agricultural Production" once again emphasized the dominant role of private farming and reiterated that increasing production was the priority of ordinary peasants and was what the party should focus on. The editorial devoted space to the issue of incorporating the small peasant economy into China's centralized planned economy. It reminded CCP cadres that since the small-peasant economy was very widely dispersed, incorporating it into a planned economy was a long-term task that could not be achieved in a short period. The main way of supporting peasant farmers was through reasonable commodity prices, supplemented by viable economic and political policies. The editorial denounced the practice of coercing peasants to take action according to the party's plans.[113] In essence, the editorial was asking party members to tolerate the peasants' backwardness and ignorance—a point strikingly similar to Bukharin's conviction that "the peasant should be accepted first of all for what he is, then guided along the path of self-interest toward better and more evolved social and economic structure."[114]

In several crucial respects, the Three Documents refuted the ideas of Gao Gang and Lai Ruoyu. They instructed party members to respect peasants as small producers, even at the expense of the centrally planned economy. In practice if not in intent, they also called for a halt to the rapid development of agricultural producers' cooperatives. Although it is not known who drafted them, the Three Documents were regarded as authentic pronouncements issuing from the Central Committee of the CCP. The North China Bureau immediately adopted new guidelines. On March 20, 1953, it issued the "North China Bureau's Directive on Reinforcing the Party's Guidance on Agricultural Producers' Cooperatives (Draft)," which explicitly called for "severely restricting the number of cooperatives, immediately halting the formation of new agricultural producers' cooperatives, and organizing cadres to inspect the established ones." It urged local cadres to use the

---

112. "Zhongguo gongchandang zhongyang weiyuanhui guanyu chungeng shengchan gei geji dangwei de zhishi" (A directive [from the Central Committee] to Party committees at all levels on the Spring plowing and production), *Nongye juan*, 24–29.

113. "Lingdao nongcun shengchan de guanjian suozai" (The key to leading agricultural production), *People's Daily*, March 26, 1953.

114. Moshe Lewin, *Russian Peasants and Soviet Power*, 335.

criteria set out in the "Resolution on Mutual Aid and Cooperation in Agriculture" to examine all existing cooperatives, one by one. Those that failed to meet all the criteria should be discontinued and converted back to mutual aid teams.[115] To ensure that local cadres honored these directives, on April 6, Liu Lantao took the unusual step of writing to county heads in Changzhi prefecture, asking that each of them report to him on their progress.[116]

By this time, former provincial secretary Lai Ruoyu had left Shanxi to take up a new post in Beijing. Lacking a leader like Lai who could stand up to Liu Lantao, Shanxi provincial leaders complied with the North China Bureau's directives, even though they were not fully convinced. On March 1, vice-secretary Tao Lujia placed a ban on the building of new collective farms in Shanxi and asked his colleagues to respect the diversity and conservative nature of the small-peasant farmers.[117] A document dated March 26 shows that Tao was still planning to establish 2,500 new producers' cooperatives in Shanxi, but that he would proceed with caution.[118]

However, a week later on April 3, the Shanxi party branch abruptly drafted "An Urgent Directive on Inspecting Agricultural Producers' Cooperatives" and distributed it to the counties. This directive instructed party heads at all levels to follow the orders of the North China Bureau and to carry out their inspections in person. The language used in this urgent directive was unusually harsh, even crude. It urged cadres who had not yet acted to disband unauthorized cooperatives to do so immediately and firmly: "If these [unauthorized cooperatives] are converted [to mutual aid teams] now, it will be easier to wipe one's arse; if not, in the future it will be very difficult to wipe an outsized arse."[119] This abrasive tone re-

---

115. "Huabeiju guanyu jiaqiang dang dui nongye shengchan hezuoshe de lingdao de zhishi" (The North China Bureau's directive on reinforcing the Party's guidance on agricultural producers' cooperatives) (March 20, 1953), SPA, C54.1005.34.
116. The reports from various county heads to Liu Lantao are held in JMA, 146.1.1.
117. Tao Lujia, "Tao Lujia zai di, zhuan lianxi huiyi shang de jielun" (Tao Lujia's concluding remarks at the conference of prefectures), in *Shanxi sheng nongye hezuo shi wenjian huibian juan*, 330–331.
118. Ibid., 331.
119. "Guanyu zhengdun nongye shengchan hezuoshe de jinji zhishi" (An urgent directive on inspecting agricultural producers' cooperatives) (April 3, 1953), SPA, C54.1005.34.

vealed both the pressures from above and the reluctance, if not resistance, shown by lower-ranking cadres to implement the rectification directives.

In late March 1953, Changzhi prefecture convened a meeting of county heads to discuss the rectification campaign under the rubric, "Stopping Building the New, Inspecting and Rectifying [the Old], Consolidating and Improving." Following the meeting, it dispatched 125 district cadres to villages to begin their inspections. In early April, each county in Changzhi convened cadre meetings at county, district, and village levels to study the Three Documents.[120]

The campaign was carried out in great haste. According to a report issued by the prefecture, in just twenty days it had completed a comprehensive inspection of 1,349 cooperatives, of which 338 were found to be unauthorized. Oversized cooperatives were divided into smaller units, and peasants were given the option to withdraw. In dealing with collectivized livestock and tools, the principle of "not infringing on the peasants' personal interests while at the same time facilitating the management of the cooperatives" was upheld, although the report did not elaborate on how such inherently contradictory principles were to be harmonized. The report concluded that most peasants were choosing to stay in cooperatives or mutual aid teams of their own volition; that their incentives to work had been successfully restored; and that local cadres, after studying the Three Documents, had made substantial improvements in their political consciousness and work methods. In the end, the Changzhi report warned that when combating "leftist" errors, it was equally important to avoid the "rightist" error of failing to organize the peasants.[121]

However, Tao Lujia remained unconvinced by these reports. On May 4, 1953, he undertook a critical review of the history of the Mutual Aid and Cooperation movement in Shanxi. He acknowledged that cadres at various levels had overstated increases in agricultural production, that the success of the first ten experimental cooperatives in Changzhi prefecture had been exaggerated, and that the peasants' enthusiasm for collective labor had been overestimated. Tao Lujia also acknowledged that from the very be-

---

120. "Guanyu xianweihui hou jinyibu jiuzheng huzhu hezuo yundong zhong mangmu maojin qingxiang de zonghe baogao" (On further rectifying rash tendencies in the mutual aid and cooperation movement following the county conference) (April 15, 1953), JMA, 1.1.50.

121. Ibid.

ginning party cadres in Shanxi had failed to take opposing opinions into account, and that "rash tendencies" were thus an outgrowth of the mentality exhibited by many rural cadres. Tao Lujia asked rural cadres to focus on agricultural production and downplay the ideological role of mutual aid teams and cooperatives. He also warned them against conducting a merely superficial education program on socialism, as had occurred in 1952. Tao Lujia told cadres that they were to undertake intensive study of the Three Documents and to work on increasing agricultural productivity.[122]

Tao Lujia's critical remarks cast a pall over Shanxi's quest for collectivization over the previous three years. It seemed as if Shanxi's cadres were about to give up their pioneering role in the agricultural sector and were ready to comply with the North China Bureau's new set of demands. After learning of the evidence that set out how model laborers and cooperative heads had falsified production data, Tao had good reason to act as he did.

Doctored Production Reports

When spring famine broke out across China in 1953, the steep drop in agricultural production in the year was irrefutable. Thus the high productivity figures claimed by model mutual aid teams and cooperatives were put in question. Indeed, as early as December 1952, Shanxi provincial leaders had noticed a number of falsified accounts and issued a directive condemning misreporting. It directed that any model laborer or cadre who had intentionally falsified an organization's accounts or intentionally covered up falsified reports would be severely censured, and in serious cases punished. This directive questioned the practice of only praising, never censuring, model laborers, and it encouraged cadres to keep a close watch on all model laborers under their control.[123]

As the rectification campaign in 1953 proceeded, a large number of falsified reports were discovered. The situation was especially grave in Wuxiang County. In April, thirteen producers' cooperatives in Wuxiang, in-

---

122. Tao Lujia, "Zai 190 ci sheng changwei shang de fayan," 333–336.

123. "Huabeiju zhuanpi shanxi shengwei guanyu zhengque zhixing peiyang nongye laodong mofan zhengce de jueding" (The North China Bureau's comments on Shanxi's decision on the right way of educating agricultural model laborers) (December 19, 1952), *Huibian*, 629–630.

cluding the well-known Wang Jinyun cooperative, were discovered to have falsified their accounts.[124] By June 1953, 135 out of 408 units that had been awarded in 1952 were exposed as having fabricated production data. It was likely that these cases were merely the tip of the iceberg. Nearly all the county's celebrated model laborers were involved—falsifying reports had become endemic across the region. Local residents all knew about the practice; as they said, "From the villages to central government, one level is cheating another." The peasants reacted to the disclosures with an air of resignation: "It is useless—you are only cheating yourself." Cadres at district and county levels were heavily implicated in the scam; in many cases, they were controlling things behind the scenes.[125]

Li Shunda cooperative offers a typical example of how production figures were manipulated. An official report showed that the cooperative's unit yield in 1952 was 442 catties per mu. How was this figure determined? In the fall of 1952, an investigation team composed of cadres from Shanxi Province, Changzhi prefecture, and several neighboring counties was dispatched to Li Shunda cooperative to check its production levels. As the crop had not yet been fully harvested, the investigators estimated an average unit yield of 442 catties per mu. To make Li Shunda eligible for the national competition for high-producing model laborers, chief county cadre Chen Jie used this estimated figure as the cooperative's actual yield and submitted it to Shanxi Province. As a result, Li Shunda won top prize in that year's contest. However, it turned out that the eventual yield was only at best 372 catties per mu. Chen Jie decided to conceal this fact, arguing that "if we correct the figure, Shunda's reputation throughout the nation would be tarnished."[126]

In the first round of "checking falsified accounts" conducted by cadres from the same county in April 1953, Chen Jie managed to have Li Shunda cooperative spared. In May, when the Agricultural Ministry in Beijing sent its own agents to investigate, Chen Jie worked with the cooperative's treasurer and other county cadres to doctor the old accounts and finally got the cooperative through the inspection. Only in June, when Changzhi prefec-

124. "Guanyu jiefa jibao fengchan qingkuang de buchong baogao ji chuli yijian" (Additional reports and comments on the problems of exposing falsified accounts of grain harvests) (July 4, 1953), JMA, 1.1.124.

125. *Neibu cankao*, May 14, 1953.

126. Ibid., July 23, 1953.

ture dispatched cadres to settle the issue of compensation for collectivized livestock and to finalize a new annual production plan that aimed at an even higher yield, did Chen Jie and Li Shunda confess their deception.[127] In their case, their dishonesty had gone undetected during several rounds of inspections. It was only exposed when the material interests of cooperative members came to the fore.

Well aware of the degree of deception being practiced, the Changzhi prefecture took steps that prevented the counties from punishing the perpetrators. It was emphasized that only those who had *intentionally* cheated the party *and* had very bad reputations *and* were opposed by the masses were to forfeit the title of model laborer and to return their prizes; in most cases, a public apology was the only punishment sought. In the event, most model laborers came through the scandal unscathed. The principle enunciated by Changzhi prefecture was "to protect and nurture model laborers, stand by them, educate them, and correct them."[128] Contrary to the directives issued by Shanxi Province, falsifying accounts was rarely punished in practice. At this time, peasants were not yet required to pay additional taxes for increases in production, whether claimed or real. However, it would not be long before model laborers, together with millions of Chinese peasant farmers, would pay a heavy price for their inflated harvests, as discussed in the next chapter.

Shanxi's peasant activists learned a number of important lessons from this episode. First, cadres at prefecture level were usually unwilling to punish model laborers, unless the latter had committed very serious violations. Second, without strong pressure from above, prefectural cadres seldom focused on unfavorable circumstances in the areas under their control. Because cadres dispatched from the townships, and even those of higher ranks, tended to encourage farmers to exaggerate the yields, the same officials would have found it almost impossible to stop peasants from engaging in the very behavior that they had encouraged. Third, local governments, for whom rural stability was a major concern, were willing to aid those who had suffered from "progressing too fast" if they had the resources at their disposal.

---

127. Ibid.
128. "Guanyu jiefa jiabao fengchan qingkuang de buchong baogao ji chuli yijian."

Conclusion

This chapter has demonstrated how the Mutual Aid and Cooperation movement was profoundly affected by the Three-Anti movement, leading to a change in its nature and direction. Between summer 1952 and spring 1953 the Mutual Aid and Cooperation movement was politicized. Often using coercion and even violence, rural cadres forced peasant farmers to surrender their private property to form agricultural producers' cooperatives. The events that unfolded in Shanxi Province exemplified the ways in which local cadres responded to political pressure from above.

By the spring of 1953, the damage done to China's agricultural and economic fabric was widespread and severe. A major spring famine wreaked havoc across the nation. In response, the Central Committee of the CCP sought to curb the "excesses" of the Mutual Aid and Cooperation movement and issued as a corrective measure the Three Documents, which were studied in Beijing and in villages all across China. While not overtly questioning the theoretical basis of the movement, the party's rectification campaign placed substantial constraints on the movement and went a long way to vindicating the long-held desire of China's peasant farmers to be small producers. Gao Gang's anticapitalist manifesto was thrown out, the peasants' character as small producers was once again acknowledged, and the old Three-Anti movement was replaced by the new Three-Anti movement, which aimed at protecting peasants from the abuses meted out to them by rural cadres. The political winds appeared to have changed direction completely.

At this juncture, Gao Gang was promoted to the chair of the Central Planning Committee and was relocated from Northeast China to Beijing. Preoccupied with the need to develop China's heavy industry, he no longer had much to say about the peasants. Lai Ruoyu was also transferred out of Shanxi Province and began working for the National Labor Union Department. Shanxi's provincial leaders had lost their enthusiasm for the Mutual Aid and Cooperation movement; at least, they no longer dared to challenge the flow of central directives that sought to curb the movement. Agricultural production rather than socialist ideology became the chief priority of the CCP's rural policy. In the summer of 1953 the Mutual Aid and Cooperation movement had virtually come to a standstill. It seemed that the party leaders had decided to postpone the peasants' march toward socialism and give them a rest break. The question to be asked in the final chapter is, Did they succeed?

6

The Politics of Grain

<hr style="width:30%" />

The peasants are living in hell while the workers are living in heaven.

—liberal intellectual Liang Shuming, 1953[1]

The peasants have appalling spontaneous tendencies.

—CCP member Li Xiannian during the grain crisis of 1953[2]

If necessary, kill people.

—Liu Lantao's comment in the implementation of the
"United Purchase, United Sell" policy, 1953[3]

Resistance to the Rectification Campaign

At first sight, the dossier known as the Three Documents appeared to be well balanced. It demanded that those poorly run cooperatives be disbanded, that inefficient ones be overhauled, and that well-founded ones be

<hr style="width:25%" />

1. Li Hua-yu, *Mao and the Economic Stalinization of China,* 140. For a study of Liang Shuming, see Guy Alitto, *The Last Confucian.* Liang Shuming's remarks accurately summarized conditions in the countryside as reflected in documents in local archives uncovered during my research for this book.

2. Shangyebu dangdai liangshi gongzuo bianji bu, *Dangdai liangshi gongzuo shiliao,* 168.

3. Ibid., 166.

consolidated. The voluntary principle was to be honored, and members were allowed to withdraw at any time, along with their assets. Yet, considering that so much property had been pooled, so much zeal and emotion invested, and in many cases so much debt accumulated, any initiative at this stage would arouse reactions and expose the personal interests of all involved. Rectification was not going to be an easy task.

In practice, the more balanced the policies were, the more difficult it proved to be to implement them. For most local cadres, understanding the Three Documents was a challenge in itself. To find out how much rural cadres had learned from their study of the dossier, several prefectures in Shanxi Province did tests. The scores were surprisingly low. For example, of 193 cadres in Wutai County, only 19 passed the test; 177 did not know the difference between mutual aid teams, agricultural producers' cooperatives, and collective farms. Some cadres had never even heard of the "Three Documents." Of forty cadres from Yucheng prefecture, only two had read the "Directive to Party Committees at All Levels on the Spring Plowing and Production." In addition to factors such as low literacy and insufficient study time, lack of motivation also contributed to this poor level of performance.[4]

According to Changzhi prefecture's reports, the rectification campaign was proceeding smoothly. However, the report drafted by "the spring plowing inspection team," dispatched by the provincial authorities, demonstrated otherwise. In Changzhi, rural cadres resisted the rectification campaign by instinct. While leading cadres from the counties did study the Three Documents, most cadres at district level failed to understand the directives at all. Confusion prevailed. Fearing that they would be labeled as rightists who had "left the peasants to their own devices," many rural cadres were unwilling to step in and rectify leftist mistakes. Deviation from the official line was common. For example, in Pingshun and Gaoping counties cooperative heads returned collectivized livestock to its former owners, a point that the Three Documents had insisted on. However, they retained other public assets, controlled their members' trading activity, and continued to attack the small-peasant economy. In Qin, Yangcheng, and Jincheng counties, county heads were still wavering on whether or not to support the rectification campaign and thus acted slowly and reluctantly. For example, in Wuxiang County various methods were devised to intimidate households that had

---

4. *Neibu cankao*, June 22, 1953.

asked to exit. In addition, for good reasons, rural cadres often claimed that their cooperatives were well founded and had no problems. Some did not want to lose their status as model laborers and the rewards; others simply did not want to lose face. Bolder ones complained to their superiors, "You shit, we wipe your arse. Only your words matter. I cannot take back what I have said [to the peasants]. You go ahead and make the correction."[5]

In reality, conditions were complicated. In many cases, collectivized livestock had died or been sold off, farm implements had worn out, fertilizers had been ready mixed for application, and land had been sown collectively. More often than not, agricultural producers' cooperatives were in deep debt, so what share of the debt should each farmer shoulder?[6] Such conflicts were routinely papered over. For example, after Hedong cooperative in Jincheng County halted its activities, conditions there were extremely chaotic, yet this did not stop the village head from stating in his report to the district, "We did well."[7]

Resistance to the rectification movement was by no means limited to Shanxi Province. For example, in Hebei Province, many cadres were angry about the campaign. As they saw it, they had made enormous efforts to persuade or coerce peasants to form producers' cooperatives. Now, because of these new orders from above, their efforts had all been in vain. They felt ashamed, even betrayed, and reacted with cynicism:

- "Is it legal to form a cooperative? If it is legal, we are going to hold on—if not, take me to court."
- "If you say so, it's a cooperative; if you don't say so, it's a mutual aid team. It is what it is and I'm not going to change it."
- "If we're converting [cooperatives] to mutual aid teams now, I won't be setting up any more cooperatives for the rest of my life. And I won't allow my sons to form one either."[8]

---

5. "Guanyu xianweihui hou jinyibu jiuzheng huzhu hezuo yundong zhong mangmu maojin qingxiang de zonghe baogao."

6. Ye Yangbing, *Zhongguo nongye hezuohua yundong yanjiu*, 270.

7. "Guanyu changzhi qu jiuzheng huzhu yundong zhong mangmu maojin qingxiang qingkuang yu cunzai de wenti" (Report on the problems and circumstances involved in rectifying rash tendencies in the mutual aid and cooperation movement in Changzhi prefecture) (May 13, 1953), SPA, C29.1.16.

8. Ye Yangbing, *Zhongguo nongye hezuohua yundong yanjiu*, 271.

In brief, correcting reckless actions in the Mutual Aid and Cooperation movement required much more than simply acknowledging errors. Some local cadres were concerned that because there were so many problems waiting to be solved, it was better not to tackle them immediately. Some of the concerns emanating from below were well grounded, such as the fear that if livestock were returned to their owners, they might be sold or slaughtered on the spot, with predictably adverse effects on agricultural production. However, such concerns fell on deaf ears.[9]

The resistance to the rectification did not come entirely from below. In Beijing, discontent was also brewing. In November 1952, the CCP decided to set up the central Rural Work Department to take charge of the party's rural strategies, Mao personally promoted Deng Zihui to serve the director. At the second National Rural Work Conference on April 18, 1953, Deng Zihui argued that agricultural producers' cooperatives should be the norm in the older liberated regions and that cadres in the newly liberated areas should make greater efforts to assist established mutual aid teams and to prepare them for cooperatives. While Deng Zihui criticized the "rash tendencies" that had developed in the Mutual Aid and Cooperation movement, he supported the acceleration of the movement. For him, the key goal of the first and second five-year plans was the establishment of agricultural producers' cooperatives.[10] He extolled the virtues of efficient cooperatives and warned against simply disbanding poorly run units. Deng openly asserted that the notion of "ensuring private ownership" was wrong, and he opposed the unqualified encouragement of the "four freedoms."[11]

Deng Zihui was to become the leading Communist official in charge of rural issues. In 1955, he would bravely confront Mao Zedong over Mao's plans to push the peasants into advanced agricultural producers' cooperatives that resembled Soviet collective farms, and he risked his political career in defense of China's peasants, as the epilogue will discuss. Historians

---

9. "Guanyu xianweihui hou jinyibu jiuzheng huzhu hezuo yundong zhong mangmu maojin qingxiang de zonghe baogao."

10. Deng Zihui, "Dui nongye hezuohua yundong de zhidao yuanze" (Principles for guiding the mutual aid and cooperation movement) (April 18, 1953), *Nongye juan*, 135–144.

11. Deng Zihui, "Deng Zihui zai quanguo diyici nongcun gongzuo huiyi shang de zongjie baogao" (A summary report by Deng Zihui of the first national conference on rural work (April 23, 1953), Ibid., 34–50.

have lauded him as a propeasant and anti-cooperativization activist. As a result, the likelihood that Deng Zihui at one time was a strong supporter of Mao has been overlooked. However, if Deng Zihui had not supported Mao in the beginning, why did Mao Zedong choose him in the first place? Deng's addresses in April 1953 confirm this speculation. The divergence between Deng's sentiments expressed in his speeches and the Three Documents reflected a split among the CCP leadership, with Mao Zedong and Deng Zihui on one side, and other leaders, probably including Liu Shaoqi and Bo Yibo, on the other. Above all, the biggest obstacle to the rectification campaign was Mao Zedong himself.

Between 1952 and 1953, Mao Zedong devoted himself to promoting "the General Line for Socialist Transition" (the General Line).[12] As Mao took a firm position on the necessity and urgency of transforming China into a socialist country, he became more obsessed with his vision of China's socialist future, and his optimism about that future grew accordingly. Several other factors also helped foster his sanguine outlook. In October 1952, Soviet Politburo member Georgy Malenkov announced that the Soviet Union had solved the grain problems through collectivization. Mao welcomed the news and, in October 1953, used it to encourage the CCP to adopt similar policies.[13] In February 1953, Mao had revised the "Resolution on Mutual Aid and Cooperation in Agriculture" which had originally been promulgated in December 1951. In place of setting mechanization as the precondition for collectivization, the text now stated that collectivization could begin "with the complete consent of the peasants and suitable economic conditions," which in effect expanded the option to begin collectivization whenever peasants wished.[14] In the 1920s, the Soviet Union had witnessed the deification of the machine.[15] In the relative absence of a mechanized agricultural regime in China, Mao and his followers deified the policy of "getting peasants organized."

In February 1953, when a flood of negative reports on the Mutual Aid

---

12. Why Mao chose this particular time to promote this ideological program has been the subject of much research in China and is not a topic that can be explored fully here. The most recent contribution is Li Hua-yu's *Mao and the Economic Stalinization of China*.

13. Ibid., 163.

14. Ibid., 124.

15. Moshe Lewin, *Russian Peasants and Soviet Power*, 366.

and Cooperation movement was reaching Beijing, Mao launched his first formal inspection tour of South China since 1949. As he traveled from place to place in his personal train, Mao met with party leaders at all levels as well as with ordinary Chinese. He learned—or more accurately, was supposed to learn—about the negative as well as positive aspects of mutual aid teams and agricultural producers' cooperatives. He was told by local cadres that the idea of mutual aid teams had become firmly rooted in the minds of the people.[16] Mao was also told that experimental agricultural producers' cooperatives in Xingtai prefecture had proved successful. Mao was delighted to hear these reports and commented, "Mutual aid and cooperation is better than farming on one's own," and also, "It is possible to achieve collectivization without mechanization, and therefore China does not have to follow the Soviet way of doing things."[17]

The first directive in the Three Documents dossier was issued by the Central Committee of the CCP on February 15, the same day Mao Zedong was due to start his tour of South China. The other two documents were released after Mao had returned to Beijing. These documents were not in keeping with the optimism that had been confirmed in Mao's mind during the tour—their contents stood in stark contrast to what he had observed with his own eyes. Shortly afterward, in April 1953, the Central Committee instructed party members to study the *Short Course*. Two days later, this directive appeared in the *People's Daily*, sending a clear signal to the nation that precisely that form of Stalinism—and Stalin's path to socialism—was favored by the party.[18] The political and economic ideology manifested in the *Short Course* dominated Mao's thinking. By June 1953, Mao had his vision of China's transition to socialism, drawn mainly from the key features of the Stalinist road to socialism as presented in *Short Course*, ready: industrialization, collectivization in the countryside, and an all-out war on the capitalist economy.[19]

In summer 1953 Mao started to push for this agenda, first attacking the notion of preserving the capitalist economy. On June 15, 1953, at a Politburo meeting, Mao took a hard line, criticizing what he characterized as three

16. Li Hua-yu, *Mao and the Economic Stalinization of China*, 127; Zhang Yumei, "Wo xiang Mao zhuxi huibao nongye hezuohua," 104.

17. Zhang Yumei, "Wo xiang Mao zhuxi huibao nongye hezuohua."

18. Li Hua-yu, *Mao and the Economic Stalinization of China*, 132.

19. Ibid., 134.

"rightist deviations"—"the consolidation of the New Democratic Order," "walking toward socialism from New Democracy," and "protecting private property" in the countryside. Mao also attacked the notion of the small-peasant economy and condemned those who supported it. In effect, he was refuting the fundamental ideas underlying the Three Documents.[20] From June to August 1953, the National Conference on Financial and Economic Work was convened in Beijing. Mao announced that the main purpose of the conference was to discuss the General Line and to redirect the thinking of the party leadership from building an economy based on New Democracy to making an immediate transition to socialism.

In addition to citing Lenin and Stalin, Mao enlisted the help of Gao Gang to make an initial attack on those leaders who disagreed with Mao's economic agenda, mainly Liu Shaoqi and Bo Yibo, both of whom already had a history of conflict with Gao Gang. Although most senior party figures at the conference were skeptical about the General Line, after two months of persuasion and coercion they acquiesced. In fall 1953, Mao won acceptance for the General Line from the party's top leaders.

Mao's next move was to "consult" with leading non-Communist national figures and business leaders. In a meeting of the Chinese People's Political Consultative Conference held in September 1953, Mao released his plan. Liang Shuming, a well-known liberal scholar who had conducted extensive social experiments in rural China prior to 1949, questioned Mao's General Line. Liang made two memorable critiques of the party's rural policy: he asserted that "the peasants are living in hell while the workers are living in heaven," and he believed that the party had forgotten the peasants.[21] Stung by Liang's public rebuttal of his position, Mao immediately launched a brutal counterattack. This response was also designed to suppress dissent by creating an atmosphere of intolerance.[22] Ironically, while Liang was blaming Mao and the party for having forgotten the peasants, Mao was blaming the peasants for having forgotten the party.[23] Liang's eloquent defense of the peasants triggered a knee-jerk response in Mao. Two years earlier in fall 1951, Mao had accommodated the novelist Zhao Shuli's objections to the Draft (see Chapter 3); however, in September 1953, con-

---

20. Ibid., 132–139.
21. Ibid, 140.
22. Li Hua-yu, *Mao and the Economic Stalinization of China*, 141.
23. Feng Xianzhi and Jin Chongji, *Mao Zedong zhuan*, 355–356.

vinced by what he had been shown by local cadres with a stake in the status quo, Mao was no longer open to ideas emanating from people he described as "the discontented."

Soviet comrades also contributed to Mao's unfolding plans. On September 7, 1953, Khrushchev drafted a report on measures that aimed at reforming Soviet agriculture. Approving the report and acknowledging both the positive and negative features of collectivization, the Communist Party of the Soviet Union (CPSU) decided to maintain collectivization and to enhance it. Despite Mao's determination to find a distinctively Chinese road to socialism, he must have felt encouraged by the Soviet decision to maintain the collective system that Stalin had established several decades earlier.[24]

As we have seen, most central government officials accepted Mao's grand vision with a certain amount of reluctance. It seemed that they lacked the enthusiasm to carry it out. What Mao Zedong needed was a platform from which to announce formally his plans and then to have them implemented with the full range of resources and administrative powers at his disposal. The grain crisis that hit China in the summer of 1953 provided him with a timely opportunity to roll out his plans. Mao was not alone among CCP leaders in becoming increasingly disenchanted with the Chinese peasantry over the years. In the party's eyes, the peasants had failed to supply the CCP with sufficient grain for the needs of the state. The following section examines the politics of supply and demand of grain under the PRC.

The Politics of Grain

As Charles Tilly points out, controlling the food supply is crucial in statebuilding.[25] In the CCP's view, the peasants' primary function was to supply the state and particularly the cities with grain. There can be no doubt that after 1949, grain production formed the most important bond between the CCP-led state and Chinese peasants. Unfortunately, this subject is understudied, mostly as a result of a dearth of reliable statistics.[26]

---

24. Li Hua-yu, *Mao and the Economic Stalinization of China*, 163.

25. Charles Tilly, *The Formation of National States in Western Europe*.

26. Scholars have focused mostly on issues relating to grain production during the Great Leap Forward and have in general neglected the early years. One of the best studies of the subject is Kenneth Walker, *Food Grain Procurement and Con-*

Two questions are often asked in relation to grain production: How much grain did peasant farmers actually produce? How much grain did the state collect? These two seemingly simple questions are not at all easy to answer. Details about the quantity of grain production and taxes were considered sensitive, risking giving rise to accusations that the party was exploiting the peasants. Numbers from different sources did not add up to commonly accepted figures. Scholars have long questioned the accuracy of statistics published by the Chinese governments, not to mention the possibility that even the CCP did not know the real numbers given the widespread inflation of data in reports as already discussed above. While retaining a healthy skepticism regarding the accuracy of the statistics examined, this chapter focuses on *relative* figures, analyzing significant patterns and changes over time. Statistics are from two resources, *Zhongguo nongmin fudanshi* and *Neibu cankao*.[27] The former was a multivolume project sponsored by the Chinese government, and thus was granted special access to the CCP's internal archives; the latter was aimed to provide unfiltered information for high-ranking party members.

First we examine the kinds of taxes levied on peasant producers by the CCP. Between 1949 and 1951, the CCP attempted to levy the regular state tax (*zhengshui*) based on how much peasants had produced. In addition to that tax, a "local surcharge" was added, ranging from 15 to 25 percent of the state tax, to finance the operation of village and township administration. Both were categorized as state agricultural taxes (*gongliang*). In addition to these levies, local governments were empowered to impose miscellaneous taxes on the peasants (*difang tanpai*), which were known in various forms and by a number of names: an "education grain" tax, donations, levies on local irrigation projects, expenses deducted for local ceremonies, and so on. These miscellaneous taxes were not counted as part of the state agricultural tax, which made it difficult for the central government to know what they were let alone control their collection and use. This was important because they could be extremely high. For example, an investigation into thirty townships in eight provinces in 1951 showed that on average, miscellaneous taxes constituted 24 percent of state agricultural taxes; in extreme cases they

---

sumption in China, although it has little to say about the situation pre-1954. A more recent study is Liming Wang and John Davis, *China's Grain Economy*.

27. Zhongguo nongmin fudanshi bianji weiyuan hui, *Zhongguo nongmin fudanshi*.

could exceed the state tax by as much as 460 percent.[28] Besides state and local taxes on agricultural products, the state also charged taxes on transactions such as the sale of craft work or farm animals, which were not categorized as agricultural taxes.

Supplementary to these grain and other taxes, the CCP also purchased grain on the market at prices set by the government, known as "state-purchased grain" or grain procurement. The CCP established the China National Grain Corporation to take charge of the purchase and the sale of grain in the market.

The second question to be considered is: Beyond the stipulated amounts of taxes, how much grain did the state actually collect? The CCP kept its grain-related records according to fiscal years, running from July 1 to the end of June the following year. In the new government's first fiscal year, 1949–1950, tax collection proved to be a difficult exercise. Military expenditure remained extremely high, and the demand for grain in the cities was critical. Although the CCP planned to collect 29.2 billion catties in grain tax, it failed to meet this goal and ended up with only 24.8 billion catties. The older liberated regions were the first to come under a heavy taxation regime. Even party cadres admitted that peasants living in these areas had made great sacrifices to ensure victory for the CCP. As the Communist armies marched south and conquered new territory, the party turned to the newly liberated peasants for their grain. While the army commanders who entered these areas likely knew little about their inhabitants, they did not hesitate to set ambitious goals and push the peasants hard. The People's Liberation Army's (PLA) advance into Southwest China, including Guizhou, Yunnan, and Sichuan provinces, provides a typical case study of this phenomenon.[29]

It took the liberation army only fifty-seven days to gain control over Southwest China, from November 1949 to December 1949. The initial takeover was smooth, and the majority of local residents accepted the new CCP government without protest. Only sporadic cases of local opposition were reported. Deng Xiaoping, who took charge of the administration of the re-

---

28. Ibid., vol. 4, 110.

29. As the result of being granted special access to classified local archives, Chinese scholar Wang Haiguang recently published a valuable study of the relationship between taxation and peasant rebellions in 1950. Wang Haiguang, "Minbian yu 'feiluan.'"

gion, was optimistic. But before long the relationship between the CCP and local residents soured as the new government began demanding grain from the peasants.

Beijing asked for 2 billion catties of grain from the southwest—the same amount as the Guomindang had levied in agricultural taxes there. But the regular tax season—the summer and fall—had passed, and in many counties, the Guomindang had already collected agricultural taxes; the peasants had nothing left but grain for their own sustenance, so-called mouth grain (*kouliang*). Deng Xiaoping, preoccupied with the urgent need for grain both in Beijing and in his own administrative region, doubled the projected tax to 4 billion catties. The tax burden was intended to be imposed according to the ability to pay. To meet the new goal, CCP cadres, most of whom were outsiders, coerced landlords, rich peasants, middle-ranking peasants, and even poor peasants to give up their grain.

This approach triggered massive resistance. By the end of February 1950, bands of rebels were active everywhere in the southwest. The situation was particularly serious in Guizhou Province where, over 460 large gangs roamed the countryside, involving more than one hundred thousand insurgents. Using slogans like "Beat the CCP and don't pay taxes for three years" and "We would rather fight to the death than starve," local residents blocked roads, hijacked cars, killed CCP's grain collection teams, murdered local party officials, and even stormed government headquarters in various counties. Of the seventy-nine counties in Guizhou Province, gangs and rebel groups took over thirty-one. In the next two months, over two thousand CCP soldiers and officials were killed in Guizhou alone. Similar rebellions broke out in Sichuan and Yunnan provinces. These tax revolts were finally put down by the PLA.[30]

Despite the turmoil in the countryside, Deng Xiaoping was unwilling to lower the tax threshold. He believed that 4 billion catties of grain amounted to less than one-fifth of farmers' total yield and was a lesser amount than the Guomindang had collected in the past. He simply blamed the peasants, especially landlords, for hoarding grain. By May 1950, the tax collection season was over, accompanied by much bloodshed, but only 40 percent of the projected total had been achieved. Faced with the reality of the situation, Deng Xiaoping eventually lowered the figure to 3 billion catties and gave

---

30. Ibid.

farmers a period of grace before they would have to hand over any out-standing dues following the 1950 summer harvest.[31]

Deng Xiaoping was certainly not pleased by the failure of his tax scheme. For reasons that remain unclear, he believed that landlords in the southwest had held back 8 billion catties of grain and that they had simply refused to turn it over. Deng concluded that this group was inadequately taxed and had engaged in a large amount of clandestine cultivation. Surviving official documents, however, indicate that on average, rich peasants in the south-west handed over 223 catties of grain per person in state taxes and landlords turned in 780 catties per person. Given that the average grain holding was 521 catties per person per year in Sichuan Province, and likely lower in Guizhou, the tax burden on rich peasants and landlords was anything but light.[32] Nonetheless, Deng refused to consider the possibility that he had over-estimated grain output in the southwest and continued to blame the peasants for hoarding surplus grain. This mentality was not rare among CCP leaders.

What happened in the southwest was also not exceptional. In early 1950, rebellion and armed resistance were widely reported in the newly liberated regions. Much of this opposition arose not during the military campaigns, but after the battles were over and the party had implemented its taxation policies.[33] While Chinese scholarship has traditionally blamed the Guomin-dang for these outbreaks, recent research points to the CCP's grain expro-priation policy as the main cause.[34] This first post-1949 encounter between peasant farmers and the CCP erupted in a conflict over grain, an indicator of stormy times ahead.

In 1950, the CCP developed two separate tax regimes. In the older liber-ated regions where land reform had been completed and few if any land-lords remained, a proportional tax was levied. Tax rates ranged between 15 and 25 percent of the output, varying by region. In the newly liberated areas, a progressive tax was levied, based on class status. Tax rates for landlords ranged from 35 to 50 percent, and it was not uncommon for landlords to

31. Ibid.

32. Ibid.

33. Shangyebu dangdai liangshi gongzuo bianji bu, *Dangdai liangshi gongzuo shiliao*, 85.

34. Wang Haiguang, "Minbian yu 'feiluan.'"

surrender half or more of their output in taxes.[35] In extreme cases, landlords were required to pay taxes that exceeded their total production.[36] Rich peasants were usually taxed at 20 to 40 percent of their production. Middle-ranking peasants paid 10 to 15 percent; tax rates for poor farmers were between 0 and 8 percent. Local administrations had a virtually free hand when it came to appropriating landlords' property. As planned, landlords and rich peasants shouldered most of the tax burden. Such a progressive tax system itself constituted land reform of a kind: landlords strove to change their class status by selling land, by simply giving it away, or by dividing family plots into smaller units.[37]

When the CCP began setting its taxation goals for the fiscal year 1950–1951, the leadership agreed to reduce agricultural taxes and give farmers some breathing space. With his persistent disdain for taxation consistent with a long Chinese tradition of favoring light governance, Mao Zedong in particular pressed for the formal agricultural tax rate to be lowered. Chen Yun, the head of the Financial and Economic Committee, which was responsible for drawing up the national budget, confirmed that the state's agricultural tax would not be increased during the next three to five years. He suggested setting the 1950 tax take at 20 billion catties, over 10 percent less than the amount collected in 1949.[38] Presumably in response to pressure to balance the budget, the figure was later raised to 25.7 billion.

In September 1950, the State Council released new tax regulations, which gave some relief to landlords and wealthy peasants. It capped taxes for landlords at 50 percent, for rich peasants at 25 percent, for middle peasants at 15 percent, and for poor peasants at 10 percent. The new regulations provided that taxes would be levied only on agricultural products and would exclude sideline income and income earned from raising livestock.[39] Confident of increasing grain production, the CCP offered incentives to farmers to plant cash crops, especially cotton; these included applying a uniform tax

35. Zhongguo nongmin fudanshi bianji weiyuan hui, *Zhongguo nongmin fudanshi*, vol. 4, 34–35.
36. *Neibu cankao*, multiple issues 1952.
37. Xiaojia Hou's discussion with Cao Shuji, Shanghai, May 2011.
38. Zhongguo nongmin fudanshi bianji weiyuan hui, *Zhongguo nongmin fudanshi*, vol. 4, 87.
39. Ibid., 42.

rate for cash crops and grain, increasing the value of cotton as compared to grain, and collecting taxes on cotton in kind.

To encourage efficient collection practices, Beijing allowed local administrations to retain 80 percent of any grain collected in excess of the central government's targets, with the remaining 20 percent going to Beijing.[40] As for the grain procurement, so optimistic was the CCP in 1950 that the China National Grain Corporation was worried about how it would deal with a projected glut in the market. It proposed that farmers be encouraged not to sell all their surplus grain on the market, but to store it at home instead. At the same time, the corporation was working on a plan that would enable it to sell large quantities of grain on the market.[41]

In the end, the 1950 tax target of 25.7 billion catties was exceeded by 1.3 billion catties. Satisfied, the Central Committee of the CCP announced that local cadres should also strive to exceed their taxation targets.[42] However, the state grain procurement did not go as well as the China National Grain Corporation had anticipated: it collected only 2.4 billion catties, less than two-thirds of its original target of 3.9 billion catties.[43] Before long, optimistic predictions for China's grain supply evaporated—and were never to be repeated during the entire Mao era. The outbreak of the Korean War suddenly began siphoning off a large proportion of state revenue. Table 2 divides state expenditure between 1950 and 1952 into three categories.

Table 2. State Expenditure, 1950–1952 (billion RMB)[44]

	Total state expenditure	Defense expenditure	Economic reconstruction expenditure
1950	6.8	2.8	1.7
1951	12.3	5.2	3.5
1952	17.6	5.8	7.3

---

40. Shangyebu dangdai liangshi gongzuo bianji bu, *Dangdai liangshi gongzuo shiliao*, 83.

41. Ibid., 102.

42. Ibid., 92–93.

43. Ibid., 104.

44. *Zhongguo tongji nianjian 1992*, 215–220.

Compared with the 1950 figures, state expenditure doubled in 1951 and almost tripled in 1952. Where did the revenue come from? The CCP substantially raised taxes in nearly all sectors, monopolized the sale of liquor and cigarettes, and launched the Three-Anti and Five-Anti movements, in part to extract more revenue.[45] However, the most crucial source remained the tax on grain. Table 3 shows the amount of grain the CCP managed to obtain from peasants between 1949 and 1953.

Table 3. China's Tax Regime, 1949–1953 (billion cattie)[46]

	1949–1950	1950–1951	1951–1952	1952–1953	1953–1954
Proposed state tax	29.2	25.7	unknown	40.7	37.0
Tax collected, with local surcharge	24.8	27.0	36.1	34.8	37.1
Planned state procurement	unknown	unknown	18.6	unknown	34.0
Actual State procurements	unknown	11.5	22	24.3	unknown
Miscellaneous taxes, collected	Unknown	Unknown	6.4	3.4	unknown
Total grain state collected and purchased	>24.8	38.5	58.1	61.8	unknown

Between 1949 and 1953, the state more than doubled its grain acquisition from peasant farmers. How did the CCP accomplish it?

In 1950, the government first decided to raise the agricultural tax target by 10 percent,[47] but that proved to be far from adequate. As the Korean War

---

45. Dong Zhi-kai, "The 'War to Resist America and Aid Korea.'"

46. Numbers are drawn from Zhongguo nongmin fudanshi bianji weiyuan hui, *Zhongguo nongmin fudanshi* and Shangyebu dangdai liangshi gongzuo bianji bu, *Dangdai liangshi gongzuo shiliao*.

47. Zhongguo nongmin fudanshi bianji weiyuan hui, *Zhongguo nongmin fudanshi*, vol. 4, 40.

continued, some leaders became alarmed about the incapacity of the grain supply to keep up with rapidly increasing demands. Chen Yun prescribed two solutions. The first was to encourage farmers not to plant more cash crops, and the second was to implement the compulsory purchase of surplus grain.

Chen's first suggestion was adopted immediately. In 1952, farmers were forbidden to enlarge the area set aside for the growing of cash crops. The compulsory purchase option proved more difficult to execute and was shelved, as discussed below. To meet its fiscal needs, the CCP had to raise both state agricultural taxes and state grain procurement. Surprisingly, in the fiscal year 1951–1952, most regions not only fulfilled their grain tax targets, but also exceeded them. The state collected more than 36 billion catties of grain, a 33 percent tax hike compared with the previous year; that same year some farmers also experienced a 70 percent surge in local miscellaneous taxes.[48]

To facilitate the collection of these taxes, Beijing did not impose unified tax rates across the nation. It continued to levy proportional taxes in the older liberated regions and maintained a progressive regime in the newly liberated regions. It allowed local governments to submit their own tax plans provided that they had exceeded their assignments for the previous fiscal year. This approach worked. In addition, state purchases of grain nearly doubled.

While achieving the targets was not easy, Chinese farmers succeeded for two main reasons. First, the tax hike coincided with land reform in the newly liberated regions. It is likely that the burden was disproportionately shouldered by wealthier families in the countryside, directly or indirectly. As had happened before, during the land reform process, poor peasants and sometimes middle-ranking peasants had obtained "struggle fruits" through the confiscation of property belonging to wealthier families. As a result, they possessed extra cash in hand that enabled them to cope with the tax hike. Second, at this time, peasants were still able to purchase grain from government grain retailers, at prices only slightly higher than they charged the state. In 1950, government grain retailers sold 9.3 billion catties of grain, and in 1951, this figure rose to 16.9 billion; at least half the increase went to peasants and residents of small towns.[49]

---

48. Ibid., 119.

49. Shangyebu dangdai liangshi gongzuo bianji bu, *Dangdai liangshi gongzuo shiliao*, 23.

The state's tax take for the fiscal year 1951–1952 was a big success, and the central government drew up a similar plan for 1952–1953. It proposed collecting 40.7 billion catties of grain in state taxes (excluding miscellaneous local levies) and purchase yet more grain. But this time, its plans turned sour. The land reform process was complete and no more "struggle fruits" were available to distribute to poor peasants. Middle-ranking peasants now predominated in the countryside, while few wealthier families remained. It was no longer feasible for the government to levy taxes based on class status, since landlords and rich peasants had largely vanished from the rural scene. The tax burden would need to be shouldered by middle-ranking and poor peasants, who were used to paying their taxes at much lower rates.

To secure the income it needed, the central government confronted the need to extract more from peasant farmers. The question was how. The most effective solution was to raise tax rates. But these rates were already high, and many CCP leaders, especially Mao Zedong, were not comfortable with high agricultural taxes, which they had vehemently opposed during the revolutionary years. Another solution was to enlarge the tax base—for example, by identifying more taxable land and by increasing taxable agricultural output. The CCP chose the latter route.

In 1951, the party had already planned to launch a national campaign under the rubric Surveying Land and Fixing *Production* Quotas (*chatian dingchan*) with the aim of identifying more "hidden land" and making an accurate assessment of agricultural output. Because actual land yield fluctuated each year and was extremely difficult to assess, the party decided to change the tax base from actual land yield to estimated average perennial land yield. The ostensible reason for this change was to encourage peasants to improve productivity by allowing them to retain surplus yields when they occurred.[50] The real reason was to stabilize the government's income and to facilitate tax planning. Although the campaign was designed to run its course over three to four years,[51] in 1952 one after another local government rushed to implement the campaign and attempted to complete it within a year. The campaign did much to harm peasant farmers, and the agricultural tax target for 1952 remained unmet. The state succeeded in collecting only 34.8 billion

---

50. "Nongye shui chatian dingchan gongzuo shishi gangyao."
51. Ibid.

catties of grain, 15 percent short of its target. The state's grain purchase plan fell even farther behind in nearly every region.[52]

The fiscal year 1951–1952 delivered a particularly large hike. In 1952, the figure reached 60 billion catties, combining the taxes and procurement. What do these numbers mean in comparative terms? Did the CCP collect more in grain tax than the Guomindang government had done? Unfortunately, accurate figures for the Guomindang's agricultural tax system are hard to find. The Guomindang government, with its high-flying financial minister Song Ziwen, had developed alternative methods—deemed more "modern"—of financing itself. The Guomindang's state revenue relied heavily on tariffs, taxes on urban business enterprises and industrial products, and national bonds. Agricultural taxes were insignificant in terms of the income stream flowing into the central government's coffers because the Guomingdang never controlled much of the countryside and actually had to subsidize regional regimes to purchase their loyalty to Nanjing. Indeed, in 1928, tax reform allowed provincial administrations to retain a good proportion of their agricultural taxes. This did not mean that peasants were relieved from the burden of extraction by the state. They were squeezed by local administrators and warlords alike, sometimes for years in advance. Nevertheless, under the Guomindang regime, peasant farmers did not directly shoulder the major expense of the central government. Further, with access to world markets prior to the Anti-Japanese War, each year China imported grain, ranging from 0.4 billion to 4 billion catties.[53]

When the CCP came to rule China, it lacked the variety of sources for its state revenue that the Guomindang had enjoyed and it was determined to restore the rural economy that had long served as the chief fiscal base for Chinese states. Agricultural taxes thus became an important source of revenue; in 1950, nearly 30 percent of state revenues came from agricultural taxes.[54] In other words, in the early years of the PRC, peasant farmers effectively financed a large proportion of the expenses incurred by the massive new CCP administration. Nicholas Lardy estimates that in the 1930s, total government revenues, including at the central, provincial, and local levels,

---

52. Shangyebu dangdai liangshi gongzuo bianji bu, *Dangdai liangshi gongzuo shiliao.*

53. Ibid., 33.

54. Zhongguo nongmin fudanshi bianji weiyuan hui, *Zhongguo nongmin fudanshi,* vol. 4, 138.

amounted to only 5 to 7 percent of GNP. But the CCP raised this figure to 30 percent, approaching levels of other, so-called modern, states.[55] To make the burden on farmers worse, the Communist state reversed the practice of importing grain from world markets; instead, it began to export grain, averaging around 3 billion catties per year to fund the import of industrial goods.[56]

It is difficult to estimate how much local administrations collected from farmers under the Guomindang. One possible figure is suggested by the fact that in 1949, when the CCP assigned tax quotas to the newly liberated regions, it by and large based its estimates on the tax rates set by the previous regime, as happened in Southwest China.[57] So if we assume that the amount that the CCP planned to collect in 1949 and 1950 was close to the figure collected by the Guomindang to fund both their central and local administrations, Chinese peasants surrendered much more grain to the CCP government following the tax hike in 1951 than they had to the Guomindang. As the new PRC became established, the CCP central state found that it needed to extract more grain from the peasants than the Guomindang had ever done. It succeeded in this task.

While CCP leaders understood that tax rates for peasant producers were already heavy, they justified the 1951 tax hike through a simple rationale: in previous years, peasants had had to pay rents as high as 50 percent of their yield to landlords; now that the CCP had eliminated landlords as a class and given farmers land to boot, farmers would now be in a good position to supply more grain to the state.[58] However, the reality was much more complex than this simple calculation. The CCP tended to overestimate the number of landlords and the extent of the land they owned. It also overestimated their exploitation of the peasants and ignored the fact that in most cases, rents included agricultural taxes. Further, it was the landlords and rich peasants, not the middle-ranking or poor peasants, who had traditionally supplied the most surplus grain to the market.

The third major question to be asked is, Were farmers producing more

---

55. Nicholas Lardy, "Economic Recovery and the 1st Five-Year Plan," 151.

56. Shangyebu dangdai liangshi gongzuo bianji bu, *Dangdai liangshi gongzuo shiliao*, 102.

57. Wang Haiguang, "Minbian yu 'feiluan.'"

58. Zhongguo nongmin fudanshi bianji weiyuan hui, *Zhongguo nongmin fudanshi*, vol. 4, 60–66.

grain to match the accelerating pace of taxation? How did small producers cope with rapidly increasing demands from the state? Given the distorted channels of communication, inflated production reports, and the unpredictable nature of agriculture, it is virtually impossible to give an accurate account of the amount of grain Chinese peasants produced in the early 1950s—although the CCP's official records indicate that agricultural output increased by over 40 percent from 1949 to 1952 and that between 1952 and 1957, output increased by a further 24 percent.[59]

For the agricultural sector, these growth rates were unusual.[60] No major technological breakthrough had occurred during this period. Between 1949 and 1952, Chinese peasant farmers were struggling to recover from decades of war. While the government asserts that in 1952 total agricultural production did reach levels on a par with those achieved prior to the Anti-Japanese War, some scholars have reservations. Wu Hui, the leading Chinese scholar on China's commercial history, points out that on average, the unit yield per mu in 1957 was still lower than the highest one in the 1930s. Only in late 1960s, with breakthroughs in seeds and technology, did it surpass the 1930s.[61] Liming Wang and John Davis point out that grain yield was 1.32 tons per hectare in 1952; it rose only by a very small amount to 1.47 tons per hectare in 1957.[62] Nature did little to help boost production. The period 1952–1957 witnessed two good years (1952 and 1955), two average years (1953 and 1957), and two bad years (1954 and 1956).[63] So how are we to explain the consistent agricultural growth? The chief explanation was the increase in sown land, or more precisely, the increase in registered sown land under CCP rule. This leads us to consider one of the CCP's most solid accomplishments in managing rural China: its completion of a national cadastral survey, the first one since the early Qing period.

For centuries, China's imperial states had struggled to compile an accurate cadastre, and most had failed. As the twentieth century dawned, the

---

59. Ibid., 138–144.

60. In the ninety-four developing market economies studied by Kenneth Walker between 1961 and 1976, grain production increased by an average of only 2.6 percent per year. Kenneth Walker, *Food Grain Procurement and Consumption in China*, xiii.

61. Wu Hui, *Zhongguo lidai liangshi muchan yanjiu*, 217.

62. Liming Wang and John Davis, *China's Grain Economy*, 14.

63. Kenneth Walker, *Food Grain Procurement and Consumption in China*, 31.

cadastre in numerous localities across China had not been reviewed for decades and in some places for centuries. It was common knowledge that many fields that had been cultivated for generations had never been registered, and thus they had escaped taxation. This unregistered land was often known as "black fields" (*heitian*). Lack of knowledge about the true ownership of land, the real size of landholdings, the value of land, and its tax registration status was the source of an enormous loss of earnings for local and national administrations, as well as inequalities between taxpayers. After the collapse of the Qing in 1911, first Yuan Shikai, president of the Republic of China and then the Guomindang government, undertook successive campaigns to survey land and to register black fields, but they achieved little success. Both met fierce resistance and were confronted with rural rebellions.[64]

According to the Guomindang's official records, prior to the Anti-Japanese war, taxable land in China was 1.02 billion mu, only 73 percent of arable land estimated at 1.4 billion mu. The reasons for this disparity were complex. The continuing widespread existence of black fields was probably the primary cause. The gap was also a reflection of regional differences in ways of measuring land area. It also had to do with rural customs. For example, areas of dry land adjoining rice paddies were often not counted as taxable land; in some regions amalgamated or "fiscal mu" were customarily smaller than the real acreage under cultivation.[65]

Well aware of the great extent of the black fields, the CCP was determined to increase its revenue by registering this "hidden" land. Land reform itself constituted a means of updating the cadastre. In 1951, the party set about planning the Surveying Land and Fixing *Production* Quotas campaign. In the older liberated regions where land reform had been completed, the state had compiled a fairly accurate cadastre, so the primary task of the campaign in these areas was to calculate the average perennial yield. In the newly liberated regions where land reform was still under way, the campaign had a dual function: to resurvey the land (taking advantage of the land reform process) to establish ownership, and to fix the perennial yield for tax purposes.

While the party had accumulated abundant experience in surveying the land, it had little knowledge of how to estimate average perennial yield. In

---

64. Lucien Bianco, *Wretched Rebels*, 110–113.

65. Zhongguo nongmin fudanshi bianji weiyuan hui, *Zhongguo nongmin fudanshi*, vol. 4, 84.

this project, the central government was no longer keen to enlist the services of poor peasants, and it emphasized that the necessary investigations should be conducted by county cadres. It warned that the "democratic assessments" by the masses at the village level could not be fully trusted. Beijing required that the local administration at each rung below the provincial level form a committee dedicated to the Surveying Land and Fixing *Production* Quotas campaign, to be headed by the chief local administrator. Each county-level committee should determine the standard perennial yields for land of different quality in its area, check reports originating from lower administrative levels, and then compile a register of agricultural taxes for each village. In the villages and townships, a committee for agricultural tax investigation and assessment was formed, composed of representatives drawn from all social classes. Its task was to survey the population, measure agricultural land, and assess its quality. Then, based on the standards set by the Surveying Land and Fixing *Production* Quotas county committee, it was to assess the perennial yield for each household.[66] This arrangement granted considerable authority to county cadres, who had the power to set the standard perennial yield arbitrarily.

By the end of 1952, taxable land in China had risen to 1.62 billion mu, a dazzling success compared with Guomindang's figure of 1.02 billion mu.[67] But this campaign hit the newly liberated regions particularly hard, where farmers had a large amount of unregistered land. The South Central region was one of those areas, for example. Internal reports from the South Central China Bureau revealed that the campaign had brought to light almost 350 million mu of unregistered arable land in the region, 20.4 percent more than the figure for 1950. The estimated agricultural perennial yield was increased by 34.3 percent compared to 1950. As the tax base expanded, so did the state tax regime. In 1950 the South Central China Bureau had collected 5.64 billion catties of grain; in 1952 it collected 9.9 billion catties, a tax hike of 76 percent—a much higher figure than the increase in arable land and agricultural perennial yield.[68]

---

66. "Nongye shui chatian dingchan gongzuo shishi gangyao."

67. Zhongguo nongmin fudanshi bianji weiyuan hui, *Zhongguo nongmin fudanshi*, vol. 4, 87–88.

68. Shangyebu dangdai liangshi gongzuo bianji bu, *Dangdai liangshi gongzuo shiliao*, 95–96.

When land surveys uncovered additional tracts of unregistered land, and the state moved to levy taxes and increase its tax revenue, the CCP claimed that as more land was brought under cultivation, farmers' incomes would rise accordingly. The flaw in this argument was that peasant farmers had already worked their black fields for decades without paying taxes on them. Thus, the CCP campaign did not really uncover new land and find new income for peasant producers. The increased taxes came directly from farmers' pockets—or rather, their previously unreported pockets. What made the situation more confused was the poor quality of the Surveying Land and Fixing *Production* Quotas campaign. Eager to wrap up the campaign, local CCP officials did not carry out their work with sufficient care and attention. In many cases, cadres ignored local customs when surveying land, thus misestimating the land's potential output. The use of inflated production data by the Mutual Aid and Cooperative movement compounded the problem.

Many of these tendencies were apparent in the case of Xia County in Shanxi Province. As the Surveying Land and Fixing *Production* Quotas campaign rolled out in fall 1952, the county sent out thirty cadres tasked with surveying and fixing quotas. First, they asked village cadres to measure local landholdings and submit an estimate, which they considered too low. So they simply raised the figures and submitted them. Although county cadres were aware of the difficulties involved in these surveys, they swept them under the carpet. As a result, Xia County discovered 54,000 mu of black fields, which raised the amount of taxable grain by an average of one-third. In all the villages in the county, regardless of their ability to pay, the tax burden mounted, with increases ranging between 5 and 100 percent. The peasants complained, with many visiting the county headquarters to argue their case, but little was changed. They came to resent model laborers, who inevitably raised the party's estimates of grain production. One model laborer passionately denied that he had been selected for the role and concealed his prize.[69]

The high unit yields reported at the height of the Mutual Aid and Cooperation movement had given the CCP the illusion of substantially increased rural productivity and it led to the assumption that farmers had hoarded large quantities of surplus grain. Excited by the prospect of high

---

69. *Neibu cankao*, July 17, 1953.

unit yields, the central government raised its expectations for overall agricultural production and increased its extraction quotas to claim its share of the supposedly "increased" productivity.

Agricultural Cooperativization Recharged Amid Crises

With burgeoning taxes, the Three-Anti movement, the Mutual Aid and Cooperation movement, and the Surveying Land and Fixing *Production* Quotas campaign to contend with, peasant farmers were exhausted and fearful for their future. The Three-Anti movement had wiped out most private traders; the peasants had to turn to state grain retailers to maintain a basic food supply. The state agencies were not prepared for such a large spike in demand and ran short of grain. Some state retailers simply closed their stores. Panicked over the scarcity of grain on the market and deprived of their tax-free income from black field production, farmers reacted in two ways: on the one hand, they declined to surrender their grain to the market, and on the other, they sought to purchase grain from the state and hoard it.

From late 1952, panic buying of grain spread like wildfire throughout China. Peasants queued outside state grain retailers for days and nights on end. When spring famine broke out in 1953, the central government had to draw on emergency grain supplies. To ease the situation, the state encouraged private merchants to engage in grain trading and allowed them greater flexibility in pricing. The Three-Anti movement waned. Some private traders went back into business. To extract more grain from peasant producers, private traders raised the price, which had the immediate effect of reducing state purchasing. Nevertheless, the spring famine was temporarily ameliorated.

Beijing was certainly not pleased by this whole episode. In April 1953, officials from the Ministry of Food engaged in acts of self-criticism over grain sales. The ministry admitted that in the past, state grain retailers had treated purchases and sales equally, sold grain anywhere there was business, and had sold it to whoever wanted to buy. As a result, a great deal of the state's hard-won grain stocks had been consumed in the countryside and small towns. The lesson the ministry learned was that the state could not supply all the people's food needs; it should attend exclusively to the needs of urban residents, while leaving others to be serviced by cooperatives and private traders.[70] The ministry should certainly not be serving the peasants, who were supposed be supplying the state with grain, not removing it.

Beijing was acutely aware of the difficulties caused by the increasing demand for grain at a time of rapidly decreasing supply. When the new grain collection season began in summer 1953, the state was faced with repeating the whole painful cycle once again. This time, however, things were to get much worse.

In the summer of 1953, marketable grain stocks plummeted. In every region of China, local administrations exhausted themselves trying to fulfill their grain tax quotas. State grain retailers were frequently tardy in fulfilling the grain procurement plans that they were assigned; instead, many sold more grain than they purchased. Between July and September 1953, the traditional harvest season, while the state purchased 9.9 billion catties of grain, it had already sold 12.4 billion catties.[71] In Henan Province, in October, the traditional grain-buying season, the state sold nine times more grain than it purchased. In the big cities, the people remained calm, but "grain panic" quickly emerged in the towns and smaller urban centers.[72]

Chen Yun, responsible for drawing up the national budget, appreciated the gravity of the situation better than any other CCP leader. The projected grain procurement figure for 1953 was 34 billion catties, which Chen knew the state would likely fail to meet; on the other hand, state sales were set to rocket to 56 billion catties or more. If agricultural taxes were included in the calculation, the deficit between state taxes and procurement combined and government sales was at least 8.7 billion catties of grain.[73] Shortages on this scale were daunting. The government's grain reserves had dropped by one-third as a result of the spring famine. What made the situation even more dangerous was that much of the grain that the state had purchased was acquired from poor peasants who would come to the government asking for grain the following year.[74] Publicly, the government blamed the crisis on private traders' speculation. Internally, it blamed the peasants for hoarding grain and consuming too much. Again, Chen Yun put forward his plan for

---

70. Shangyebu dangdai liangshi gongzuo bianji bu, *Dangdai liangshi gongzuo shiliao*, 65.

71. Ibid., 151–163.

72. Ibid., 153.

73. Ibid., 151.

74. Ibid., 163.

the nationalization of the grain market. This time his suggestion was given serious consideration.

Three explanations have been commonly advanced to explain the party's decision to nationalize the grain market. The first holds that this policy was originally a temporary solution to the grain procurement crisis, but was then kept in place for decades. The second is that it was part of Mao Zedong's General Line. The third explanation is that it was implemented as part of the agricultural cooperativization movement.[75] Recently published documents have shed light on a fourth explanation: although long advocated by the Financial and Economic Committee, the nationalization of the grain market was opposed by several CCP regional leaders. The grain crisis of 1953 provided the Financial and Economic committee with a golden opportunity to put its plan into practice.

As we have seen, from the founding of the PRC, extracting grain from peasant farmers had proved to be a challenge, despite the CCP's long history of mobilizing the peasants. The responsibility for resolving this problem fell on the Financial and Economic Committee. As early as 1951, Chen Yun had suggested forcing farmers to sell their surplus grain to the state alone. The forced requisitioning of grain by the Soviet Bolsheviks was certainly one inspiration for this policy. Chen Yun also had a number of other models to draw on: China's experience of the Japanese grain extraction system in Manchuria during the Anti-Japanese war (1937–1945); the rationing system put in place by the Nationalist government in wartime Chongqing; and his own experience of taking control of Manchuria in the late 1940s. Because the Soviet, Japanese, and Chinese Nationalist models were notoriously harsh, Chen Yun sought to differentiate his vision from these undesirable historical precedents by giving his plan a different name.

In early 1952, Chen Yun and his colleagues in the Financial and Economic Committee submitted a proposal to the Central Committee in which they asserted that there would be a shortfall in the nation's grain supply for a long time to come. Because the urban population and the state reserve would have an increasing need for grain, the committee recommended that the government adopt the compulsory purchase of surplus grain. The proposal was opposed by a few regional leaders and was not adopted. In September 1952, at the national grain conference, the compulsory purchase option was again discussed. In October, the official report on the First Na-

---

75. Wang Danli, "Tonggou tongxiao yanjiu shuping."

tional Grain Conference suggested that it be tried; however, the idea was shelved because it was too late in the year to be implemented.[76] During the spring famine of 1953, the policy was brought up again. Fearing the chaos it might bring to the countryside, the Central Committee did not approve it.[77] However, in certain regions, such as Sichuan, the compulsory purchase of surplus grain was introduced on a trial basis later in the year.[78]

Overall, the Financial and Economic Committee was the main advocate of nationalizing the grain market. As Chen Yun said, if the free market was allowed to continue, the central government would have to beg for grain each day, so that every day would be painful. He considered that nationalization would be a long-term solution.[79]

The grain crisis of 1953 provided Chen Yun with a prime opportunity to promote his plan. As he said, he was tired of being a beggar and asking for grain each day. The simple solution was to make it compulsory for farmers to supply their surplus to the state.[80] In early October 1953, an emergency meeting was convened in Beijing to discuss the operation of a nationalized grain market. At the provincial level, complaints surfaced even before the final decision was made. For example, provincial officials in Guangdong and Guangxi opposed the policy, Henan provincial officials were hesitant, and Jiangxi had some vague reservations.[81] But as the pressure mounted, one after another they consented.

Moreover, Li Xiannian, the head of the South Central China Bureau, who had not initially supported the policy, made some remarks later in the meeting on what he saw as the dual nature of the peasantry. He admitted that in the past, the CCP had been afraid to comment on the peasants' underside, but he had since come to learn about their "appalling spontaneous tendencies." According to Li Xiannian, the peasants' spontaneous tendencies were manifested in their involvement in grain speculation and their reluctance to join the Mutual Aid and Cooperation movement. He believed

---

76. Chen Yun, *Chen Yun wenxuan*, 160; Jin Chongji and Chen Qun, *Chen Yun zhuan*.

77. Tian Xiquan, *Ge'ming yu xiangcun*, 25.

78. *Dangdai Zhongguo liangshi gongzuo shiliao*.

79. Tian Xiquan, *Ge'ming yu xiangcun*.

80. Shangyebu dangdai liangshi gongzuo bianji bu, *Dangdai liangshi gongzuo shiliao*, 153.

81. *Dangdai Zhongguo liangshi gongzuo shiliao*.

that the time had now come to actively resist these tendencies.[82] Zhang Xiu-shan, the new head of the Northeast China Bureau following Gao Gang's departure to Beijing, told those attending that since 1949 the Chinese people had consumed too much fine grain. He suggested selling fine grains and coarse grains in proportion so to save more fine grains.[83]

In the end, Chen Yun's proposal was passed; Mao approved it before the meeting was over. Now the policy of "United Purchase, United Sell" (*tong-gou tongxiao*) was officially on the government agenda. The government was to monopolize the trade in grains and demanded that peasants sell their surplus grains on market. The state grain procurement plan was daunting in its scope: in addition to the state grain tax, a new quota of 70 billion catties of grain was approved, more than double the original procurement plan.[84]

When we compare Chen Yun's plan with the Three Documents issued early in the year, the contrast is striking. It is an excellent example of the blinkered approach so often taken by the CCP leaders: they tended to focus narrowly on their own spheres of interest while overlooking how their policies and decisions would affect other sectors. After three years of the CCP ruling China, it was clear that the everyday living conditions experienced by the masses were no longer a priority for the CCP; probably they never had been. But by introducing the United Purchase, United Sell, the party made a conscious decision that the people needed to sacrifice more to create a "stronger China."

Prior to October 1953, Chen Yun had made little mention of anything related to the party's Mutual Aid and Cooperation movement. For the first week of the emergency conference on grain, discussions rarely touched on Mao's General Line or issues to do with the Mutual Aid and Cooperation movement. But after that, the party decided to requisition the surplus grain and to set the high quotas, actions that would take away grains saved by the peasants from the current year plus their savings from past years,[85] and the

---

82. Shangyebu dangdai liangshi gongzuo bianji bu, *Dangdai liangshi gongzuo shiliao*, 168.

83. Ibid., 169.

84. Ibid., 171.

85. *Dangdai Zhongguo liangshi gongzuo shiliao*, 150–167.

CCP leaders foresaw stiff resistance. It was expected that there would be bloodshed. As Liu Lantao urged, "If necessary, kill people."[86]

It was very clear to the leadership that United Purchase, United Sell would have serious political implications. To their dismay, the immediate objections came from within the party itself. For example in Hubei, when the provincial party congress was convened to discuss the new policy, most representatives at lower levels of the administration opposed it. A common reaction was, "This is nothing less than an attack on the peasants by the CCP."[87] Many were unwilling to carry out the policy. At county and district levels, discontent was strong as well.

This reaction represented a serious challenge. The cadres who opposed the new policy were regarded as the backbone of the party. Li Jingquan, who was charged with testing the policy in Sichuan Province and who was known for his loyalty to Mao Zedong, suggested combining the United Purchase, United Sell with the propaganda campaign for the General Line as a way of getting older cadres on their side. By shifting the focus onto China's bright socialist future, Li Jingquan reasoned that it would be easier for these cadres to overcome their reservations. Mao agreed and affirmed that in future propaganda campaigns, United Purchase, United Sell would go hand in hand with promotion of the General Line. By making it an integral part of the General Line, it would be more likely that the whole party would embrace the nationalization of the grain market and be more willing to implement it. When promoting the policy, the peasants should be fed material about socialism and industrialization and also about the prosperous future awaiting the Soviet Union. After discussing the issue with Mao, Chen Yun confirmed that United Purchase, United Sell would indeed be presented as an integral part of the General Line.[88] This decision was implemented in November, 1953. From now on, the stakes had risen for anyone expressing discontent with the decision on United Purchase, United Sell: "Are you questioning the Chairman's line?"

In October, the Third National Mutual Aid and Cooperation Confer-

---

86. Shangyebu dangdai liangshi gongzuo bianji bu, *Dangdai liangshi gongzuo shiliao*, 166.

87. *Neibu cankao*, October–December 1953.

88. Shangyebu dangdai liangshi gongzuo bianji bu, *Dangdai Zhongguo liangshi gongzuo shiliao*, 150–168.

ence was convened. Seeking to set an appropriate tone for the conference, Mao consulted Chen Boda and Liao Luyan, vice-ministers of the Rural Work Department. With full faith in the high productivity levels achievable by agricultural producers' cooperatives, Mao asserted: "The room for individual farmers to increase productivity is very limited. [We] must rely on mutual aid teams and cooperatives." In the face of the grain procurement crisis, Mao attributed the shortfall in supplies to the contradiction between private ownership and efficient production forces: "The relations of production in a system of individual ownership are totally in conflict with [the goal of] large-scale supply. A transition must be made from a system of individual ownership to a system of collective ownership to socialism."[89] Mao urged the necessity of building agricultural producers' cooperatives; the more, the better.[90] For him, the rectification campaign in the spring of 1953 had only hampered the progress of the Mutual Aid and Cooperation movement. Mao chastised the Rural Work Department for saying nothing about socialism and overvaluing the small peasant economy.

Driven by what he considered the urgent need to increase agricultural productivity, Mao had become obsessed with the virtues of large-scale cultivation. The two main excesses that the earlier rectification campaign targeted were building too many agricultural producers' cooperatives and mouthing slogans like "Bigger is better." Mao was guilty on both counts. Given a choice between mutual aid teams and agricultural producers' cooperatives, Mao apparently favored the latter. To him, the general rule was to proceed from mutual aid teams to cooperatives, but jumping directly from private family farming to building a cooperative should be allowed. And again: "Developing agricultural producers' cooperatives is not only necessary, but possible—their potential is enormous." Where conditions permitted, he even suggested building collective farms. Mao also valued size as a virtue and believed that building larger cooperatives was one important way of practicing socialism. He encouraged the building of larger units whenever possible. In his mind, many of the problems found in the countryside would be automatically remedied in large cooperatives. He also be-

---

89. Mao Zedong, "Speech on Mutual Aid and Cooperativization in Agriculture" (October 15, 1953), in Michael Kau and John Leung, *The Writings of Mao Zedong, 1949–1976*, 416.

90. Gao Huamin, "Guanyu hezuohua yundong bufa jiakuai yuanyin de lishi kaocha."

lieved that cooperatives consisting of hundreds of households would be the ideal solution to the problem of impoverished families, so that all the problems would be solved.[91]

Beginning in November 1953, a campaign to study the General Line was rigorously enforced at each level of the party. In the countryside, the two major arms of the campaign were, first, to encourage farmers to sell their grain to the state, and second, to draw a firm line between capitalism and socialism. The peasants' "spontaneous tendencies" were to be curbed and any further manifestations firmly dealt with. Joining mutual aid teams and agricultural producers' cooperatives thus emerged as the only correct path to follow. Under pressure from Mao and in an intensified political atmosphere with the General Line taking center stage, the effects of the rectification movement in the spring of 1953 had evaporated entirely. Although likely unintended, United Purchase, United Sell paved way for the revival of agricultural producers' cooperatives. By the end of 1953, the CCP officially announced the launch of Agricultural Cooperativization nationwide, a move aimed at encouraging all Chinese peasants to join agricultural producers' cooperatives as a key part of the socialist transformation of the countryside.

In the years to come, what had happened in Shanxi in late 1952 and early 1953 would be repeated in other regions, on a larger scale and with more catastrophic results, as the epilogue will discuss.

---

91. Ibid.

Epilogue

Recipe for Tragedy

The Aftermath

Following the nationwide launch of agricultural cooperativization in December 1953, the Central Committee of the CCP set the goal of establishing 35,300 agricultural producers' cooperatives by the end of 1954 and a nationwide total of 800,000 by 1957. Just after the announcement, the target was exceeded—by spring 1954 there were already 90,000 cooperatives in existence. Needless to say, Beijing was very pleased with this level of progress. In April 1954, the proposed number was raised to 300,000–350,000 in 1955. In October 1954, the figure was revised again and raised to a total of 600,000 in operation before the 1955 spring plowing. At the same time, established producers' cooperatives were encouraged to progress to a higher stage of development in which farmers' land was given to the cooperative and the distribution of profit according to land share was abolished—in essence becoming Soviet collective farms.[1]

As Beijing boosted the numbers, local cadres came up with increasingly ambitious plans and competed vigorously with each other. As had happened in Shanxi, local cadres rode roughshod over the principle of voluntarism, publicizing slogans like "Working by oneself is against the law" and "Failing to join cooperatives is [pursuing] capitalism."[2] They created a variety of methods to punish those who refused to join cooperatives. By the end of 1954, 480,000 agricultural producers' cooperatives had been established

---

1. Lin Yunhui, Fan Shouxin, and Zhang Gong, "Selection from China 1949–1989," 82–85.

2. Ibid., 85.

throughout China, and the momentum was growing stronger by the day. However, both the extent of the damage to agricultural production and the souring of relations between the party and the peasants were ringing alarm bells in Beijing, especially in the Central Rural Work Department. As their colleagues in Shanxi had done, peasant farmers across China began selling or slaughtering their livestock in large numbers. For example, in Northeast China, livestock prices dropped between one-third and a half, and the number of farm animals plunged, with drastic consequences for production. The peasants were rapidly losing interest in farming, and their discontent with the party was reaching a crisis point.[3]

Aware of the growing resistance in the countryside, Deng Zihui, director of the Central Rural Work Department, consulted with Liu Shaoqi and Zhou Enlai in January 1955 to seek ways of regulating the movement. Seemingly in Mao's absence, the party leadership endorsed Deng Zihui's proposals. Between January and March, the party issued four urgent directives calling for caution and prudence in developing agricultural producers' cooperatives. However, this did little to slow the progress. As it had happened in 1953, attempts from the top to "rectify" excesses, however worthy in their intentions, were not well received among those who were below.

In early March 1955, Mao Zedong returned to Beijing from a tour. After seeing the report from the Central Rural Work Department, Mao summarized the party's response in a simple three-part dictum: first, stop; second, contract; third, develop. With his characteristic optimism, Mao placed the emphasis on the third term, "develop," whereas other leaders stressed the first two. Breaking his silence on peasant issues, Liu Shaoqi once again voiced his opinions. In a meeting with Deng Zihui, Liu urged the necessity of eliminating one hundred thousand agricultural producers' cooperatives in order to stabilize the situation. Deng consented. In reality, Mao's three-word maxim had become "stop, contract, and overhaul." In Zhejiang Province alone, 15,607 cooperatives were decommissioned.[4]

Mao Zedong, however, chose to conduct several inspection tours in the countryside, as he had in 1953. Once again he encountered a good deal of "staged" enthusiasm for producers' cooperatives. Having witnessed these apparently positive responses from below, Mao was dismayed by the conservative attitudes in Beijing. On his return to the capital, he warned Deng

---

3. Ibid., 87–90.
4. Ibid., 99.

Zihui, "Do not repeat the mistake made in 1953 of dissolving large numbers of cooperatives. Otherwise, you will have to make another act of self-criticism."[5] Mao urged the party both to take full advantage of the peasants' aspirations to lift themselves out of poverty and to guide them toward socialism. Mao also approached several provincial governors and harshly criticized negative approaches to agricultural producers' cooperatives. Aware of Mao's attitude, local leaders swiftly abandoned their plans of stopping the construction of new cooperatives.[6]

Mao condemned Deng Zihui's "right deviationist" errors and ridiculed him, calling him "a woman with bound feet." In October 1955, at the enlarged Sixth Plenary of the Seventh Central Committee, Deng Zihui's viewpoint was officially declared an error of "right-deviationist opportunism." With the central party leadership solidly behind Mao, the provincial leaders returned home to pass on Mao's views. From this time on, the target figures for agricultural producers' cooperatives skyrocketed. One after another, the provinces revised their plans upward. The actual growth of new cooperatives even outpaced these ambitious projections. By the end of 1955, more than 1.9 million agricultural producers' cooperatives had been established throughout the country, covering over 60 percent of peasant households. By May 1956, 110 million households, accounting for 91 percent of total peasant households, had joined the cooperative movement. Increasing numbers of producers' cooperatives developed into more advanced cooperatives. By the end of 1956, private ownership of land had been virtually abolished in China.[7]

This is the so-called High Tide of agricultural cooperativization. The peasants sacrificed much for the breakneck pace of these developments. In the spring of 1957, mass starvation struck Guangxi Province—a disaster that even local CCP cadres attributed to accelerated cooperativization and to the state monopoly on grain purchasing and marketing. Zhou Enlai, Chen Yun, and Bo Yibo agreed that the party's excessively high targets had done much damage in the countryside and called for "rash advances" to be curbed. As in 1953 and again in 1955, these efforts paradoxically stimulated another resurgence

---

5. Bo Yibo, *Ruogan zhongda juece yu shijian de huigu*, vol. 1, 326–355.

6. Frederick C. Teiwes and Warren Sun, "Editor's Introduction," *The Politics of Agricultural Cooperativization in China,* 5–27.

7. Lin Yunhui, Fan Shouxin, and Zhang Gong, "Selection from China 1949–1989," 114–118.

in the cooperativization movement. Small units were merged to form large cooperatives, and tens of millions of laborers were deployed to work on irrigation projects across the country. In April 1958, the first people's commune was established in Henan Province. In the following months, people's communes—where the peasants "ate from one big pot"—were established throughout China. The Great Famine was on its way.[8]

An Entangled Bureaucracy

While history often repeats itself, people are capable of learning from their past mistakes. Why did the CCP leaders fail, repeatedly, to learn from their earlier experiences, and why did they instead keep pushing cooperativization? Why did the efforts to remedy the excesses of the cooperativization movement instead produce further excesses? Much of the responsibility must be laid at Mao Zedong's door. However, Mao was not the only actor in the tragedy that unfolded across China. Our attention must also be directed to those who inspired, aided, or simply accepted Mao's decisions.

In the creation of those experimental agricultural producers' cooperatives in 1950–1951, Mao himself was a rather passive actor. Mao did not clarify his own position until he was presented with what appeared to be well-documented reports demonstrating the efficiency and popularity of agricultural producers' cooperatives. Far from being a "top-down" initiative, it was Shanxi party members—often from relatively low levels in the administrative hierarchy—who provided Mao with the inspiration, evidence, confidence, and even theoretical backing, which convinced the chairman to support a nationwide cooperative movement in the countryside.

What happened in Shanxi demonstrates how official reports were modified and distorted to meet the specific agendas of particular interest groups. Although China's rural reality was complex and varied, the images presented to higher-level party leaders were simplified and one-dimensional, often disguised as the voice of the peasants. The phenomenon can be traced back to Mao Zedong's constant use of the term "mass line" (*qunzhong luxian*) as a means of legitimizing the party's elite leadership. Following Leninist tradition, the people "were in the end to be made to embrace, and to interiorize, ideas which if left to themselves, they were quite incapable of

---

8. Yang Jisheng, *Tombstone*.

elaborating in systematic form."[9] This need to seek legitimacy explains in some ways Mao's willingness to embrace concrete examples of participation from below and to publicize such initiatives widely. Such circumstances in turn created a powerful impetus for local cadres to distort reality in their favor, usually presented as the voice of the peasants.

Mao was not blind to this "filtering" process, and on several occasions he insisted on conducting investigation tours of the countryside in person, where he was welcomed by staged performances. Such distorted presentations were not sporadic activities—rather, they were built into the system. "The more coercive the regime, the more what passes upward is what leaders want to hear. Negative information is suppressed and its agents repressed."[10]

Ironically, in the political system that developed under Mao, support from below and the endorsement of the masses rarely mattered because, for the most part, such appeals were little more than rhetoric. In Communist China, the promotions of party cadres and government officials were nominated by the superiors, often checked by the Organizational Department, and sometimes formally approved by the official meeting or congress. The most crucial requirement of promotion was to develop the support of a network, preferably including superiors and even leading politicians, by cultivating patron–client ties.[11] Another requirement was the ability to produce results and to fulfill, or overfulfill, instructions from above—at least on paper if not in reality. Thus, cadres answered to their superiors—likely to be their patrons—rather than to those they were supposed to be serving. A good cadre took care of his people; a successful cadre took care of his superiors.

Of the two major requirements for promotion, personal networking was subtle and private so that efficiency and success in delivering results became the most obvious measure of a cadre's ability—at least in public. The simplest evidence that a task had been completed was the writing of reports, many of which were compiled by the cadres themselves. It was not uncommon for cadres at lower administrative levels to present their superiors with plans and projects far in excess of what was expected of them—and to fabricate data in their subsequent reports to prove their success. Party leaders could gain access to "reality" only through the information passed upward by various levels of subordinates following additional layers of distortion.

---

9. Stuart R. Schram, *The Thought of Mao Tse-Tung,* 98.

10. David Apter and Tony Saich, *Revolutionary Discourse in Mao's Republic,* 27.

11. Frederick C. Teiwes, *Leadership, Legitimacy, and Conflict in China,* 96–97.

This process would reach the apogee of absurdity during the Great Leap Forward, but it had started long before this time. In this sense, the CCP became a victim of its own power structure.

Prior to filing reports, however exaggerated, cadres had to find ways of fulfilling the tasks with which they were charged, a process that often involved the abuse of power and coercion. Lower-ranking cadres were frequently given ambitious, even conflicting instructions and sometimes assigned unattainable goals. Teiwes aptly reminds us of the contradiction between task (*renwu*) and policy (*zhengce*). The task usually involved a quantitative target set by the party, which was easy to measure, while the policy, which prescribed the proper methods for fulfilling these tasks, was difficult to quantify and limited cadres' means of achieving their goal. In reality, violations of the policy were often the easy—or even the only—way to accomplish the task.[12] For cadres, the successful completion of their tasks would aid them in their path to success. However, outsiders, researchers included, were better informed about policies, which were more accessible in published documents, than about tasks, the details of which were restricted to the party's inner circles.

The pressures on cadres were compounded by factionalism. The CCP, a Leninist party in its basic character, insisted on collective leadership and majority rule and banned factional activities. However, the reality was very different. Collective leadership ran up against Mao's charismatic authority; majority decision-making, and the insistence that orders be strictly implemented regardless of one's own views, sat uneasily with the complexity of Chinese society. As discussed in Chapter 2, the party was riven by a number of splinter groups. The ban on factional activities certainly conflicted with the reality within the party.[13] When the CCP denied the existence of factionalism, it could not be openly discussed or negotiated, and policymaking became a major arena for factional struggles. At the same time, these internal conflicts could magnify alternative policy positions into matters of right and wrong, left and right, socialist and capitalist. In China, political competition swiftly morphed into ideological struggles and ended up with winners and losers, with the latter becoming "traitors." This made attempts at correction even more difficult and risky than they might otherwise have been, as the repeated failures of rectification campaigns in the 1950s bore witness.

---

12. Frederick C. Teiwes, *Politics & Purge in China*, 118.
13. Frederick C. Teiwes, *Leadership, Legitimacy, and Conflict in China*, 92–98.

Indeed, the gulf between the operation of a system in principle and in reality is the norm in any political system, but denying the existence of the gulf is positively destructive. Because the CCP refused to acknowledge the imperfections of its system, it failed to develop mechanisms to deal with intrinsic problems, which would inevitably lead to breakdowns. When these breakdowns became too pressing to overlook, the CCP chose to blame individual malpractice, typically launching a campaign to suppress certain individuals and to protect the party's purity. More often than not, these campaigns turned into battlegrounds for factional struggles and only planted the seeds of future conflicts.

In a modern state, effective bureaucracy is supposed to replace personal connections with impersonal, rule-governed administration.[14] The Communist system under Mao was not: it relied on personal networks rather than an impersonal bureaucracy. How did it happen? Some of this phenomenon must have been derived from history. In China's imperial past, power had been vested in a system run by personnel, although China was among the first polities to develop bureaucracy. But in addition to its dynastic past, China's Communist system was rooted in the "mobile networks of personal links," a feature characteristic of the Soviet Union and other socialist countries.[15] In this system, promotion decisions were made by superiors; local cadres were responsible to higher authorities in the party hierarchy rather than to their local subjects. Not surprisingly, abuse of power was endemic in this system—a situation that continues today.

At the very end, we reexamine what happened in Mao's China in light of the fate of the Soviet Union.

The Allure of the Soviet Model

Fundamentally, this book explores the question of how the Chinese Communists came to adopt the Soviet collectivization model and launched their own agricultural cooperativization movement in 1953. Today, many agree on the failures of collectivization, and, with the advantage of hindsight, we are inclined to ask why the party adopted Soviet collectivization despite the many black marks in its track record. However, the question that really mat-

---

14. Joseph Strayer, *On the Medieval Origins of the Modern State*.

15. Gail Kligman and Katherine Verdery, *Peasants under Siege*, 189.

tered for Communists in the 1950s was, Why shouldn't we adopt Soviet-style collectivization?

Scholars have long noted the differences between the experiences of collectivization in China and in the Soviet Union, in particular, the relative lack of popular resistance during China's transition to agricultural collectivization. Most recently, Yu Liu has isolated five factors that facilitated the movement in China:

- the effects of land reform;
- a newly created class system;
- an effective system of social control;
- the imposition of a basic-level party apparatus;
- the existence of a legitimizing discourse.

In sum, he argues that in China, even before the introduction of agricultural cooperativization, the Communist Party had fundamentally altered the rural status quo, established its basic political apparatus, and penetrated the countryside. Thus agricultural cooperativization was erected on these preexisting building blocks. In Russia, on the other hand, the Bolsheviks created their party apparatus *through* the collectivization movement.[16]

Despite these evident differences, the parallels between the two countries are still striking. Russia (in 1921) and China (in 1949) had both emerged from a civil war and then briefly adopted moderate economic policies. In Russia, it was Lenin's NEP; in China, it was New Democracy. Both strategies were designed to encourage a mixed economy, which in the agricultural sector, acknowledged the dominant role of private farming. To assure the state's control of the rural economy, Lenin recommended the formation of cooperatives, a concept that Bukharin elaborated in terms of Supply and Marketing Cooperatives (SMCs) to serve as the state's channel to control the individual peasant economy. In China, Liu Shaoqi and Zhang Wentian proposed the establishment of commercial cooperatives, a form rooted in Bukharin's SMCs, to provide an economic conduit between the state and individual peasant farmers. Following these prescriptions, numerous commercial cooperatives were set up in both countries; and in both countries they failed to serve their intended purpose as channels between the state and individual peasants.

---

16. Yu Liu, "Why did it go so high?"

In both the Soviet Union and China, following a few years of moderate policies, peasant farmers had improved their living standards and become socially stratified. The majority of peasants desired to be left alone by the state, to prosper as farmers, and to dispose of their produce as they saw fit.[17] At the same time, new circumstances arose that the Communists did not necessarily like. Rural productivity remained low; peasants had little, if any, incentive to employ new technology. In both countries, earnings from off-farm work and craft products were sharply reduced.[18] The peasants complained about state taxes and the gap between the hard conditions endured by rural folk and the easier life of urban workers.[19] Peasants were reluctant to supply their surplus grain to the state. Because both governments intentionally kept grain prices low, the supply of marketable grain fell sharply. In the Soviet Union, the quantity of grain marketed by farmers fell from a pre-war figure of 26 percent of total output to 13.3 percent in 1928, almost half.[20] The same happened in China. Statistics gathered from villages in Changzhi prefecture show that the amount of marketable grain dropped by half in 1950 (see Chapter 3).

As the state sector was steadily developing in the direction of centralization and national planning, it came into conflict with decision-making in the peasant economy, which mainly occurred at the level of the household.[21] Under the shadow of war—the war scare of a capitalist coalition against the *USSR* in 1926–1927,[22] the Korean War in the case of China—industrialization became imperative, and heavy industry was prioritized. Both states put a five-year plan on their agendas. Russian and Chinese leaders were coming under increasing pressure to reform the existing economic structures to strengthen the polity vis-à-vis other states.

Underlying these projected changes was the pressure of grain supply. From their respective inceptions, both regimes had struggled to extract suf-

---

17. Viola Lynne, *Peasant Rebels under Stalin,* 15.

18. Sheila Fitzpatrick, *Stalin's Peasants,* 25.

19. According to Fitzpatrick, in the Soviet province of Novgorod, agricultural tax was 14 percent of net profits. Ibid. In China, between 1950 and 1952, it ranged from 15 to 20 percent for most regions.

20. Moshe Lewin, *Russian Peasants and Soviet Power.*

21. Ibid.

22. John P. Sontag, "The Soviet War Scare of 1926–27"; Alfred G. Meyer, "The War Scare of 1927."

ficient grain to support the state and feed the cities. When their grain procurement difficulties reached a crisis point, they triggered fundamental
transformations in rural policies. In the Soviet Union, the grain crisis of
1927–1928 caused the Communist leadership to reinstate the requisition
system. In 1929, a contract system was introduced that obligated all villages
to set aside specified quotas of grain for the state. In 1929, Stalin announced
the decision to collectivize. In China, the grain crisis of 1953 resulted in the
"United Purchase, United Sell" policy in October 1953. The state informed
each farming household how much of its grain surplus the state would purchase and at what price—essentially a contract system. At the same time,
Mao Zedong launched the agricultural cooperativization movement across
China.

After these new approaches had been announced, their implementation
outpaced planning and went far beyond the initial schemes devised by the
central authorities, producing substantial damages in both nations. In 1930,
Stalin had warned the party against becoming "dizzy with success" and
called for the disciplining of wayward cadres; this was followed by a massive
outflow of peasants from Soviet collective farms. In 1955 China, the Central
Committee of the CCP attempted to slow the pace of cooperativization and
called for consolidation, resulting in hundreds of thousands of agricultural
cooperatives being dissolved. However, the situation was reversed shortly
after. The goals of collectivization had been achieved much more rapidly
than either Stalin or Mao had originally anticipated, albeit accompanied by
the heavy use of coercion and violence.[23] Famines of catastrophic propor-
tions wracked both countries: the Soviet Union in 1932–1933 and China in
the late 1950s.[24] Following the famines, both countries loosened state con-
trols over the private economy. Before long, however, Stalin and Mao both
set about targeting their former comrades. Stalin waged his Great Purge in
1935–1938, fourteen years after the close of the civil war; Mao launched the
Great Proletarian Cultural Revolution (1966–1976) at least partly as a personal crusade aimed at purging his rivals within the party, sixteen years after
the CCP's victory over the Guomindang.

In terms of the process, the parallels are similarly illuminating. In both
countries, although violence was forbidden in principle, it was widely exer-

---

23. Viola Lynne, *Peasants Rebels under Stalin*, 27.
24. Ibid.

cised with the government's full knowledge. Fulfilling the plan was deemed more important than using "correct" methods. Both governments used similar tactics to enforce the collectivization/cooperativization. Quotas were set by the center and progressively made their way down to the villages. Cadres at different levels arbitrarily amended these figures to suit their own interests. They competed with one another to set up more and bigger collective farms and to exceed the schedules set for them.

Both governments adopted similar pedagogies to persuade peasants to join the movement. The most widely used methods were propaganda and teaching by example. Propaganda tools included party newspapers, wall gazettes, and media such as literature, music, radio, film, and drama. In the Soviet Union, the party established model collective farms by way of heavy investments, tax privileges, and fabricated statistics. In addition to these methods, Chinese Communists were able to draw directly on Soviet precedents. Chinese comrades, from top party leaders down to peasant representatives, were invited to visit model collective farms in the Soviet Union and to witness the benefits of collectivization for themselves. A form of socialist competition was introduced to encourage members to greater efforts; titles such as model peasant and model collective farm were handed out, along with economic incentives and political privileges. The government solicited letters and petitions from peasant farmers expressing their loyalty to the party and their ardor for collectivization. Peasants submitted their own requests to join collective farms as proof of their consent, as well as providing examples of initiatives from below and exhibiting the wisdom of the people in line with the party's image of itself.

Fear and coercion formed a constant backdrop to these campaigns. To "persuade" peasants to join up, cadres would hold meetings that went on for several days and nights and disseminated a variety of threatening slogans, many clearly in violation of the law. In pursuit of their aims, rural cadres devised various forms of intimidation directed against private farmers and their families, ranging from verbal abuse and excessive tax levies to physical attacks. Beatings and detention were also regularly used against those who opposed the party's wishes.[25] Nevertheless, three notorious methods used in the Soviet collectivization were largely absent from China, at least in the

25. Gail Kligman and Katherine Verdery, *Peasants under Siege*.

public record: the deportation of rich peasants, imprisonment, and executions.

Both governments adopted military imagery to propel their campaigns: the language of wars, fronts, enemies, sabotage, and battles was commonplace. In the case of the Soviet Union, this martial language had been introduced during the civil war period, maintained during the allied intervention in Siberia, and retained as the result of the party's need to maintain a "combat" environment in light of hostility from the United States and its allies. China's use of military rhetoric derived from unbroken decades of civil war, the war of resistance against Japan, and the war to resist the U.S. invasion of Korea.

In both the USSR and China, farmers sought to resist state policy in a variety of ways, including "weapons of the weak," such as working at less than full capacity in the fields, slaughtering or selling off their draught animals, writing petitions, and spreading rumors about the negative effects of collectivization.[26] The most common of the rumors was that members of collective farms would be forced into "eating from one big pot." (In China, this particular rumor was soon to be realized in the communes in 1958.) But it was rare that dissident villagers progressed to open rebellion.[27]

In writing this book, I kept asking the same question: Is it possible to measure the Soviet impact on China with any degree of precision? On the one hand, it is hard to exaggerate the profound Soviet influence on China with respect to norms and perceptions of socialism and socialist institutions. Several key Soviet values were deeply ingrained in the CCP's conceptions of China's socialist future. One crucial question was, What is socialism? Indeed, finding the answer to this question had been the central quest of the CCP leadership since 1949. Right up to the 1990s, the CCP continued to puzzle over the nature of a socialist society and sought ways of reinterpreting the term itself. Unable to provide any definitive answer, Mao Zedong and his colleagues had a vague, even instinctive, perception that socialism was simply the antidote to capitalism. As historian Stephen Kotkin

---

26. James Scott, *Weapons of the Weak*.

27. For a detailed comparison of collectivization in Romania and the Soviet Union, and analyses of strategies adopted by both governments and peasant farmers, see Gail Kligman and Katherine Verdery, *Peasants under Siege*.

puts it, "One achieved socialism by eradicating capitalism."[28] Above all, the distinguishing characteristic of socialism was the elimination of private property in the means of production and of class-based exploitation.[29] It also involved a commitment to social justice: no one should be left to starve, education should be available to all, the sick should receive medical treatment, and everyone should have a job. The failure to achieve a welfare society generated the guilt that drove the CCP constantly to attack capitalism whenever socioeconomic conditions seemed to require it—that is, whenever they were not on the verge of collapse. The CCP shared the faith with its Soviet comrades that control of the means of production, along with the development of "productive forces," would automatically yield a communist future that would provide the solution to all possible problems.[30] Moreover, both states adopted Leninist systems of government under Communist parties, and both operated through multilayered bureaucratic hierarchies. The similarities between state–peasant relations in the Soviet Union and China can be explained by examining the decision-making process at all levels of these bureaucratic hierarchies.

On the other hand, in regard to specific policies and actions, the Soviet model had to be treated with extreme caution, given Chinese leaders' sensitivities about sovereignty, China's fluctuating relationship with the Soviet Union, the complexities of Chinese domestic politics, and, ultimately, the gap between the policy prescriptions adopted by the CCP and their actual implementation. One additional factor that further contributes to the complexity of the Soviet impact on China is that at times there was more than one Soviet model available for emulation; even a single model appeared in more than one version, and that version was almost always subject to a variety of interpretations. The question of which model to choose and how to apply it was always settled within the policy framework erected by the Chinese Communist Party.

Perhaps it was a case of dreaming Soviet dreams and experiencing Chinese nightmares.

---

28. Stephen Kotkin, *Magnetic Mountain*, 152.

29. Ibid.

30. Maurice Meisner, "Stalinism in the History of the Chinese Communist Party," 187.

Bibliography

Sources in English

Alitto, Guy. *The Last Confucian: Liang Shu-ming and the Chinese Dilemma of Modernity.* Berkeley: University of California Press, 1986.

Apter, David, and Tony Saich, eds. *Revolutionary Discourse in Mao's Republic.* Cambridge, MA: Harvard University Press, 1998.

Benton, Gregor. *Mountain Fires: The Red Army's Three-Year War in South China, 1934–1938.* Berkeley: University of California Press, 1992.

Bernstein, Thomas. "Keeping the Revolution Going: Problems of Village Leadership after Land Reform." *China Quarterly* 36 (1968): 1–22.

_____. "Leadership and Mass Mobilization in the Soviet and Chinese Collectivization Campaigns of 1929–30 and 1955–56: A Comparison." *China Quarterly* 31 (1969): 1–47.

_____. "Stalinism, Famine, and Chinese Peasants." *Theory and Society* 13 (1984): 339–377.

Bernstein, Thomas. "Introduction." In *China Learns from the Soviet Union, 1949–Present,* eds. Thomas Bernstein and Hua-yu Li, 1–26. Lanham: Lexington Books, 2010.

Bianco, Lucien. *Peasants without the Party: Grass-Roots Movements in Twentieth-Century China.* Armonk, NY: M.E. Sharpe, 2001.

_____. *Wretched Rebels: Rural Disturbances on the Eve of the Chinese Revolution.* Cambridge, MA, and London: Harvard University Press, 2009.

Brown, Jeremy. *City versus Countryside in Mao's China: Negotiating the Divide.* Cambridge: Cambridge University Press, 2012.

Buck, John. *Land Utilization in China,* 3 vols. Chicago: University of Chicago Press, 1937.

Chan, Anita, Richard Madsen, and Jonathan Unger. *Chen Village under Mao and Deng.* Berkeley: University of California Press, 1992.

Chang, Chung-li. *The Chinese Gentry: Studies on Their Role in Nineteenth-Century Chinese Society.* Seattle and London: University of Washington Press, 1955.

Chang, Jung, and Jon Halliday. *Mao: The Unknown Story*. New York: Alfred A. Knopf, 2005.

Chen Hansheng. *Landlords and Peasants in China: A Study of the Agrarian Crisis in South China*. New York: International Publishers, 1936.

Chen Yung-fa. *Making Revolution—The Communist Movement in Eastern and Central China, 1937–1945*. Berkeley: University of California Press, 1986.

———. "The Blooming Poppy under the Red Sun: The Yan'an Way and the Opium Trade." In *New Perspectives on the Chinese Communist Revolution*, eds. Tony Saich and Hans van de Ven, 263–298. Armonk, NY: M.E. Sharpe, 1995.

Christensen, Thomas. *Useful Adversaries*. Princeton, NJ: Princeton University Press, 1996.

Ci Jiwei. *Dialectic of the Chinese Revolution: From Utopianism to Hedonism*. Stanford, CA: Stanford University Press, 1994.

Crook, Isobel, and David Crook. *Mass Movement in a Chinese Village: Ten Mile Inn*. New York: Routledge & Kegan Paul, 1979.

Dikötter, Frank. *Mao's Great Famine*. London: Walker Books, 2011.

Dirlik, Arif, Paul Healy, and Nick Knight, eds. *Critical Perspectives on Mao Zedong's Thought*. Trenton, NJ: Humanities Press, 1997.

Duara, Prasenjit. *Culture, Power and the State: Rural North China, 1900–1942*. Stanford, CA: Stanford University Press, 1988.

Eyferth, Jacob. *Eating Rice from Bamboo Roots: The Social History of a Community of Handicraft Papermakers in Rural Sichuan, 1920–2000*. Cambridge, MA, and London: Harvard University East Asia Center, 2009.

Fairbank, John, and Albert Feuerwerker, eds. *The Cambridge History of China Cambridge*, vol. 13. Cambridge: Cambridge University Press, 1986.

Fitzpatrick, Sheila. *Stalin's Peasants: Resistance and Survival in the Russian Village after Collectivization*. New York: Oxford University Press, 1994.

———. *Everyday Stalinism: Ordinary Life in Extraordinary Times: Soviet Russia in the 1930s*. New York: Oxford University Press, 1999.

Friedman, Edward. *Backward Toward Revolution: The Chinese Revolutionary Party*. Berkeley and Los Angeles: University of California Press, 1974.

Friedman, Edward, Paul Pickowicz, and Mark Selden. *Chinese Village, Socialist State*. New Haven, CT, & London: Yale University, 1991.

Gao Huamin. "Rectifying the Problems of Impetuosity and Rash Advance in the Agricultural Mutual Aid and Cooperativization movement in 1953." In *The Politics of Agricultural Cooperativization in China*, eds. Frederick C. Teiwes and Warren Sun, 61–64. Armonk, NY: M.E. Sharpe, 1993.

Gao, James. *The Communist Takeover of Hangzhou: The Transformation of City and Cadre, 1949–1954*. Honolulu: University of Hawaii Press, 2004.

Gao, Mobo. *Gao Village: A Portrait of Rural Life in Modern China*. Honolulu: University of Hawaii Press, 1999.

Goodman, David. *Social and Political Change in Revolutionary China: The Taihang Base Area in the War of Resistance to Japan, 1937–1945*. New York: Rowman & Littlefield, 2000.

Han Xiaorong. *Chinese Discourses on the Peasant, 1900–1949*. Albany: State University of New York Press, 2005.

Hartford, Kathleen. *Step by Step: Reform, Resistance and Revolution in China's Chin-Ch'a-Chi Border Region, 1937–45*. Ph.D. dissertation, Stanford University, 1980.

_____. "Fits and Starts: The Communist Party in Rural Hebei, 1921–1936." In *New Perspectives on the Chinese Communist Revolution*, eds. Tony Saich and Hans van de Ven, 144–173. Armonk, NY: M.E. Sharpe, 1995.

Hayford, Charles W. *To the People: James Yen and Village China*. New York: Columbia University Press, 1990.

Heilmann, Sebastian. "Policy-Making through Experimentation: The Formation of a Distinctive Policy Process." In *Mao's Invisible Hand: The Political Foundations of Adaptive Governance in China*, eds. Sebastian Heilmann and Elizabeth Perry, 62–73. Cambridge, MA: Harvard University Asia Center, 2011.

Heilmann, Sebastian, and Elizabeth Perry, eds. *Mao's Invisible Hand: The Political Foundations of Adaptive Governance in China*. Cambridge, MA: Harvard University Asia Center, 2011.

_____, and Elizabeth Perry. "Embracing Uncertainty: Guerrilla Policy Style and Adaptive Governance in China." In *Mao's Invisible Hand: The Political Foundations of Adaptive Governance in China*, eds. Sebastian Heilmann and Elizabeth Perry, 1–29. Cambridge, MA: Harvard University Asia Center, 2011.

Hinton, William. *Fanshen: A Documentary of Revolution in a Chinese Village*. New York: Random House, 1966.

Holquist, Peter. "'Information is the Alpha and Omega of Our Work': Bolshevik Surveillance in its Pan-European Context." *Journal of Modern History* 69 (1997): 415-450.

Hou, Xiaojia. "'Get Organized': The Impact of the Soviet Model on the CCP's Rural Economic Strategy, 1949–1953." In *China Learns from the Soviet Union, 1949–present*, eds. Thomas Bernstein and Hua-yu Li, 167–196. Lanham: Lexington Books, 2010.

Howe, Christopher. "China's High Tide of Socialism of 1955: Strategic Choices and Paths Not Taken, Some Changing Perspectives." *China Quarterly* 187 (2006): 754-762.

Huang, Philip C. *The Peasant Economy and Social Change in North China*. Stanford, CA: Stanford University Press, 1985.

Huang Shu-min. *The Spiral Road: Change in a Chinese Village through the Eyes of a Communist Party Leader*. Boulder, CO: Westview, 1989.

Hughes, James. *Stalin, Siberia, and the Crisis of the New Economic Policy*. New York: Cambridge University Press, 1991.

_____. *Stalinism in a Russian Province: A Study of Collectivization and Dekulakization in Siberia*. New York: St. Martin's Press, 1996.

Jae Ho Chung, "Central–Local Dynamics: Historical Continuities and Institutional Resilience." In *Mao's Invisible Hand: The Political Foundations of Adaptive Governance in China*, eds. Sebastian Heilmann and Elizabeth Perry, 297–320. Cambridge, MA: Harvard University Asia Center, 2011.

Kau, Michael and John Leung, eds. *The Writings of Mao Zedong, 1949–1976*. Armonk, NY: M.E. Sharpe, 1986.

Keating, Pauline B. *Two Revolutions: Village Reconstruction and the Cooperative Movement in Northern Shaanxi, 1934–1945*. Stanford, CA: Stanford University Press, 1997.

Kingston-Mann, Esther. *Lenin and the Problem of Marxist Peasant Revolution*. New York: Oxford University Press, 1983.

Kligman, Gail, and Katherine Verdery. *Peasants under Siege: The Collectivization of Romanian Agriculture, 1949–1962*. Princeton, NJ: Princeton University Press, 2011.

Knight, Nick. *Rethinking Mao: Explorations in Mao Zedong*. Lanham, MD: Lexington Books, 2007.

Kotkin, Stephen. *Magnetic Mountain: Stalinism as Civilization*. Berkeley: University of California Press, 1995.

Kotsonis, Yanni. *Making Peasants Backward: Agricultural Cooperatives and the Agrarian Question in Russia, 1861–1914*. New York: St. Martin's Press, 1999.

Kueh, Y.Y. "Mao and Agriculture in China's Industrialization: Three Antitheses in a 50-Year Perspective." *China Quarterly* 187 (2006): 700–723.

Kuhn, Philip. *Rebellion and Its Enemies in Late Imperial China: Militarization and Social Structure, 1796–1864*. Cambridge, MA: Harvard University Press, 1970.

_____. *Origins of the Modern Chinese State*. Stanford, CA: Stanford University Press, 2002.

Lamley, Harry J. "Liang Shu-ming, Rural Reconstruction and Rural Work Discussion Society, 1933–1935." *Chung Chi Journal* 8 (1969): 50–61.

Lardy, Nicholas. "Economic Recovery and the 1st Five-Year Plan." In *The Cambridge History of China, vol. 14: The People's Republic, Part I: The Emergence of Revolutionary China, 1949–1965*, eds. Roderick MacFarquhar and John K. Fairbank, 144–183. Cambridge: Cambridge University Press, 1987.

Ledovsky, Andrei. "Mikoyan's Secret Mission to China in January and February 1949." *Far Eastern Affairs*, no. 3 (1995): 72–94.

_____. "Two Cables from Correspondence between Mao Zedong and Joseph Stalin." *Far Eastern Affairs*, no. 6 (2000): 89–96.

Lenin, V.I. "On Cooperation." In *Collected Works*, V.I. Lenin, vol. 33, 2nd English Edition. Moscow: Progress Publishers, 1965.

Levine, Steven. *Anvil of Victory: The Communist Revolution in Manchuria, 1945–1948*. New York: Columbia University Press, 1987.

Lewin, Moshe. *Political Undercurrents in Soviet Economic Debates: From Bukharin to the Modern Reformers*. Princeton, NJ: Princeton University Press, 1974.

_____. *Russian Peasants and Soviet Power—A Study of Collectivization*. New York. London: W.W. Norton, 1975.

Li Hua-yu. *Mao and the Economic Stalinization of China, 1948—1953*. Lanham, MD: Rowman & Littlefield, 2006.

Li Huaiyin. *Village China under Socialism and Reform: A Micro-History, 1948-2008*. Stanford, CA: Stanford University Press, 2010.

Lieberthal, Kenneth. *Revolution and Tradition in Tientsin, 1949-1952*. Stanford, CA: Stanford University, 1980.

Lin Yunhui, Fan Shouxin, and Zhang Gong. "Selection from China 1949-1989: The Period of Triumph and Advance." In *The Politics of Agricultural Cooperativization in China*, eds. Frederick C. Teiwes and Warren Sun, 82-120. Armonk, NY: M.E. Sharpe, 1993.

Little, Daniel. *Understanding Peasant China: Case Studies in the Philosophy of Social Science*. New Haven, CT, and London: Yale University Press, 1989.

Liu, Yu. "Why Did It Go So High? Political Mobilization and Agricultural Collectivization in China." *China Quarterly* 187 (2006): 732-742.

Ma Junya and Tim Wright. "Industrialization and Handicraft Cloth: The Jiangsu Peasant Economy in the Late Nineteenth and Early Twentieth Century." *Modern Asia Studies* 44 (2010): 1337-1372.

Manning, Kimberley Ens, and Felix Wemheuer, eds. *Eating Bitterness: New Perspectives on China's Great Leap Forward and Famine*. Vancouver: University of British Columbia Press, 2012.

Marks, Robert. *Rural Revolution in South China: Peasants and the Making of History in Haifeng County, 1570-1930*. Madison: University of Wisconsin Press, 1984.

Marx, Karl. *Communist Manifesto*, ed. Frederic Bender. New York, London: W.W. Norton, 1988.

Meisner, Maurice. *Mao's China and After: A History of the People's Republic*. New York: Free Press, 1986.

_____. "Stalinism in the History of the Chinese Communist Party." In *Critical Perspectives on Mao Zedong's Thought*, eds. Arif Dirlik, Paul Healy, and Nick Knight, 184-206. Trenton, NJ: Humanities Press, 1997.

_____. *Mao Zedong: A Political and Intellectual Portrait*. Cambridge: Polity Press, 2007.

Meliksetov, Arlen. "'New Democracy' and China's search for socio-economic development routes (1949-1953)." *Far Eastern Affairs* 1 (1996): 75-92.

Meyer, Alfred G. "The War Scare of 1927." *Soviet Union/Union Sovietique* 5, no. 1 (1978): 1-25.

Myers, Ramon. "The Agrarian System." In *The Cambridge History of China*, vol. 13, eds. Dennis Twitchett and John K. Fairbank, 230-269. Cambridge: Cambridge University Press, 1986.

Ngo, Thi Minh-Hoang. "A Hybrid Revolutionary Process: The Chinese Cooperative Movement in Xiyang County, Shanxi." *Modern China* 35 (2009): 284–312.

Oi, Jean C. *State and Peasant in Contemporary China*. Berkeley: University of California Press, 1989.

Perry, Elizabeth. *Shanghai on Strike: The Politics of Chinese Labor*. Stanford, CA: Stanford University Press, 1993.

Pomeranz, Kenneth. *The Making of A Hinterland: State, Society and Economy in Inland North China, 1853–1937*. Berkeley: University of California Press, 1993.

Prazniak, Roxann. *Of Camel Kings and Other Things: Rural Rebels against Modernity in Late Imperial China*. Lanham, MD: Rowman & Littlefield, 1999.

Rankin, Mary. *Elite Activism and Political Transformation in China: Zhejiang Province, 1865–1911*. Stanford, CA: Stanford University Press, 1986.

Rawski, Thomas. *Economic Growth in Prewar China*. Berkeley: University of California Press, 1989.

Saich, Tony. "Writing or Rewriting History? The Construction of the Maoist Resolution on Party History." In *New Perspectives on the Chinese Communist Revolution*, eds. Tony Saich and Hans van de Ven, 299–338. Armonk, NY: M.E. Sharpe, 1995.

Saich, Tony, and Hans van de Ven, eds. *New Perspectives on the Chinese Communist Revolution*. Armonk, NY: M.E. Sharpe, 1995.

Schram, Stuart R. *The Thought of Mao Tse-Tung*. Cambridge: Cambridge University Press, 1989.

Schram, Stuart R, and Nancy Hodes, eds. *Mao's Road to Power*, vols. 1–7. Armonk, NY: M.E. Sharpe, 1992–2014.

Scott, James. *The Moral Economy of the Peasant: Rebellion and Subsistence in Southeast Asia*. New Haven, CT, and London: Yale University Press, 1976.

———. *Weapons of the Weak: Everyday Forms of Peasant Resistance*. New Haven, CT, and London: Yale University Press, 1987.

———. *Seeing like a State*. New Haven, CT, and London: Yale University Press, 1998.

Schoppa, Keith. *Revolution and Its Past*. Saddle River, NJ: Pearson Education, 2006.

Selden, Mark. *The Yenan Way in Revolutionary China*. Cambridge, MA: Harvard University Press, 1971.

Shanin, Teodor. *The Awkward Class*. Oxford: Oxford University Press, 1972.

———. "Socio-Economic Mobility and the Rural History of Russia 1905–30," *Soviet Studies* vol. 23, no. 2 (October 1971): 222–235.

Shapiro, Judith. *Mao's War against Nature: Politics and the Environment in Revolutionary China*. Cambridge: Cambridge University Press, 2001.

Short, Philip. *Mao: A Life*. New York: Holt, 1999.

Shue, Vivienne. *Peasant China in Transition: The Dynamics of Development toward Socialism, 1949–1956*. Berkeley: University of California Press, 1980.

Sih, Paul, ed. *The Strenuous Decade: China's Nation-Building Efforts, 1927–37*. Jamaica, NY: St. John's University Press, 1970.

Skinner, William. "Regional Urbanization in Nineteenth-Century China." In *The City in Late Imperial China*, ed. William Skinner, 211–252. Stanford, CA: Stanford University Press, 1977.

Sontag, John P. "The Soviet War Scare of 1926–27." *Russian Review* 34 (1975): 66–77.

Spence, Jonathan. *The Search for Modern China*. New York: W.W. Norton & Company, 1999.

Strayer, Joseph. *On the Medieval Origins of the Modern State*. Princeton, NJ: Princeton University Press, 1970.

Tanaka Kyoko. "Mao and Liu in 1947 Land Reform: Allies or Disputants?" *China Quarterly* 75 (1979): 566–593.

Teiwes, Frederick C. *Leadership, Legitimacy, and Conflict in China*. Armonk, NY: M.E. Sharpe, 1984.

_____. *Politics at Mao's Court: Gao Gang and Party Factionalism in the Early 1950s*. Armonk, NY: M.E. Sharpe, 1990.

_____. *Politics & Purge in China, Rectification and the Decline of Party Norms 1950–65*. London: Routledge, 1993.

Teiwes, Frederick C., and Warren Sun, eds. *The Politics of Agricultural Cooperativization in China*. Armonk, NY: M.E. Sharpe, 1993.

Tetsuya Kataoka. *Resistance and Revolution in China: The Communists and the Second United Front*. Berkeley: University of California Press, 1974.

Thaxton, Ralph. *Salt of the Earth: The Political Origins of Peasant Protest and Communist Revolution in China*. Berkeley: University of California Press, 1997.

Thomson, James. *While China Faced West: American Reformers in Nationalist China, 1928–1937*. Cambridge, MA: Harvard University Press, 1969.

Thorner, Naniel, Basile Kerblay, and R.E.F. Smith, eds. *A.V. Chayanov on the Theory of Peasant Economy*. Homewood: Richard D. Irwin, 1966.

Thornton, Patricia. "Retrofitting the Steel Frame: From Mobilizing the Masses to Surveying the Public." In *Mao's Invisible Hand: The Political Foundations of Adaptive Governance in China*, eds. Sebastian Heilmann and Elizabeth Perry, 237–268. Cambridge, MA: Harvard University Asia Center, 2011.

Tilly, Charles, ed. *The Formation of National States in Western Europe*. Princeton, NJ: Princeton University Press, 1975.

Twitchett, Dennis, and John K. Fairbank, eds. *The Cambridge History of China*, vol. 13. Cambridge: Cambridge University Press, 1986.

U, Eddy. "Reification of the Chinese Intellectual: On the Origins of the CCP Concept of Zhishifenzi." *Modern China* 35 (2009): 604–631.

Viola, Lynne. *Peasant Rebels under Stalin: Collectivization and the Culture of Peasant Resistance*. New York: Oxford University Press, 1996.

Vogel, Ezra. *Canton under Communism: Programs and Politics in a Provincial Capital, 1949–1968.* Cambridge, MA: Harvard University Press, 1969.

Walker, Kenneth. "Collectivization in Retrospect: The 'Socialist High Tide' of Autumn 1955–Spring 1956." *China Quarterly* 26 (1966): 1–3.

Wang Liming and John Davis. *China's Grain Economy.* Burlington, VT: Ashgate, 2000.

Wingrove, Paul. "Mao's Conversations with the Soviet Ambassador, 1953–55." *Cold War International History Project Working Papers Series*, no. 36 (2002).

Wolf, Eric. *Peasant Wars of the Twentieth Century.* New York: Harper & Row, 1968.

Yang Jisheng, *Tombstone.* Farrar, Straus and Giroux, 2012.

Zhu Yonghong, "Reflections on the Party's Policy toward the Rural Individual economy during the First Seven Years of the State." In *The Politics of Agricultural Cooperativization in China,* eds. Frederick C. Teiwes and Warren Sun, 51–59. Armonk, NY: M.E. Sharpe, 1993.

Sources in Chinese

ARCHIVES

Changzhi Municipal Archive, Changzhi, Shanxi Province (CMA)
Jincheng Municipal Archive, Jincheng, Shanxi Province (JMA)
Shanxi Local History Office Library, Taiyuan, Shanxi Province
Shanxi Provincial Archive, Taiyuan, Shanxi Province (SPA)
Sichuan Provincial Archive, Chengdu, Sichuan Province
Wuxiang County Archive, Wuxiang, Shanxi Province

NEWSPAPERS

Hebei Daily
Northeast Daily
People's Daily
Shanxi Daily
Xinhua Daily

RESTRICTED CIRCULATED JOURNALS

Jianshe (Construction)
Neibu cankao (Internal References)
Zhongguo nongye hezuoshi ziliao (Documents on China's Agricultural Cooperativization)
Zhonggong zhongyang Huabeiju zhongyao wenjian huibian (A collection of important documents relating to the North China Bureau of the CCP), vol. 1 (hereafter cited as *Huibian*)

BOOKS AND ARTICLES

"Bixu jishi jiuzheng laodong huzhu yundong zhong de quedian" (We must promptly correct the mistakes of the mutual aid and cooperation movement). *Kangzhan Daily*, May 18, 1944.

"Bixu kefu zai lingdao nongye shengchan zhong de yanzhong mangmu xing" (The serious mistakes in promoting agricultural production as the result of blindness must be rectified). *Jianshe*, no. 210 (March 30, 1953).

Bo Yibo. *Ruogan zhongda juece yu shijian de huigu* (Reflections on certain major decisions and events). Beijing: Zhonggong zhongyang dangxiao chubanshe, 1991.

Cao Jiansheng. "Tudi geming chuqi de 'nongye jitihua' wenti zaitan" (Another discussion on the agricultural collectivization during the early years of land revolution). *Zhongguo nongye hezuoshi ziliao*, no. 1 (1986).

"Changzhi diqu wuge cun tugai shengchan zhong jieji bianhua de diaocha" (An investigation into changes in class status during land reform and reorganized production in five villages in the Changzhi area) (January 10, 1950). In *Changzhi diqu shiban he fazhan nongye shengchan hezuoshe de ruogan lishi ziliao* (Several historical documents regarding the establishment of experimental agricultural producers' cooperatives in the Changzhi area). Shangxi: Rural Politics Department, 1977.

"Changzhi zhuanqu huzhuzu zhong de gonggong caichan yu gongjijin wenti" (Problems relating to communal property and community funds held by mutual aid teams in Changzhi prefecture) (February 21, 1951). In *Zhonggong zhongyang Huabeiju zhongyao wenjian huibian* (A collection of important documents relating to the North China Bureau of the CCP), vol. 1 (hereafter cited as *Huibian*), 271–273. Restricted circulation.

Chen Jin, ed. *Mao Zedong dushu biji* (Reading notes of Mao Zedong). Guangdong: Guangdong renmin chubanshe, 1996.

Chen Yun. *Chen Yun wenxuan* (Collected works of Chenyun). Beijing: Renmin chubanshe, 1986.

Chen Yung-fa. "Civil War, Mao Zedong and Land Revolution—Misjudgment or Political Strategy?" *Ta Lu* (Taiwan), no. 92 (1996): 9–19.

_____. "Reconsidering Yan'an, Again." *New History* (Taiwan), vol. 8, no. 3 (1997): 95–159.

Cong Hanxiang ed. *Jindai Ji Lu Yu xiangcun* (Villages in Ji, Lu and Yu in Modern Time). Beijing: Zhongguo shehui kexue chubanshe, 1995.

Shangyebu dangdai liangshi gongzuo bianji bu, eds. *Dangdai Zhongguo liangshi gongzuo shiliao* (Historical documents relating to grain production in contemporary China). Restricted circulation, 1989.

Ding Shijun. "Liening zhuzuo zai Zhongguo de chuban he chuanbo" (The publication and spread of Lenin's work in China). In *Chuanbo zhenli, fengdou buxi—zhonggong zhongyang bianyi ju chengli 50 zhounian jinian wenji* (Spread truth, never stop working—the collection of papers in honor of the fifties anniversary of the Central Compilation and *Translation* Bureau). Beijing: Zhonggong zhongyang bianyiju, 2003.

Dong Shijin. "Dong Shijin zhixin Mao Zedong tan tugai" (Dong Shijin's letter to Mao Zedong on the issue of land reform). *Yanhuang chunqiu,* no. 4 (2011).

_____. *Lun gongchandang de tudi gaige* (On the Communists' land reform program). Hong Kong: Ziyou chubanshe, 1950.

Dong Zhi-kai. "The 'War to Resist America and Aid Korea' and the New China's Economy." *Dangdai Zhongguo shi yanjiu,* no. 5 (2011).

Du Runsheng. *Dangdai Zhongguo de nongye hezuo zhi* (Contemporary China's agricultural cooperative system). Beijing: Dangdai Zhongguo chubanshe, 2002.

Feng Xianzhi and Jin Chongji, eds. *Mao Zedong zhuan* (A biography of Mao Zedong). Beijing: Zhongyang wenxian chubanshe, 2003.

Gao Hua. "Zai dao yu shi zhijian" (Between "ideology" and "influence"). *Chinese Social Science Quarterly* (Hong Kong), no. 5 (1993).

Gao Huamin. "Guanyu hezuohua yundong bufa jiakuai yuanyin de lishi kaocha" (The historical study on the reasons for the speeding up of the cooperativization movement). *Zhonggong dangshi yanjiu,* no. 4 (1997).

_____. *Nongye hezuohua yundong shimo* (The history of the agricultural collectivization movement). Beijing: Zhongguo qingnian chubanshe, 1999.

Gao Wangling. *Renmin gongshe shiqi Zhongguo nongmin fanxingwei diaocha* (An investigation into peasant resistance during the people's commune period). Beijing: Zhongguo dangshi chubanshe, 2006.

"Gei Huabeiju zuzhibu de gongzuo baogao" (Report to the Organizational Department of the North China Bureau) (November 5, 1948). In *Dang de jianshe* (The construction of the party), 511–518. Shanxi: Shanxi renmin chubanshe, 1989.

Gu Longsheng. *Mao Zedong jingji nianpu* (An economic chronicle of Mao Zedong). Beijing: Zhonggong zhongyang dangxiao chubanshe, 1993.

Central Committee of the CCP. *Guanyu jianguo yilai dang de ruogan lishi wenti de jueyi* (The resolution on certain questions in the history of our party since the founding of the People's Republic of China). Beijing: Renmin chubanshe, 1983.

History of the Communist Party of the Soviet Union. Moscow: Foreign Languages Publishing House, 1960.

Huang Daoxuan. "Mengyou yihuo qianzai duishou?" (Ally or potential rivals?) *Journal of Nanjing University* no. 5 (2007): 82-96.

Huang Zhenglin. *Shann–Gan–Ning bianqu shehui jingji shi (1937–1945)* (Social and economic history of the Shann–Gan–Ning base area 1937–1945). Beijing: Renmin chubanshe, 2006.

"Huzhu zu zhong de jige wenti" (Some problems with mutual aid teams). *Xinhua Daily*, April 11, 1945.

"Ivan Kovalev's report to Stalin on December 24, 1949" (translated by Ma Guifan). *Zhonggong dangshi yanjiu*, no. 6 (2004): 88–92.

Jin Chongji and Chen Qun, eds. *Chen Yun zhuan* (The biography of Chen Yun). Beijing: Zhongyang wenxian Chubanshe, 2005.

Jin Guantao and Liu Qingfeng. "Zhongguo gongchangdang weishenme fangqi xin minzhu zhuyi" (Why the CCP abandoned New Democracy). *Twenty-First Century,* no. 13 (October 1992): 13–25.

Li Weihan. *Huiyi yu yanjiu* (Recollections and research). Beijing: Zhonggong dangshi ziliao chubanshe, 1986.

Lian gong (bu) dangshi jianming jiaocheng (History of the Communist Party of the Soviet Union). Beijing: Shidai chubanshe, 1949.

Liang Quanzhi, ed. *Shanxi nongzheng yaolan 1949–1989* (Key points on rural policies in Shanxi). Taiyuan: Shanxi renmin chubanshe, 1992.

Lin Pulang. *Zhongguo hezuo jingji fazhan shi* (The history of the development of cooperative economy in China). Beijing: Dangdai Zhongguo chubanshe, 1998.

Lin Yifu, Cai Fang, and Li Zhou, eds. *Zhongguo de qiji* (China's miracle). Shanghai: Sanlian chubanshe, 1999.

Liu Guiren. *Lai Ruoyu zhuan* (Biography of Lai Ruoyu). Taiyuan: Shanxi renmin chubanshe, 1994.

Liu Jianping. "Nongye hezuohua juece de guocheng jiqi zhengzhixue yiyi: xin Zhongguo 1951" (Policy decision-making in the cooperative transformation of agriculture and its political implications: New China in 1951). *Kaifang shidai,* no. 2 (2003).

Liu Kexiang. "20 shiji 30 niandai tudi jieji fenpei zhuangkuang de zhengti kaocha he guji" (A comprehensive evaluation and a mathematical analysis of land distribution in the 1930s). *Zhongguo jingji shi yanjiu*, no. 1 (2002).

Liu Shaoqi. *Liu Shaoqi lun xin Zhongguo jingji jianshe* (Liu Shaoqi on the economic construction of the People's Republic). Beijing: Zhongyang wenxian chubanshe, 1993.

Lu Zhenxiang. *Tansuo de guiji* (Trails of the exploration). Beijing: Zhongyang wenxian chubanshe, 2003.

Luo Pinghan. *Nongye hezuohua yundong shi* (A history of agricultural cooperativization). Fujian: Fujian renmin chubanshe, 2004.

Ma Shexiang. "Interview with Tao Lujia." *Dang de wenxian*, no. 5 (2008): 72–74.

Mao Zedong. "Self-Encouragement: To Fight" (1917). Available online and accessed on November 10, 2015, http://www.bangnishouji.com/html/201510/219727 .html.

———. "Report on the Peasant Movement in Hunan" (February 1927). In *Mao's Road to Power*, eds. Stuart R. Schram and Nancy Hodes, *Mao's Road to Power*, vol. 2, 429–464. Armonk, NY: M.E. Sharpe, 1992–2014.

———. *Selected works of Mao Tse-tung*. Beijing: Foreign Languages Press, 1965.

———. *Mao Zedong zaoqi wengao* (Mao Zedong's works in the early years). Hunan: Hunan renmin chubanshe, 1990.

———. "On Cooperatives." In *Jianguo yilai nongye hezuohua shiliao huibian* (A collection of historical documents on the agricultural cooperativization movement since the founding of the People's Republic China). Beijing: Zhonggong dangshi chubanshe, 1992.

———. *Mao Zedong wenji* (Collected writings of Mao Zedong). Beijing: Zhongyang wenxian chubanshe, 1996.

Miao Xinyu. *Jianguo qian 30 nian Zhongguo nongye fazhan sixiang* (The philosophy of agricultural development in China, 1919–1949). Unpublished dissertation, Fudan University, 1997.

Nongye juan. See *Zhonghua renmin gongheguo jingji dang'an ziliao xuanbian, 1949–1952, nongye juan.*

Nongye jitihua zhongyao wenjian huibian (A collection of important documents relating to agricultural collectivization). Beijing: Zhonggong zhongyang dangxiao chubanshe, 1981.

"Nongye shui chatian dingchan gongzuo shishi gangyao" (Guidance on carrying out Surveying Land and Fixing *Production* Quotas)(July 5, 1951). In *Zhonggong caijing zhengce faling huibian* (Collection of financial policies and laws). Beijing, restricted circulation.

North China Bureau, eds. *1948 nian yilai zhengce huibian* (A collection of policies since 1948). Restricted circulation.

Ren Ziming and Zhao Mingze, "1944 nian Jia Baozhi chuangban tudi yunshu hezuoshe" (How Jia Baozhi formed his land and distribution cooperative in 1944). *Zhongguo nongye hezuoshi ziliao*, no. 2 (1988).

Shanxi nongcun zhengzhi gongzuo bu, eds. *Changzhi diqu shiban he fazhan nongye shengchan hezuoshe de ruogan lishi ziliao* (Several historical documents regarding the establishment of experimental agricultural producers' cooperatives in the Changzhi area). Shangxi: Shanxi nongcun zhengzhi gongzuo bu, 1977.

"Shanxi sheng 1952 nian shang bannian jianli yu fazhan nongye shengchan hezuoshe de qingkuang he jingyan" (Problems encountered and lessons learned by Shanxi Province in establishing and developing agricultural producers' cooperatives in the first half of 1952). In *Shanxi sheng nongye hezuoshi huzhu zu juan*, eds. Shanxi sheng nongye hezuoshi bianji weiyuan hui, 315–320. Restricted circulation, 1999.

Shanxi sheng difang zhi bangongshi, eds. *Shanxi tongzhi* (History of Shanxi). Beijing: Fangzhi chubanshe, 1999.

Shanxi sheng nongye hezuoshi bianji weiyuan hui, eds. *Shanxi sheng nongye hezuoshi huzhu zu juan* (Agricultural cooperativization in Shanxi: volume on mutual aid teams). Restricted circulation, 1999.

Shanxi sheng nongye hezuoshi bianji weiyuan hui, eds. *Shanxi sheng nongye hezuoshi wenjian huibian juan* (Agricultural cooperativization in Shanxi: volume on collection of documents). Restricted circulation.

Shanxi sheng shizhi yanjiu yuan, eds. *Shanxi nongye hezuohua* (Agricultural cooperativization in Shanxi). Taiyuan: Shanxi renmin chubanshe, 2001.

"Shanxi sheng zuzhi qilai de lishi qingkuang" (The historical facts on "getting organized" in Shanxi Province). In *Shanxi sheng nongye hezuoshi huzhu zu juan*, eds. Shanxi sheng nongye hezuoshi bianji weiyuan hui (Agricultural cooperativization in Shanxi: volume on mutual aid teams), 593–596. Restricted circulation, 1999.

Shanxi sheng shizhi yanjiu yuan, eds. *Dangdai Shanxi zhongyao huiyi* (Important meetings in contemporary Shanxi). Beijing: Zhongyang wenxian chubanshe, 2002.

Shen Congwen. *Shen Congwen wenji* (Writings of Shen Congwen). Guangzhou: Huacheng chubanshe, 1982.

"Shengwei kuoda huiyi" (Enlarged meeting of the provincial branch) (May 28, 1950). In *Dangdai Shanxi zhongyao huiyi*, 63.

Shi Jingtang, ed. *Zhongguo nongye hezuohua yundong shiliao* (Historical documents on China's agricultural cooperativization movement). Beijing: Sanlian chubanshe, 1957.

Shinji Yamaguchi. "Lun Mao Zedong fangqi xin minzhu zhuyi de zhanlue yanbian" (Discussion on how Mao Zedong abandoned New Democracy). *Zhonggong dangshi ziliao*, no. 4 (2008).

Tang Zhiqing. *Jindai Shandong nongcun shehui jingji yanjiu* (Research on social economy in modern rural Shandong). Beijing: Renmin chubanshe, 2004.

Tao Lujia. *Mao zhuxi jiao women dang shengwei shuji* (Chairman Mao taught us how to be provincial governors). Beijing: Zhongyang wenxian chubanshe, 1996.

———. "Zai di 190 ci shengwei changweihui shang de fayan" (A talk given at the 190th meeting of the provincial committee). In *Shanxi sheng nongye hezuoshi wenjian huibian juan* (Agricultural cooperativization in Shanxi: volume on collection of documents), eds. Shanxi sheng nongye hezuoshi bianji weiyuan hui, 333–334. Restricted circulation.

_____. "Mao zhuxi zhichi Shanxi sheng shiban hezuoshe" (Chairman Mao suported Shanxi Province in the establishment of trial cooperatives). In *Shanxi nongye hezuohua* (Agricultural cooperativization in Shanxi), eds. Shanxi sheng shizhi yanjiu yuan, 635–654. Taiyuan: Shanxi renmin chubanshe, 2001.

Tian Xiquan. *Geming yu xiangcun* (Revolution and villages). Shanghai: Shehui kexueyuan chubanshe, 2006.

Vladimirov, Peter. *Yan'an riji* (Dairy in Yan'an). Beijing: Dongfang chubanshe, 2004.

Wang Danli. "Tonggou tongxiao yanjiu shuping" (Summary of research on the nationalization of the grain market). *Dangdai Zhongguo shi yanjiu*, no. 1 (2008).

Wang Haiguang. "Zhengzheng yu quanzheng—Gao Rao shijian qiyin zai jiedu" (Political struggles and power struggles—Another interpretation of the cause of Gao-Rao affair). *Leaders* 26 (2009).

_____. "Minbian yu 'feiluan': yi zhonggong jieguan guizhou ji xinan shi de zhengliang weili" (Mass riots and 'bandit rebels': case of the CCP's takeover of Guizhou and southwest). *Leaders*, 28 (2009).

Wang Qian. "Zai changzhi qu huzhu daibiaohui shang guanyu shiban nongye shengchan hezuoshe de baogao" (Report on establishing experimental agricultural producers' cooperatives at a meeting of representatives of mutual aid teams in Changzhi) (March 27, 1951). In *Shanxi sheng nongye hezuoshi wenjian huibian juan*, (Agricultural cooperativization in Shanxi: volume on collection of documents), eds. Shanxi sheng nongye hezuoshi bianji weiyuan hui, 274–276. Restricted circulation.

_____. "Weishenme yao shiban nongye shengchan hezuoshe" (Why we tried to establish agricultural producers' cooperatives). In *Shanxi nongye hezuohua* (Agricultural cooperativization in Shanxi), eds. Shanxi sheng shizhi yanjiu yuan, 656. Taiyuan: Shanxi renmin chubanshe, 2001.

Wen Rui. *Mao Zedong shiye zhong de Zhongguo nongmin wenti* (The Chinese peasant problem in Mao Zedong's vision). Nanchang: Jiangxi renmin chubanshe, 2004.

Wen Tiejun. *Zhongguo nongcun jiben jingji zhidu yanjiu* (Research on the basic economic principles of the Chinese countryside). Beijing: Zhongguo jingji chubanshe, 2000.

Weng Youwei, Xi Fuqun, and Zhao Jinkang. *Dangdai Zhongguo zhengzhi sixiangshi* (History of political thoughts in contemporary China). Henan: Henan daxue chubanshe, 1999.

Wu Hui. *Zhongguo lidai liangshi muchan yanjiu* (Research on the grain unit yield in history). Beijing: Nongye chubanshe, 1985.

Wu Yong. "1941 nian Shann-Gan-Ning bianqu jiuguo gongliang zhengjiao jiqi yinfa de shehui wenti fenxi" (Analysis on the grain collection in the Shann-

Gan-Ning border regions and social problems it raised in 1941). *Zhonggong dangshi yanjiu,* no. 147 (2010): 59.

Xin Ziling. "Nongye jitihua lilun shi zenyang shizu de" (How did the theory of agricultural collectivization stumble). *Yanhuang chunqiu,* no. 10 (2007).

Xing Leqin. *20 shiji 50 niandai Zhongguo nongye hezuohua yundong yanjiu* (A study of China's agricultural cooperativization movement in the 1950s). Zhejiang: Zhejiang daxue chubanshe, 2003.

Xinhuashe pinglun (Xinhua News Agency Comments) (July–September 1948). In *1948 nian yilai zhengce huibian,* 346–358.

Yang Deshou, ed. *Zhongguo hezuoshe jingji sixiang yanjiu* (Research on the thoughts of cooperative economy in China). Beijing: Zhongguo caijing chubanshe, 1998.

Yang Kuisong. *Zhonghua renmin gongheguo jianguo shi yanjiu* (Research on the history of the founding of the People's Republic of China). Nanchang: Jiangxi renmin chubanshe, 2009.

_____. "Jianguo chuqi zhonggong ganbu renyong zhengce kaocha" (A research on the CCP's appointments of cadres in the early years of the PRC). *Zhongguo dangdaishi yanjiu,* no. 1 (2009): 3–38.

Yang Mengfu. *Minguo caizheng shi* (Financial History of the Republic of China). Beijing: Zhongguo caizheng jingji chubanshe, 1985.

Ye Yangbing. *Zhongguo nongye hezuohua yundong yanjiu* (A study of China's agricultural cooperativization movement). Beijing: Zhishi chanquan chubanshe, 2006.

Yu Guangyuan and Han Gang. *Xin minzhu zhuyi shehuilun de lishi mingyun* (The fate of New Democracy's social theory). Wuhan: Changjiang wenyi chubanshe, 2005.

"Zai Zhonggong shanxi shengwei kuoda huiyi shang de zongjie baogao" (Summary report of the enlarged meeting of the Shanxi Provincial committee of the CCP) (October 10, 1952). In *Shanxi sheng nongye hezuoshi huzhu zu juan* (Agricultural cooperativization in Shanxi: volume on mutual aid teams), eds. Shanxi sheng nongye hezuoshi bianji weiyuan hui, 321. Restricted circulation, 1999.

Zhang Guoxiang. "Xin Zhongguo nongye shengchan hezuoshe de youlai" (The beginning of China's agricultural productive cooperatives). *Bainian chao,* no. 1 (2010): 31.

Zhang Ming. *Xiangcun shehui quanli he wenhua jiegou de bianqian* (Changes in cultural and power structures in villages). Guangxi: Guangxi renmin chubanshe, 2001.

Zhang Peisen. *Zhang Wentian nianpu* (Chronicles of Zhang Wentian). Beijing: Zhongyang dangshi chubanshe, 2000.

_____. "Zhang Wentian he liening de xin jingji zhengce" (Zhang Wentian and Lenin's NEP). *Yanhuang chunqiu,* no. 5 (2007).

Zhang Wentian. *Zhang Wentian xuanji* (Selected works of Zhang Wentian). Beijing: Renmin chubanshe, 1985.

_____. *Zhang Wentian jinshann diaocha wenji* (Collection of Zhang Wentian's investigation of Jin and Shann). Beijing: Zhongyang dangshi chubanshe, 1994.

_____. "Guanyu dongbei jingji goucheng ji jingji jianshe jiben fangzhen de tigang" (Outline of the basic guidelines for economic reconstruction and organization of the economy in the northeast region) (September 1948). In *Zhang Wentian wenji* (Works of Zhang Wentian), 32–33. Beijing: Zhonggong dangshi ziliao chubanshe, 1995.

Zhang Yumei. "Wo xiang Maozhuxi huibao nongye hezuohua" (My report to Chairman Mao on agricultural cooperativization). *Zhonggong dangshi ziliao,* 48 (1993): 104.

Zhao Fasheng, ed. *Dangdai Zhongguo de liangshi gongzuo* (The work on grain in contemporary China). Beijing: Zhongguo shehui kexue chubanshe, 1988.

Zhao Jialiang and Zhang Xiaoyun. *Banjie mubei xia de wangshi—Gao Gang zai Beijing* (The past under the half of the *tombstone*: Gao Gang in Beijing). Hong Kong: Dafeng chubanshe, 2008.

Zhonggong caijing zhengce faling huibian (Collection of financial policies and laws). Beijing: restricted circulation.

"Zhonggong Shanxi shengwei di 19 ci changwei huiyi" (The 19th meeting of the standing committee of Shanxi Province). In *Shanxi sheng nongye hezuoshi nongye huibianjuan*, 258.

"Zhonggong Shanxi shengwei xiang Huabeiju zhuanbao nongyeting guanyu 1950 nian shengchan huzhu yundong de zongjie baogao" (A report from the Shanxi branch of the CCP to the North China Bureau on the development of mutual aid teams in 1950) (December 30, 1950). In *Shanxi nongye hezuohua* (Agricultural cooperativization in Shanxi), eds. Shanxi sheng shizhi yanjiu yuan, 49–57. Taiyuan: Shanxi renmin chubanshe, 2001.

"Zhonggong shanxi shengwei shuji Lai Ruoyu guanyu sheng di'erci dang daibiao huiyi zhuyao neirong xiang Huabeiju bing Mao zhuxi de baogao" (Lai Ruoyu's report to the North China Bureau and Chairman Mao on the second congress of the CCP in Shanxi) (March 5, 1951). In *Shanxi nongye hezuohua* (Agricultural cooperativization in Shanxi), eds. Shanxi sheng shizhi yanjiu yuan, 63–64. Taiyuan: Shanxi renmin chubanshe, 2001.

Zhonggong zhongyang Huabeiju zhongyao wenjian huibian (A collection of important documents relating to the North China Bureau of the CCP). vol. 1. Restricted circulation.

Zhongguo nongmin fudanshi bianji weiyuan hui, eds. *Zhongguo nongmin fudanshi* (The history of Chinese peasants' burden), 4 volumes. Beijing: Zhongguo caizheng jingji chubanshe, 1991.

Zhongguo tongji nianjian 1992 (China statistical yearbook, 1992). Beijing: Zhongguo tongji chubanshe.

Zhonghua renmin gongheguo jingji dang'an ziliao xuanbian, 1949–1952, nongye juan (A selection of economic archives from the People's Republic of China, 1949–1952, volume on agriculture). Beijing: Shehui kexue chubanshe, 1991.

"Zhongyang renmin zhengwuyuan guanyu 1952 nian nongye shengchan de jueding" (The State Council's decision on agricultural production for 1952) (February 15, 1952). In *Zhonghua renmin gongheguo jingji dang'an ziliao xuanbian, 1949–1952, nongye juan,* 43 (A selection of economic archives from the People's Republic of China, 1949–1952, volume on agriculture). Beijing: Shehui kexue chubanshe, 1991.

Index

CORNELL EAST ASIA SERIES

CORNELL
East Asia Series

CPSIA information can be obtained
at www.ICGtesting.com
Printed in the USA
LVHW111907111119
637017LV00007B/39/P